THEOLOGY OF
CREATION in an EVOLUTIONARY
WORLD

D1570187

THEOLOGY OF
CREATION IN AN
EVOLUTIONARY WORLD

Karl Schmitz-Moormann

in collaboration with

James F. Salmon, S.J.

The Pilgrim Press · *Cleveland, Ohio*

The Pilgrim Press, Cleveland, Ohio 44115
© 1997 by Nicole Schmitz-Moormann

Printed in the United States of America on acid-free paper

02 01 00 99 98 97 5 4 3 2 1

Library of Congress Cataloging-in-Publication Data

Schmitz-Moormann, Karl.
    Theology of creation in an evolutionary world / Karl Schmitz-Moormann ; in
collaboration with James F. Salmon.
        p.   cm.
    Includes bibliographical references and index.
    ISBN 0-8298-1215-6 (pbk. : alk. paper)
    1. Creation.   2. Evolution—Religious aspects—Christianity.   I. Salmon, James F.
II. Title.
BT695.S35   1997
231.7'652—dc21

97-13379
CIP

I happen to think that the religious conservatives are wrong in what they believe, but at least they have not forgotten what it means to believe something. The religious liberals seem to me to be not even wrong.

Very strange, that the existence and nature of God and grace and sin and heaven and hell are not important! I would guess that people do not find the theology of their own supposed religion important, because they cannot bring themselves to admit that they do not believe in any of it.

—STEVEN WEINBERG, *Dreams of a Final Theory: The Search for the Fundamental Laws of Nature*

CONTENTS

ILLUSTRATIONS

PREFACE

This book took a very long time to write, and thus the persons who helped me shape it are numerous. Having given many lectures on the subject around the world, in Europe, Australia, Japan, New Zealand, and the United States, I find it impossible to name all who by their feedback helped to clarify my ideas. But there are a number to whom I must address my special gratitude for helping me to give the text its final form.

The book would never have been written if I had not found the hospitality of the Center of Theological Inquiry in Princeton and the strong encouragements of its director, Daniel W. Hardy.

I am deeply indebted to the Lutheran School of Theology at Chicago, the Chicago Center for Religion and Science, and especially to its director, Philip Hefner, who invited me to use my manuscript for a course with his graduate students. Their comments, and especially Philip Hefner's suggestions for revising the text, were very helpful. I have to thank as well the German Academic Exchange Service in Bonn for supporting my stay in Chicago.

Another opportunity to present my text in a course was offered to me by Brian McDermott, S.J., dean of Weston Jesuit School of Theology in Cambridge, Massachusetts. I am grateful to him and his staff for the many ways I could test the arguments in friendly conversations, and I thank my students for their critical comments.

My deepest gratitude goes to three persons. First to my collaborator, James F. Salmon, S.J., who revised the text thoroughly, tested it with undergraduates at Loyola College in Maryland, brought it into readable English, and eliminated some less acceptable statements. Without his cooperation this book would not have been printable. Second, to William Davish, S.J., who edited very carefully the text for printing, while suggesting on the way a number of essential changes. He worked hard on the manuscript, making it consistent in its notes and in its bibliography. Third, and not least, I especially thank my wife, Nicole, who has supported my long struggle with this text and has taken a very active role in incorporating the corrections. Without the support of these three, I would not have been able to present this text to Pilgrim Press, whom I thank for publishing it.

Karl Schmitz-Moormann
Center of Theological Inquiry, Princeton, New Jersey
October 27, 1996

INTRODUCTION

If in the common scientific understanding of this world one point is generally accepted, it is the fact that this universe as a whole is in the process of evolution. Christians perceive this same universe as God's creation. Following the inspiration of Pierre Teilhard de Chardin, we take the fact of evolution for granted.[1] Though in this book Teilhard is rarely quoted, his ideas are present throughout. The goal here, however, is not to expound the thinking of Teilhard, but to present a theological vision of creation within this evolutionary world.

The debate over creation or evolution has ceased. Hence the task of theology is to read the evolving universe as creation. In this text we accept the fact of evolution as the way creation is.

"Creation" is a term that designates a double aspect of the universe: on the one hand, it points to the created reality; on the other hand, it speaks of the act of the Creator. The latter is traditionally more often than not conceived primarily as the act that brought this universe into existence. The quest for the divine is therefore linked to the question of the origin of the universe, even though theologians have always spoken of *creatio continua*, the continuing act of creation.

In recent years a large number of books have been published on cosmology that made explicit statements about the Creator and more generally about religion. Either they do away with religion as nonscientific, or they see it as a necessary part of human existence. These approaches can be distinguished most clearly by their understanding of the meaning of this world-process. Thus Steven Weinberg in his book *The First Three Minutes*[2] does not see any meaning in this universe, as he adopts a kind of atheistic existentialism. On the other hand, Paul Davies[3] seems to believe that this world cannot be explained without a Creator. Relying on a scientifically sophisticated level of modern physics, Davies revives the argument from design that physico-theologians had used during the seventeenth and eighteenth centuries. Both approaches are essentially apologetic: they want to disprove or to prove the existence of God.

The phenomenon is undeniable: scientists in growing numbers raise quasi-theological questions, mostly without asking theologians for advice about the quality of theological statements and quite often with little respect for existing theological traditions. And the question of God is often treated without reference to any of the great world religions. Some of the scientists have a clear Christian theological background and training.[4] They are more often than not strongly influenced in their theology by their scientific background. They certainly bring new ideas to theology, but one can hardly say that they have a profound influence among theologians.

As scientists had turned away from religion in the second half of the nineteenth century, so had theologians turned away more and more from science. The beginnings of the universe were taught in theological manuals as if nothing new had been discovered. We might find reference to the "order" of nature, but it is difficult to find systematic references to the created world known through the sciences.[5] In this text, however, creation is seen as an evolving universe, which ontologically is not a world of determined static beings but a world of dynamic becoming: a change barely perceived in traditional theologies. The importance of science for any theological reflection will be sketched in the first chapter, when it treats the question what theology is about.

For many theologians, at least as we have encountered them by reading and talking, scientific data are of little relevance. If they approach the problem of science and theology, they do so from the point of view of epistemology. As is well known, philosophy over the last three hundred years had a tendency to explore the possibilities of knowledge rather than the philosophical significance of the known. Thus we find relatively few theologians who address questions about scientific data as relevant for theology and for the theologian's understanding of science. Interesting as the epistemology involved in science and theology may be, such an approach seems to ignore the reality of science. Outside a few isolated issues in theoretical physics, epistemological considerations have had relatively little influence on science. Scientists seem to generally adopt a kind of undefined critical realism. One accepts the existence of the world out there and believes at least some relevant information about it has been elaborated by science. This knowledge is tested in all kinds of applications, which often engage human lives. This is the case whenever an airplane full of passengers takes off and lands. If the scientific knowledge on which the technology is based were not realistic, there would be no aircraft.

Epistemology will not give us assurance about the reality of the world investigated by science despite some interesting suggestions.[6] Even less will an epistemological approach be able to establish theological truth. Theology is essentially based on faith. Christian theology is based essentially on faith in the Creator and in the Incarnation of the Word of God in Jesus, the Christ. The first aspect, faith in the Creator, forces the theologian to look at creation. This book is essentially an attempt to understand this universe as God's creation.

To understand our world in this way, we shall need to look at reality as it is known to us. To gain knowledge about this world, one turns to scientists who explore it, since theologians do not have special inspiration about the concrete reality of the universe. The disastrous condemnation of the Copernican worldview by theologians has made this more than evident. Therefore, this book will draw extensively on information established by the sciences. Thus a solid theological tradition is followed, as will be shown in the first chapter. In scholastic times nobody was admitted to study theology without having acquired a solid scientific background. The myth of warfare between science and religion created in the second half of the nineteenth century, as well as the myth of the Dark Ages created by the Enlightenment, will be briefly demythologized.

A short outline of the basic method followed in this book will make up the second part of the first chapter. Briefly, it is stated as follows: having faith in the Creator, we look at the universe as the work of God. Since this universe is evolving, we look at the history of the creation in order to seek the intentions of the Creator. We shall touch upon the basic changes in our thinking brought about by the shift in view from a static to an evolving world. Evolution has brought into our world an inevitable relativity of perceived truths, and so the first chapter will close with a delimitation of this relativity for Christian dogmas in their historicity.

The second chapter will first review briefly the so-called proofs of God's existence, without claim to treat this subject exhaustively. This text is not about such proofs. Turning to the question of how theology may see this universe as God's creation, we are confronted with the difficulty that most theologians and many Christians do not have adequate knowledge about the history of the universe, that is, of God's creation. Therefore, we offer a short overview of the history of the universe. An interpretation of our world that starts with its beginning and includes the traditional understanding of an originally perfect place, which later deteriorated through sin, does not offer meaningful results and is not supported by scientific data. Instead we propose, with Teilhard, the human as key to understanding the universe. This is an essential point for discussion in the following chapters and is a practical application of the methodological point made in the first chapter regarding the lack of explanatory value if one starts with the beginnings. In other words, all our arguments begin with human experience.

To interpret the history of this universe up to the present, we will look for parameters that allow us to probe the evolving process. If there were no such criteria, the process would not be accessible to any inquiry and could appear irrational. We will analyze the most often advanced criterion—quantitative superiority, that is, what is most numerous is most important. Having shown this quantitative parameter to be of little explanatory value, we will propose in the following chapters a number of qualitative parameters. All discussions will start with aspects of our human reality, which can then be followed back into their history. The second chapter will start with our human experience of unity, and will treat union as the main feature of the evolutionary process. The analysis points to a metaphysics of union that transcends the metaphysics of being. The third chapter will explore consciousness and its relevance for understanding evolutionary creation. The fourth chapter turns to the parameter of information, which will include a critical analysis of classical theories of information as stored bits. Information will be seen as a general feature of the evolutionary process that involves meaning at all levels. The fifth chapter will begin with the human experience of freedom and will trace its evolution to its beginnings. The parameters of union, consciousness, information, and freedom will be analyzed because of their relevance for measuring the direction, if there is one, of the evolutionary process. Each chapter will then ask how the particular qualitative parameter makes intelligible God's intention in creation. The parameters become a way in which the universe becomes diaphanous, translucent of the reality of the Creator.

The first five chapters necessarily emphasize what science tells us about our world, God's evolving creation. We hope in the future, when theologians and Christians will be better informed about the universe, as educated Christians were in the thirteenth century, knowledge of this scientific kind will be presumed. But for the present it appears an unavoidable necessity to insist on a large database for purposes of the discussion.

The sixth chapter will pull together the results of the first five chapters in preparation for theological reflection. We will then develop the idea of what we call *creatio appellata*, along with the notion that the process of union in an evolving creation is not incompatible with a triune Creator. This process of union might be seen as the reflection of the eternal union in the Trinity in which God exists. It is not the intention of the text to present a comprehensive theology of the Trinity. Rather, we limit ourselves to insights about the triune God gained from our knowledge of the evolving creation. Seeing more clearly the triune God in relation to the known created universe may help modern Christians to experience their world as a constant invitation to praise its Creator.

1 THEOLOGY OF CREATION AS A PERMANENT TASK

Before we address the question of theology of creation in the evolving world, we shall sketch a picture of theology as it presents itself today. We try to clarify the notion of theology as *fides quaerens intellectum* to explore how this view of theology becomes relevant for understanding creation and requires the use of science as essential information. This is, as we will show by the example of medieval theologians, a traditional procedure, which was lost during the last century. A changed world, an evolving universe, needs new theological approaches. Not everything is at the theologian's disposal: there are limits to historically conditioned theological statements, which a Christian theologian must respect.

Today we live in a universe that is perceived as evolving. Theology, as we know it, developed in the context of a universe that was perceived as stable and fundamentally unchanging. Though in the world of the eighteenth century the word of the theologian was generally accepted as valuable information to securely structure one's life, we no longer find such a clear attitude as acceptable to a large number of persons. During recent centuries, and especially for nineteenth-century academia, the concrete world became less and less relevant in theology, as theology distanced itself from nature and became more and more an abstract and bookish subject. Today theology often appears to be an exercise of reading biblical texts according to the historical-critical method. This method has helped us to obtain more reliable texts and to interpret them more adequately, and has offered a better understanding of the biblical world. Yet it seems that modern theology often fails in its purpose to reach people in this world. Even though strong religious needs appear in our time, creating all sorts of New Age religions that require persons to search for answers in religions that are exotic to them, people show little interest in the theology of the Christian churches. For example, in European universities the number of students of theology declines more or less steadily; the number of priests in the Roman Catholic Church is insufficient to serve still existing parishes; in Germany some Protestant churches are being transformed into Islamic mosques.

The trend of a diminished worldwide mainline Christian population, at least in industrialized countries, is accompanied by the rise of fundamentalist movements like scientific creationism and Islamic fundamentalism, which promise to their adherents great security within the limited framework of a dogmatist worldview. Theologians can be at a loss if they have to discuss fundamentalist positions with which they rarely agree. The post–sixteenth-century limitation of discussion to historical texts and especially to biblical texts, as most clearly articulated by the *sola scriptura* formulation, becomes the source for excessively individual interpretations given by theologians. The practical idea of establishing a text representing the verbally inspired Bible—for example, as Osiander tried to do in the sixteenth century—cannot be realized. And even so, we have no way of knowing exactly what interpretation should be given to the text. Realizing there are a number of errors about physical facts—such as calling the hare a ruminant[1]—theologians have been forced to give up the idea of a literally inspired text.

But what are the criteria for understanding correctly the biblical text? Actually, there seems to be no *via absoluta* to overcome this basic difficulty of theology, especially if the interpretation is based on the biblical text alone. In this latter case theology becomes a philological enterprise, a more or less fanciful interpretation of texts coming to us out of another world, or a fundamentalist theology that seems barely credible to modern humanity. Theology needs to address the question what it is about.

WHAT IS THEOLOGY ABOUT?

In the second article of his *Summa Theologica* Thomas Aquinas distinguished two kinds of sciences:

> [Some] proceed from principles known by the natural light of the intellect, such as arithmetic and geometry and the like. There are also some that proceed from principles known by the light of a higher science: thus the science of optics proceeds from principles established by geometry, and music from principles established by arithmetic. So it is that sacred doctrine is a science because it proceeds from principles made known by the light of a higher science, namely, the science of God and the blessed.[2]

The essential point of this statement is that theology is a science based not on natural knowledge but on revealed knowledge as grasped in faith. "Theology, *intellectus fidei*, is rooted in faith."[3] It is not a higher form of philosophy, as natural theology might have appeared in the late eighteenth century;[4] rather, theology is the endeavor to understand the revealed content of faith. It is *fides quaerens intellectum*, faith seeking understanding. Therefore, theology is not philosophical reflection about God. Such reflection is not impossible, so long as a rational universe is presumed. Philosophy, like any science, is limited by its presuppositions. Often presumed presuppositions of the natural sciences, incidentally, limit the possibility of asking other appropriate questions about the universe: for example, the presupposition that everything can be explained by the laws of physics and by material causes.[5] It is, to use Sir Arthur Eddington's metaphor about science, like using a two-inch fishing net as a method to detect all of reality. On the one hand, reality is identified with the oceans; on the other hand, with a two-inch net one does not catch fish smaller than two inches, which therefore do not exist for science. As Eddington's ichthyologist states haughtily: "Anything uncatchable by my net is *ipso facto* outside the scope of ichthyological knowledge, and is not part of the kingdom of fishes which has been defined as the theme of ichthyological knowledge. In short, what my net can't catch isn't fish."[6] We may extend Eddington's metaphor: not only the net but the universe of the ichthyologist is limited to the ocean. Therefore, he knows nothing about birds and stars. Actually, the materialistic science of our time denies the existence of anything escaping physical examination. Thus science, though highly effective, has become an exclusive enterprise, allowing only a limited view of reality. This limitation is hardly justified. As Karl Rahner states, "The limitation to experimentally verifiable facts—of the natural sciences, mathematics, quantities, fields outside value-judgments—is arbitrary, a mere matter of terminology and would deprive theology only of a claim to be scientific in a way foreign to it."[7]

Scientists are more often than not unaware of this self-imposed limitation. Theology differs from science inasmuch as it is very conscious of the presuppositions to which it is bound. Giving up these presuppositions, giving up one's faith, disables one from doing theology. "Faith must be the subjective inspiration, and not merely the object, of this operation of human reason"[8] that we know as theology. Thus theology is always linked to a specific faith: there can be Christian theology, Islamic theology, Hindu theology, or pantheistic theology; because there are strong differences between these forms of faith, there cannot be a general theology covering them all. Ideally, a general human faith may make its appearance one day. But now we live in a world with quite different traditions of faith, and it seems improbable that they can be united in an amalgam that would take the best from every religion. There are especially today, as there have often been in the past, efforts to create such a global religion, but with little success.[9]

In spite of such hopes, which seem misguided for a Christian, there seems no viable way other than to try to do theology with the presuppositions of Christian faith.[10] For the past few centuries these presuppositions have been accepted as laid down primarily in biblical texts. And theology, especially in this century, has to a large extent conceived its task as the most adequate interpretation of these texts. Within Catholic thought, besides the biblical texts, tradition has always been accepted as a source for theology. Tradition can be thought of as based "on the words and signs of the apostolic testimony," which "form the permanent basis of all Christian tradition."[11]

The concept of tradition for many centuries, especially since the Council of Trent, was understood as the handing down of the original Christian faith, which was to be kept unchanged. This corresponds to the classical definition, in the sense of post-Tridentine classicism, of the *depositum fidei* in the words of Vincent of Lerins:

> What is the deposit? It is that which has been entrusted to you, not invented by you, what you have received not what you have thought up; a matter not of personal ingenuity but of doctrine, not of private acquiring but of public tradition, a matter handed down to you not brought out by you, of which you should be not the author but the guardian, not the starter but the joiner, not leading but following. "Guard," he says, "the deposit" (1 Tim. 6:20); conserve the treasure of the Catholic faith inviolate and unmarred . . . especially careful must we be to *hold what everywhere, always, and universally has been believed*. . . . Let there be a clearer understanding of what was somewhat obscurely believed earlier. . . . Teach the same you have learned so that while speaking in a new way you may not speak new things.[12]

Taking this definition seriously, Catholic theologians especially were at a disadvantage in developing new theological visions: they were permitted to clarify but not to add anything to the content of faith. With these guidelines theology became an enterprise to show that the proposed interpretation of faith was concordant with interpretations given by the church fathers. To a very large extent, tradition in Catholic theology was understood as using patristic literature to corroborate one's theology. This understanding of tradition was complemented by "clarifications" from the magisterium of the church, which "functions merely as hearer and servant of the tradition of the primitive church, as inspired by God and committed to writing in Scripture."[13]

This limited concept of tradition, seemingly unaware of any cultural developments in history, has been largely overcome, in principle at least, by the Vatican II declaration that "the books of Scripture only teach faithfully, firmly and without error that truth which God wanted put forward into the sacred writings for the sake of our salvation (*Dei Verbum*, art. 11)."[14]

This limitation of the "true" content of the biblical texts naturally applies as well to all dogmatic declarations made by the councils of the church and by its magisterium. This understanding of tradition puts before the theologian as a principal task the clarification and demarcation of the salutary affirmation made in those biblical and historical texts. "Only when this has been done can the effort be made to translate the kernel thus singled out in the truth of the faith, and to adapt it to the language of the day. To transplant inconsiderately the doctrinal utterances of the past into a later age may well be to falsify them."[15]

The difficulty with this research plan is that we have no immediate insight into which truths are necessary for salvation. As Karl-Heinz Weger points out, the notion of a "hierarchy of truths"[16] might be helpful to guide the theologian to the important points on which to build and from which to examine less important doctrines. The latter may have had only a temporal function in the history of salvation. But how can we make judgments about such a temporality? Are we bound to listen in the first place to the historians and to the exegetes to recognize what may be put aside and what must be kept? Though certainly we should pay attention to them, they do not offer a solution to the dilemma, at least not when they rely on the tools of historical criticism to identify and elaborate the most reliable texts and the historical background in which they appeared. They may show us what appeared important for salvation to persons in the early church and in the past, but what does it mean for us? When we look at pre-Tridentine theology, we cannot see this same concern. Rather, we see an immediate effort to "understand what we believe,"[17] using all the knowledge available at the time.

Theology in this vision is the effort to understand God's revelation in the context of the world in which we live. Without knowledge about the world, as it is established through philosophy and its offspring such as the sciences, we are confronted with the impossibility of understanding what we believe as related to our concrete life in this world. This becomes especially clear if we consider the Christian creed in its generally accepted Apostles' and Nicene formulations, both of which start with the Confession of Faith "in Deum creatorem coeli et terrae, visibilium et invisibilium," that is, of God as Creator of everything existing in our world. Faithful to the Christian creed, theology is thus bound to strive to understand this universe as creation. (See figure 1.) This has a number of implications, which we need to explore.

THEOLOGY OF CREATION
AS A PERMANENT TASK OF THEOLOGIANS

Christians believe that God created this world. This is not a statement to be verified or falsified by natural sciences. God the Creator is not a factor in the physical makeup of the universe. Certainly there have been times when writers tried to prove the existence of God by pointing to special features of the universe. The Newtonian settlement is one such enterprise. The argument from design by the physico-theologians of the sixteenth and seventeenth centuries[18] is another example. As Michael Buckley[19] has shown, these attempts

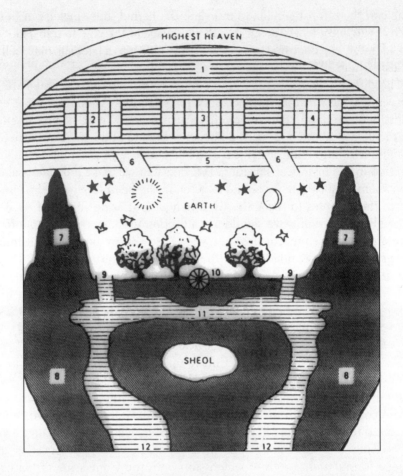

Figure 1   The image of the world according to the Bible; a well-ordered world founded on columns, as we encounter it in biblical hymns (Job 26:11; Ps. 18:2, 74:4). Everything has its assigned place: (1) waters above the firmament; (2) storage of snow; (3) storage of hail; (4) rooms for the winds; (5) the firmament; (6) cataracts; (7) the pillars of heaven; (8) the pillars of earth; (9) fountains of the abyss; (10) center of the earth; (11) the subterranean waters; (12) the rivers of the underworld. *From Annibale Fantoli,* Galileo: For Copernicanism and for the Church, *trans. George V. Coyne, S.J. (Notre Dame, Ind.: University of Notre Dame Press, 1994), 13. Reprinted by permission of the Vatican Observatory.*

to prove the existence of God with the help of the laws of nature make God subject to these laws. When one can prove God by the laws of nature, then one can as well disprove God with their help. God would become part of the natural world, a natural and explorable factor in the universe. This is at least not compatible with the Christian teaching that sees God transcendent and absolutely independent of this world, even though immanent in the world. But immanence does not make God a factor to be researched by science. Science cannot be the basis of theology, the ground on which theology should stand. This is not to say that theology can ignore what science finds about the concrete reality of this universe. Since Christians believe that God created this world, theology can hardly lack interest in this world. Moreover, a basic task of theology is to think through the implications of the Creed in more detail in order to make them preachable and understandable to people in the present world. Therefore, the theologian needs to look closely at the reality of God's creation in order to be able to speak to those who are part of it.

The need to know about creation, to know about the universe, does not in itself indicate where the theologian should look for such information. Ever since Descartes struggled for a kind of certainty that is unattainable, modern epistemologies have not proven very helpful in assuring a solid basis on which to build a systematic theology. The criteria of self-evidence and clarity are not necessary signs of truth. Within a certain tradition some points may be quite evident and clear, yet basically in error. In the medieval world it was quite evident and clear that every heavy object would tend to reach the center of the earth.[20] Even without the Cartesian methodical doubt, which contradicts itself by trying to argue without having any knowledge as the object of doubt, the experience of evidence[21] is not the most important criterion of truth. Clarity is often had with the trivial, but seldom with the more complex and significant. Only with difficulty can some understandable realities and experiences become important truths for us. Truth is not necessarily linked with clarity, though clarity of expression is desirable. Unfortunately, the truths of greatest importance for humanity often are neither self-evident nor extremely clear. The content of faith may be expressed clearly, but the content is certainly not self-evident.

Regarding clarity, the task of theology is to express the message of God's revelation in an understandable way. But the way in which this clarity of expression is achieved will always be largely conditioned by the intellectual horizon within which the message is put into words. Traditionally philosophy, as the intellectual horizon of a time bringing the knowledge of the time into unity, has been helpful for theologians. Using the philosophy of the day that was considered to be the best description of the world, medieval theologians could formulate a theology that was understandable to the people of those times. Common preachers and educated persons were able to relate this world to God as the Creator, to recognize their own place, and to understand the message of salvation as it related to them and to the world in general.

Contemporary philosophy does not offer us a comprehensive vision of the world in which we live. It is much more concerned with questions of how we may know and how human knowledge may be related to the "reality out there" than with questions about what we know and what that means for understanding our existence in the universe. Physics, an essential part of philosophy in medieval times, besides logic and rhetoric, is no longer discussed in philosophy. Cosmology, the effort to understand the structure of the universe, its origin, and the place of the human being within it, is no part of contemporary philosophy, but an important platform for "philosophizing" scientists.

Modern theologians generally do not investigate the universe or human beings in their concrete existence. From their biblical sources they may make the formal statement that this universe is God's creation, but this does not give them knowledge about details of the structure and development of the universe and the place humans have within the universe. Theology must acquire this kind of knowledge from sources available to it. The old saying that philosophy is the handmaiden of theology seems quite correct. But the handmaiden today is nobody one can push around in the style of a nineteenth-century bourgeois landlady. The services rendered are necessary to the household, but more often than not the handmaiden can do quite well without a landlady, especially if she is good at her task. And certainly, those who today create knowledge about our universe are very good at their task. Theology cannot tell them how to do their job or what they are allowed and not allowed to know. Ultimately, theology is unable to have reliable knowledge about the world without seeking help from the sciences, which act quite independently of what theologians would like to know. The sciences deliver knowledge to all members of society. Theologians will have to take the information seriously, or they will not be talking to people about concrete existence in this universe.

Theologians can and should also take a critical stance regarding what the sciences deliver. Some scientists often manifest a tendency to extrapolate beyond their knowledge and to generalize their own field as if it were all-encompassing. Critical distinctions must be made between established knowledge and undue generalizations. Theologians are in an uneasy position because typically they do not possess the necessary background and they do not know the criteria for making such distinctions. As the case of Galileo Galilei has shown clearly, references to the Bible—in this case to the book of Joshua and the battle of Gideon[22]—or to the decisions of councils have no force of conviction when information about the concrete structure of the universe is concerned. Therefore, theologians are confronted with the dilemma that on the one hand they must learn from the sciences about God's creation, the universe, but on the other hand they have not developed the critical ability to evaluate information that the sciences deliver. This is especially true of physics, where the language of science proper has become more and more sophisticated, based on the firm Pythagorean belief that what may be calculated is real. Of course, this assumption can be questioned: not all that can be calculated is real. Moreover, vast domains of reality can be neither calculated nor measured.[23] Yet what the scientific community has generally accepted is not to be neglected by a theology that desires to speak about the world and its Creator, that is, to speak about God. Thus we may state that science is a necessary source of information for the theologian. But, we may ask, is this not in contradiction to the supposed opposition between science and theology? How did theologians relate to science in the past?

The Example of the Thirteenth Century's Theologians

Classical theology before what euphemistically is called *the anthropological turn*, which started with Descartes's *Cogito ergo sum* and his quest for certitude, did know about the necessity of information coming from the sciences. Ever since the Cappadocian fathers, mastering the *quadrivium*—the study of physics, astronomy, mathematics, and music—was a necessary condition for admission to studies in theology. Future theologians prepared theses on subjects such as *de machina mundi* (on the world machine), *de orbibus caelestibus* (on the heavenly spheres), *de rerum natura* (on the nature of things), *de universo* (on the universe), *de mundo* (on the world), *de imagine mundi* (on the picture of the world), *de philosophia mundi* (on the philosophy of the world), *de divisione naturae* (on the division of nature), and *de mundi universitate* (on the totality of the world).[24] The mechanics of the heavens usually were taught according to the book by John of Hollywood on the spheres of the heavens.[25] (See figure 2.)

Together with the more technical anonymous *theoria planetarum* (theory of the planets) and the *Toledan* and *Alfonsine Tables*, this manual, many times reedited and revised, was used in practically all European schools when teaching astronomy. It was based on the Ptolemaic worldview, which allowed the exact calculation of the position of the planets, the prediction of solar and lunar eclipses, and recalculation of the modern Gregorian calendar, which required the omission of one day every *four* thousand years. The Jesuit Matteo Ricci, when contesting with Chinese astronomers at the imperial court of China, where the calendar each year was reestablished and proclaimed by the emperor, predicted a solar eclipse exactly to the minute. The Chinese astronomers were off by many hours. Naturally, in view of the importance of astronomy for the imperial calendar, Ricci won the confidence of the Chinese emperor. Astronomical clocks constructed in those times in European cathedrals, when they have been kept working, still show today

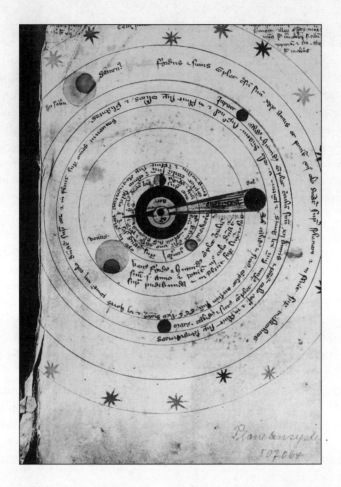

Figure 2   Medieval geocentric Ptolemaic world with the seven planets, and with an explanation of the lunar eclipse. Woodcut, thirteenth century. *Reprinted by permission of Deutsches Museum, München.*

the actual position of the planets. For the most part monks made the calculations for the clocks, such as the clock in the cathedral of Münster, which was calculated by a monk in the Hude monastery north of Münster. This successful way of understanding the movements in the skies was not easily given up without definite proof.[26] (See figure 3.) Thus the revised manual of Sacrobosco, translated into all European languages, was in use into the eighteenth century, and the astronomical atlas of the mid-eighteenth century still shows a Ptolemaic world.

Of course, the Ptolemaic vision has been falsified by now. But by scientific standards its calculations worked perfectly, and people were reluctant to

Figure 3   Medieval world. Woodcut, 1502. (From Virgil, *Opera* [Strassburg: Grueninger, 1502], fol. 69 Libri rari 318; Deutsches Museum, München.) This was still the current vision in the sixteenth century and was thus taught at the Lutheran School in Wittenberg by Philip Melanchthon in his *Initia doctrinae physicae*. (*Initia doctrinae physicae*, dictata in Academia Vuitebergensi Philip. Melanth. Iterum edita, Witebergae, per Johannem Lufft, 1550.) *Reprinted by permission of Deutsches Museum, München.*

give them up without definite proof, which Galileo still lacked.[27] But our interest is not in the Galileo case. The point is that the science of the Scholastics was quite accurate and serious and not at all as book-oriented as we are sometimes told. As Albert the Great states with precision:

> It is the function of natural science not simply to accept what has been told but in natural things to seek [their] causes.[28]
>
> This proof (through the senses) about the nature of things is most certain, and has more value than reasoning without experiment.[29]
>
> Experiment alone is valid in such things, in that for natures so particular a syllogism cannot be had.[30]

Historians of science are only starting to go into the archives of the great European libraries such as the Bodleian in Oxford, where works in medieval science are not even yet registered by their *incipits*, let alone analyzed by their content. But awareness of a very bright age is growing.[31]

Medieval theologians were aware of the need to be knowledgeable about the created world. Whereas Augustine might have considered this knowledge to be superfluous and not essential for theology so long as the right faith was upheld, Thomas Aquinas left no doubt about his stance in this matter. Aquinas criticizes a position reported by Augustine and insists on the necessity of knowledge about creatures:

> Therefore it is clear that the opinion of some is false, who held that it in no way concerns the truth of the faith what a person might perceive about creatures as long as there is a right perception about God, as Augustine narrates in his *Origin of the Soul* (c.4 and 5). For an error about creatures redounds to a false knowledge of God, and draws men's minds away from God.[32]

Sermons of the thirteenth century quite naturally used images taken from the scientifically known world. For example, monks and clergy are admonished to follow the good example of fixed stars, which are closer to God and are therefore a model for the behavior of priests. The fixed stars

> do not move by their own motion but they follow the motion of the firmament, and so true dwellers in cloister ought not to be moved by their own will but by the motion of the firmament, namely God's. . . . But many are moved by a contrary motion, following their own wills, and for this reason Daniel (8:1, 10) says he saw in a vision a ram's horn fling down stars and crush them. . . . A star . . . is fixed in one place, so religious and clerics ought to be fixed so that they do not change their places. . . . But there are some who do the contrary.[33]

This image, based on the scientific worldview of the time, was used not only by educated persons like the clergy, the only ones besides upper-class women and nuns who knew how to read and write, but also by preachers of popular sermons in the vernacular. The greatest preacher of the thirteenth century in Germany, Berthold von Regensburg, has left two sermons with the title "On the Seven Planets,"[34] in which each planet represents one of the seven chief virtues. Hearers of the sermons are to reflect on these virtues, especially during the days of the week named after the respective planets.

As is well known, the world described by modern science is not concordant with the worldview of the Bible. Theologians of the thirteenth century were quite conscious of such a discordance and had two approaches to handle it. One concerns the ability to interpret the Scriptures correctly. This time, fully agreeing with Augustine, Aquinas writes:

> In questions of this sort, two things are to be observed. The first indeed is that the truth of Scripture be firmly held. Second, since divine Scripture can be presented in many ways, no presentation should be adhered to so absolutely by any person that if by sure reasoning what this person believes to be the sense of Scripture is established as false, he would nevertheless continue to assert it tenaciously: this in order that Scripture should not be ridiculed by unbelievers and the way to belief not be foreclosed to them.[35]

The second approach to the apparent dilemma was to distinguish the book of nature from the Bible as two sources of revelation. Each book was assigned its own focus of interest. In this view Scripture is not concerned with a description of the world as it is. Rather, it speaks in such a way that the people can understand what it says, using the accepted worldview of the time. Scripture teaches us not about the stars or planets, but about salvation. Bonaventure has stated this distinction clearly:

> Scripture ordinarily *recounts* how much is necessary for doctrine, although not so explicitly describing the distinction between the spheres whether celestial or elementary, saying little or nothing about the movements and forces of higher bodies and about the mixtures of the elements and composites. . . . The reason for understanding these matters is that, as the first principle makes itself known to us through *Scripture* and through *the creature*, it manifests itself through the book of *the creature* as the *effective* principle, through the book of *Scripture* as the *restoring* principle.[36]

Thus theologians of the thirteenth century were not trying to make their understanding of the world harmonious with the biblical text. They generally accepted creation in six days because there was no evidence to the contrary.[37] The idea of the two books as separate sources of revelation did not create difficulties for theologians as it did when the principle of *sola scriptura* was introduced by the sixteenth-century reformers.[38] This principle could not remain without influence on Roman Catholic theologians, who in the case of Galileo insisted on definitive proof. We also know from the words of Cardinal Bellarmine that, if proof had been given, theologians would have had to change their reading of the biblical text.[39]

We close our short review of medieval theological praxis with the conclusion that theology was using the science of the day as an essential theological source. This approach permitted Galileo and his contemporary scientists to investigate the book of nature in which God makes God known through divine works.

Between the sixteenth and nineteenth centuries the situation changed. The traditional understanding of the cosmos gradually was undone. (See figure 4.) Theology no longer used science as a reliable source of information to read the book of nature as God's self-disclosure. But theologians did not turn away from science. Returning to the praxis of church fathers, they showed serious interest in the details of creation and its wonders.[40] Even Kepler and Newton considered themselves as having made essential theological contributions. Physico-theology and the argument from design became popular as theology and science remained at peace in spite of the condemnation of the Copernican worldview. At the same time theologians themselves were concerned primarily with internal reform: Reformation churches among themselves, and all in confrontation with the Roman Catholic Church, were striving to define their theological positions. If there was an external enemy during the eighteenth century, it was the Enlightenment, which claimed the dominance of reason as absolute judge of all questions, even those of religion. It was only in the nineteenth century that some struggle arose between the church and those atheists who claimed to be scientific and who sometimes were people of science. Actually, the church was principally opposing popularized scientism as a philosophy. In spite of these disagreements, which stigmatized the church in public opinion as opposed to science, some church representatives maintained a way of thinking that was developed in the Middle Ages and by the church fathers, namely, to look for scientific evidence in matters concerning the book of nature. The breakthrough[41] of evolutionary concepts with publication of Darwin's *Origin of Species*[42] was a greater challenge to theologians than was the heliocentrism proposed by Copernicus, because the traditional story of creation was being questioned. Even more, the ontological grounding of the church's teaching of unchangeable and eternal dogmatic truths was endangered. Pope Pius XII saw this quite clearly. When referring to evolution, he asked, "If such a doctrine were to spread, *what would become of the unchangeable Catholic dogmas, what of the unity and the stability of the faith?*"[43]

It took the churches a long time to cease fighting or ignoring evolution. The Roman Catholic Church had to wait for Pope John Paul II to ask theologians to think over what evolution means for understanding human beings, for Christology, and for the development of Christian doctrine.[44] But in the last century important churchmen were speaking like the Scholastics. Cardinal John Henry Newman was quite clear:

I cannot imagine . . . why Darwinism should be considered inconsistent with Catholic doctrine.[45]

There is as much want of simplicity in the idea of distinct species as in that of the creation of trees in full growth, or rocks with fossils in them. I

Figure 4   Competing world pictures at the end of the seventeenth century. Center above: Ptolemy (second century); below left: Copernicus (1543); below right: Tycho Brahe (1588). The best position is obviously given to Ptolemy. Tycho Brahe, to whom is given the right side, is preferred to Copernicus. The three world images are all marked by a clearly recognizable order based on the circle. Kepler's ellipses were evidently no more accepted by astronomers than was the heliocentrism of Copernicus. It even happened that the Rudolphine tables, calculated by Kepler and fitting his elliptical heliocentrism, were recalculated for use within the Ptolemaic system. *From Johannes Zahn,* Specula physico-mathematico-historica notabilium ac mirabilium scientiarum; in qua mundi mirabilis oeconomia *(Nurnberg: n.p., 1898). Reprinted by permission of Deutsches Museum, München.*

mean that it is as strange that monkeys should be so like men, with no *historical* connection between them, as that there should be no course of facts by which fossil bones go into rocks. The one idea stands to the other as fluxions to differentials. . . . I will either go the whole hog with Darwin, or, dispensing with time and history altogether, hold not only the theory of distinct species but that also of the creation of fossil-bearing rocks.[46]

Thus the need to integrate the evolutionary worldview into theology was recognized quite early. Attempts unfortunately were often repressed by church authority or by an unwillingness of theologians to consider the natural world, God's creation, as a source for theological information. This factor had some negative consequences in the case of Galileo, though in that case the actual impact on the relations between theology and the sciences is highly overestimated. This is clear if one looks at the flourishing of natural theology that followed in the seventeenth and eighteenth centuries. Darwin's story and the issue of an evolutionary worldview had more far-reaching consequences. The fundamental perceptions of the human person, the origins, the place in nature and in creation, were challenged. More, the general understanding of reality and its origins changed. Philosophical hylomorphism, for centuries the essential key to understanding nature, was no longer an adequate tool in a world of constantly changing species. If Galileo's physics did not overcome Aristotle, Darwin's biology certainly did. Ours was no longer a world of stable species. The ἀρχαί (beginnings) were no longer a sure source of knowledge. Knowing the first man and woman did not tell us much about human beings today or about the relation of a human to his or her Creator. If the new perception explained anything about human beings and their relation to the Creator, it was a different story from what we read in Genesis.

The new worldview drawn from science also raises questions about the basic structure of theologically developed doctrine. If, as science shows us, this universe is evolving and God's creation is dynamic, then we must ask about our traditional tools of thinking, tools developed in a time when a seemingly static universe was brought forth in the beginning by the Creator as *very good*.[47] What changes in our ways of doing theology are caused by this new worldview?

Doing Theology in an Evolutionary Environment

Our task here is not to enter the debate regarding theories of evolution, which have been explained elsewhere[48] and are far from satisfactory. But this lack of a theoretical explanation does not make the fact of evolution less real. And this fact of evolution is the first concern when we consider essential changes in tools for theological reflection on God's creation.

Our first and basic proposal is concerned with the classical way of reasoning in theology. Catholic theology during the last three hundred years became more and more inflexible, into a kind of "*Denziger* theology," as Karl Rahner noted in the 1950s.[49] Protestant theology during that time turned away from considering creation as a source of theological information in order to build on the biblical text alone. The Barthian "No!" to all philosophy of nature as a source of information for theology is still a dogma widely accepted among Protestants. Both Catholic and Protestant theology are based on an unchangeable, though usable, source of knowledge. The main differences arise from the perception of this basic source, roughly delivered by the two axioms: *depositum fidei* and *sola scriptura*. Both slogans are definite and complete. Nothing can be added or taken away. All theology can do is reach a better understanding of the revelation that was completed in Christ. Vincent of Lerins admonished the theologians: *cum dicas nove non dicas nova* (when you say something in a new way do not say anything new).

This teaching of the churches over the centuries was in full agreement with their perception of creation: it was a momentary act of God in the beginning, which brought into existence the whole universe with everything in it. And in the beginning the creation was perfect, *very good*. It was complete, with nothing missing and nothing to be added: "Whatever God does endures forever; nothing can be added to it, nor anything taken from it."[50] The complete truth had to be sought in the beginning. The full picture of creation was in Paradise at the origin, the fullest realization of man, *masculine and feminine*.[51] Generations of theologians reflected on the original human status. Thus in the beginning one could find the full truth. The same was true of the church. Its ideal state has again and again been identified with the early church of Jerusalem when it was closest to Jesus Christ. In this view typically the church needed reformation, not innovation.

Such an attitude among Christian theologians has been by no means atypical. We find it in all religions. The Chinese and Japanese veneration of ancestors and the Bantu-philosophy identification of forebears as closer to the invigorating Force providing life are other examples. This attitude was the same in philosophy. In Plato's Νόμοι (Laws) the παλαιοί (ancients) are said to be closer to the gods and therefore to have better laws. And Aristotle starts his metaphysics by searching for the ἀρχαί (beginnings).

The epistemological presumption of this search for the beginning was that truth in its completeness is had only there. Tertullian put this epistemological presumption into its shortest version:

> In sum, *if it is certain that the earlier is the truer*, that that is earlier which is [from the beginning], and that that is from the beginning which is from the apostles, it is equally certain surely that what has come down from the apostles is that which was held sacred among the churches of the apostles.[52]

This statement may be justified in a static universe, perfectly created in the beginning. But in an evolving creation the situation is different. The beginnings are far from perfect and complete. As we shall see later in detail, evolution seems not to be the unfolding of a complete set of beings laid out in a divine blueprint and realized only in time. At least, we have no clear indication from the side of the universe that there was an original perfect plan with full detail. Even if this were the case, revelation could not use a language of a certain moment beyond the point of realization thus far reached by God's creation.

Our evolving universe is marked by the slow but constant emergence of new realities. The new, as will be seen in more detail later, cannot be deduced from the old. Nobody who studies the earliest stages of the universe could write an algorithm that would lead with certitude to the existence of humans. The earlier does not necessarily contain the later. The new realities come into existence step-by-step, but no steps seem necessary or clearly planned. An evolving creation is not finished in the beginning: it is still emerging. One might reflect on the relation to an eternal God of the time-dominated universe, but as far as human perception is concerned, this is certainly a secondary question. Human beings always experience the universe in the flow of time.

Any revelation addressed to humans cannot disregard this fundamental condition of human existence, which evidently is the work of the Creator. Not to respect this condition would leave the Creator in self-contradiction. Such a consideration might offer one criterion for appreciating a revelation: to come from God it must at least be understandable to the human beings of the time, speaking the language of that time. The language itself is defined by the knowledge of the time and is the most complete expression of this knowledge. We can verify this easily by looking at languages of older times where the knowledge linked with words has been lost. There are words we do not understand anymore (e.g., we have little chance to identify all the plants we can find with a Latin description of the flora). In our time it is even more evident that to speak of galaxies, black holes, or neutron stars would not have made sense some hundred years ago. Revelation is in its very expression bound to the knowledge of the time in which it is given.

There is little doubt that analysis of the biblical text itself requires this constant readaptation of revelation to a changing world. There can be even less doubt that we are living through the most profound change in the perception of the universe in human history. We are becoming increasingly aware that the world is not a stable structure, basically unchanged from its beginnings. Rather, we exist within a dynamic becoming with a very dim beginning and a very open future. Predictions about the human future, even for the next hundred years, are naive.

This lack of certitude has created a widespread fear. In the last century humans were striving to conquer the earth definitively and to overcome all evils by scientific means; late traces of this attitude are still present among some behavioral psychologists and sociological schools. Today more often than not, we seem to reach the limits of the feasible. Despite enormous amounts of money spent on research investigating illnesses such as AIDS and cancer, progress is very slow. Scientists are more and more tentative about ultimate success in their struggles against illness. The population at large has become aware of some undesirable consequences of technological progress. This awareness in itself is a new phenomenon. For example, the devastation of large parts of North Africa by the cutting down of trees in Roman times and the destruction of large areas of arable land in Italy and Spain caused by the loss of forests were never linked to their causes in earlier times.

Our new awareness presents new human responsibilities. But often the reaction is that of looking for an ideal state of affairs in the past. Preservation is the main interest, and preservation in most cases means to get back to some rather romantically imagined better situation in the past. Not to permit change, and to undo changes caused by humans, reconstruction of habitats, even though they were modified by nature during the natural process of evolution, seems to be the guideline of our time. Conservative theology is quite well united with this Zeitgeist. But this Zeitgeist itself is a contradiction of evolution. The evolving creation does not allow for a world that has come to a standstill. Answers are not to be sought in a past to which we cannot return. Though we have to build on what the past has brought forth into our present, return, *re*-form,[53] is not possible. Theology cannot return to an initial perfect state. To state it bluntly, the theology of the apostles is not necessarily the best possible theology for our time. It is not the best possible proclamation in the present state of God's evolving creation. Practically, regress would be blind to the ongoing revelation manifested through God's ongoing creation.

To be taken seriously, theologians will have to work with current knowledge about this universe, which they believe to be created by God. The scientific community will make this information accessible. (See figure 5.) Theologians are in no better position than other human beings to have reliable information about the universe, God's creation. The universe itself must be studied, and science does this professionally. We orient ourselves in this world with the help of the scientific community. Its information will certainly not cover all we can know. There are other forms of knowing, for example, through poetry and art. But science, as science, ultimately has the advantage of offering a fully communicable and, to a very large extent, verifiable range of knowledge.

Naturally, we might idealize here too much. The history of science has proven that seemingly valid scientific theories and paradigms can be shown later to be wrong and then replaced or modified by new ones. But as will be shown in succeeding chapters, the overwhelming evidence from all fields of

Figure 5   Modern image of the world: photograph of the deep sky, taken by the Hubble telescope. In an unimaginable vast space about fifty billion galaxies are dispersed; their distribution does not indicate order, though local moments of order emerge within the galaxies. This order is comparable to what one sees when dust on a disk is rotated. Might this be the commencing of order in the universe? *Reprinted by permission of NASA.*

science makes it clear that God's creation is a dynamic, evolving world. Thus the credibility of a theology can be questioned. Michael Buckley commented, "And when a philosophic or theological conclusion does not explain reality, but explains it away or contradicts something unquestionably established, the premises under which the inquiry was constructed become problematic."[54]

An essential point for theology is that the creation stories do not offer definite knowledge about the physical world. Moreover, in science the earlier is by no means the more reliable. As new insights are offered, the newer seems to be the truer. And as evolution produces new knowledge, new truths are introduced into the universe. Here ontologically, too, the newer seems to be truer.

If these consequences of the fact of evolution as God's way to create are correct, then evidently the biblical revelation should be reread in the context of this changing universe. And the newer reading would be truer than the original reading. In an evolving universe the classical statement of Tertullian should then read: *id verius quod posterius*.

This change of perception can create quite a shock in theology. The importance of the biblical text as the source of theology changes from absolute to relative. Since God is the Creator of an ongoing story of creation, it is hard to understand how revelation would suddenly stop at a certain point in time. The Bible, without losing its value as the source document of God speaking to humans, has itself a place within the story of creation. The challenge is for theologians to study this new environment of the biblical text that has barely been explored. The experience and teaching of the church fathers, though valuable, can no longer hold the same kind of authority they held for many centuries.

Even more, there seems to be no possibility of having a definite Christian doctrine formulated once and for all. Pope Pius XII was quite justified in his fears for *unchangeable* dogmas. Some formulations would seem unacceptable in an evolving creation. The resistance to the notion of an evolving universe from the Christian churches therefore is seen to be quite understandable. For example, narrow interpretations of the doctrine of infallibility as a general and timeless notion are incompatible with the creation in which we find ourselves.

Taking evolution seriously forces theology and humankind in general to refrain from fixing truths in unchangeable doctrines. The time for an unleashed relativism has not arrived. But we will have to learn to accept the revelation that comes to us from God through the ongoing creation. As the universe itself has reached only a provisional state, theology must recognize itself as provisional in its historical formulations.

A dilemma appears: theologically on the one hand, we engage the whole person, even the whole of humanity, in the faith we confess, *nulla salus extra ecclesiam* or *nulla salus extra Christum* (outside the church/ Christ there is no salvation), and we often cannot avoid extrapolating to statements that engage and concern the whole universe.[55] On the other hand, we must recognize today that our generalizations in theology are subject to constant revision and can contain some error. Even more, to cling adamantly in an evolving creation to once-formulated expressions of faith might become a way of being unfaithful to that very faith. Not respecting God's ongoing revelation in creation could be a misdeed of which theologians become guilty.

Theologians, in trying to interpret an ongoing revelation as representatives of their churches and as teachers of future pastors, are confronted with a dilemma: on the one hand, they are asked to instruct their students in the accepted teaching of their church, and on the other hand, they must integrate new revelation into the church's theology. As a possible result theologians might end teaching, at least to a certain degree, a deviant theology, taking the risk of hurting themselves and the church. But there is hardly a way to avoid such a risk. The church is called to proclaim the faith in a clear and intelligible message. People just do not build their lives on a poorly stated doctrine. To say "perhaps we are saved in Christ" makes the Christian faith useless to establish a worldview. The church must always state what it wants to have proclaimed in its name. When somebody teaches other than what the church believes it should teach, then a break is inevitable.

Tensions will exist if theology is done in a way that respects the evolving structure of God's creation. New truth does not shine like a brilliant light; it can make its appearance as a heresy, as Teilhard stated in his diary before 1920. Unfortunately, this statement is not reversible. Not all of today's heresies will be the truths of tomorrow. Each will have to make its case. Truths do not become acceptable through syllogisms or algorithms as in mathematics. Studies of paradigm shifts that have occurred in the history of science make it clear that, for vital truths concerned with a new way of seeing, people will have to first adopt the new point of view. The people to be convinced will have to change before they can see. Given normal human inertia, preachers of a newly found truth will come upon hard times, especially in churches that teach the traditional doctrines.[56] Innovators may be the theologians of the future, but as long as their teaching continues to be a new truth, they will be more or less ostracized in the church communities. They may find isolated groups who support them, but they will probably have to suffer from the resistance of churches not ready to accept the new view. It is a question not only of finding a new vision but also of standing up for it. The history of the churches shows that the new truth will be accepted only if people live concretely in the world of accepted dogmas and yet suffer to keep it before others. This seems to be the only viable way to keep the truth alive and have the church community finally accept it.

Truth is only in a very restricted sense a question of epistemology. Though arguments will help to make the truth acceptable, they are rarely sufficient when questions of faith are concerned. Therefore, theologians and their theology will generally be in tension with the hierarchy of churches, which tend to protect doctrinal standpoints. One might even question theologians who never have difficulties with their church hierarchy with regard to their being open to incoming new revelations in God's creation. Theologians and churches must deal with this issue in new and more creative ways as they reflect seriously on creation as evolving. Churches will be forced to accept theologians who try new ways. Innovative theologians will not be accepted immediately, but churches will gradually learn to tolerate and not excommunicate[57] them by administrative means. Theologians will learn that few definitive doctrines might not become obsolete in the future, at least to some degree. Moreover, they must be ready to admit errors in theology. In an evolving world the human species alone, including theologians, can distance itself from its errors. Churches and theologians should be open to two possibilities: the heretics of today may be the teachers of tomorrow, the *doctores ecclesiae,* or they could just as well be the heretics, even the repentant heretics, of tomorrow.

Theologians and church officials eventually will be forced to become aware of this situation. Each must respect the rights and responsibilities of the other. Then theology will develop in an atmosphere of freedom, and church officials will not prematurely reject the work of theologians. Showing more confidence in the action of the Holy Spirit, who was promised to assist the church and to maintain it in the truth, will be necessary. At times in the past, church administrators have behaved as if they felt obliged to organize the activities of the Holy Spirit. A good model used by Orthodox churches is to permit the Holy Spirit to decide a case: if a new teaching is valid, it will survive; otherwise it will soon be forgotten. Ultimately, the message is for the church to take seriously the teaching of the Holy Spirit in God's ongoing creation.

Theology in an evolving world is going through a fundamental mutation from holding an unchanging deposit of faith to receiving an ever-renewed revelation through God's self-disclosure in creation. As we have seen, doctrines—at least to some degree—become relativized. New theological insights are always preliminary and need witnesses. They might become tomorrow the teaching of the church, or they might end in the storeroom for past errors. The church should learn to let the Holy Spirit decide.

But faced with this inevitable dogmatic relativism, we have to ask if there are limits to it.

THE LIMITS OF RELATIVISM IN CHRISTIAN THEOLOGY

Theologians have developed many methods to avoid total relativism. Rudolf Bultmann's demythologizing approach used science as a criterion to delimit myths from reality to make room for faith,[58] and then some of his followers even did away with the resurrection and interpreted it as the fact that the work of Jesus is not finished but goes on. Our approach differs from Bultmann's in that we do not accept science as an ultimate criterion of the possible or the impossible. The history of the universe is full of facts unexplained by science.[59] These gaps in our understanding should not be used as an argument for the existence of God (that would be a return to the God of the gaps); on the other hand, these gaps cannot be closed by the postulate that science will deliver full explanations for everything in the future.[60] This universe does not exclude divine action in history. Therefore, Bultmann's approach is of limited help for establishing a workable theology.

A quasi-contrary approach to Bultmann is taken by Karl Barth, who centers his theology on the self-revelation of God in Christ. Taking hardly any notice of the created universe—only philosophical-theological personalists such as Martin Buber play an important part in his thinking—Barth's theology is resolutely Christocentric. For Barth, creation is to be understood "on a special or exclusively theological level that is inaccessible to any critique by the natural sciences, for example, as an interpretation of the first two chapters of the Bible."[61] To situate our own way of proceeding within the wide spectrum of approaches offered by theologians such as Karl Rahner,[62] Thomas F. Torrance,[63] Bernard Lonergan,[64] and Nancey Murphy,[65] not to mention the wide spectrum of exegetical methods, would require a separate volume. It should be clear that our approach is not a deductive one. Such an approach might begin with the fact of revelation, apart from its content, and explore what this implies about God.

We will take an approach similar to that of theologians such as Wolfhart Pannenberg and Arthur Peacocke. Both have strong apologetic accents that try to show that theology satisfies "the criteria of reasonableness that lead us to infer the best explanation of the broader features of the natural world"[66] or to answer the question "of whether on the basis of the biblical idea of God the entirety of reality in which we live reveals itself more comprehensively than on other presuppositions."[67] Both stress the information coming from science as of great importance and even as a criterion of the possible. Peacocke makes an effort to show that the resurrection of Jesus accords with the reasonable scientific understanding of emerging realities like life and consciousness.[68]

On the other hand, we try to avoid this apologetic stance because we do not share a belief in science's unlimited capacity to make everything understandable. Science cannot know about incarnation or resurrection, as it cannot know about creation. God's action by its very nature escapes the possibility of scientific testing. Theology cannot expect from the sciences a confirmation that this world is created. Faith is based not on science, but on the authority of revelation. ἡ πίστις ἐξ ἀκοῆς: *Faith comes from what is heard* (Rom. 10:17). Faith is in search of understanding; in our understanding, the task of the theologian is not to make the world known by science more comprehensible. Rather, the task is to understand the world known by science as creation, as the work of God. In a changing understanding of the world there will be a changed understanding of the action of God creating this world. We have shown that theology will always be tarnished by a certain relativism.

But in our opinion this cannot be a limitless relativism, making the relative capacity of reason the strict criterion of acceptability of the teachings of Christian faith.[69]

Therefore, the theology we propose is always based on faith. There are not limitless possibilities of doing away with traditional doctrine. All religions have some core, which cannot be given up without giving up the religion itself. This applies as well to Christian faith. Though many issues in traditional doctrine need revision, some limits cannot be transgressed. We cannot define the limits by using an outside criterion, such as discussing the scientific possibility of the resurrection of Christ. Such a unique historical event cannot be proven or disproven by science. Thus we cannot make a statement about what is the core of our faith based on any proof. We must turn to authority.[70]

Following the tradition of the fathers of the church, a traditional trustworthy authority is Thomas Aquinas, who states, "Our faith consists principally in two things: first indeed in the true knowledge of God . . . and second in the mystery of the incarnation of Christ."[71] This statement seems to be a simple description of the most basic content of Christian faith. Neither of the two propositions can be dropped: our recognition of God as the Creator, whose identity is taught to us by the Bible, and that in Jesus, the Logos become man, salvation has come to all human beings and to the universe. These two points can under no circumstances be abandoned without ceasing to be a Christian. One might believe in God and hold on to Jesus as an exemplary human being, but this belief would not be Christian faith.

If we accept the statement of Aquinas on the hard core of Christian faith, we have a stable basis for doing theology. It should be evident that this core can be exposed continually to challenges by the ongoing creation and revelation. Theologians must respond to these challenges by showing that the new revelation does not eliminate the reality of the Creator and the Savior, but enlarges and advances the vision of our faith. Either God and the Christ will appear greater in the newly revealed creation, or Christianity will come to an end. The task of believing theologians is to clarify the relation of the universe, humanity, and other Christians to the Creator and the Christ.

SUMMARY

Starting with the traditional statement that theology is *fides quaerens intellectum*, we realized that this means reflecting on the revealed truth within the horizon of the universe, which faith confesses to be God's creation. Historically, as was shown especially in reference to the Middle Ages, theology has followed this rule through the centuries, losing its grip on the realities of creation only during the last 150 years. Theology now must adopt a new view, in which this evolving universe is perceived as the continued self-revelation of the Creator. We elaborated the relativizing effect of this change on the formulation of dogmas and finally contrasted with the core of the Christian faith, which escapes relativizing and which will be held as given truth throughout this text. Having laid this groundwork, we may now address the concrete interpretation of the universe as God's creation.

2 THE UNIVERSE AS PROCESS OF BECOMING: GOD'S CREATION

While philosophizing or religionizing scientists have recently presented proofs of the Creator, theology offers a tradition that excludes proofs of God's existence. This chapter is not about such proofs; we try instead to read the "book of nature" in order to understand the work of the Creator. Turning to creation, we are confronted with the lack of a generally accepted *Weltbild*. Therefore, we describe in a short sketch the history of the universe as far as it is known. This history is not self-explanatory; we have to look for features that permit a coherent description. We show the often advanced "quantitative" argument to be unreasonable if used as a criterion to understand evolution. Reversing Tertullian's statement to *id verius quod posterius*, we posit the human being as the key to understanding the universe. Starting from human experience, we find the becoming of unities as a basic feature of the evolutionary process. Analysis of the process of union at different levels reveals a first parameter for understanding the orientation of the process of becoming. Thus union appears as a first quality of God's way of creation.

PROOFS OF GOD'S EXISTENCE?

In recent years scientists have written a growing number of books that develop cosmological perspectives. Most of them offer reflections on theological matters.[1] The most prominent, though much less provocative than it was meant to be, is the concluding passage in Stephen Hawking's *A Brief History of Time*, where he exposes the final goal of his dream of a theory of everything:

> If we do discover a complete theory, it should in time be understandable in broad principle by everyone, not just a few scientists. Then we shall all, philosophers, scientists, and just ordinary people, be able to take part in the discussion of why it is that we and the universe exist. If we find the answer to that, it would be the ultimate triumph of human reason—for then we would truly know the mind of God.[2]

This presumptuous statement, along with Hawking's prediction of the end of theoretical physics within five years, has found manifold echoes within the world of science, whereas theologians have hardly turned their attention to it. One exception is the discussions led cooperatively by the Vatican Observatory and the Center for Theology and the Natural Sciences[3] at Berkeley. An interesting point in all these discussions is their focus on the question of proof of God's existence. The notion of God presented in the discussions is similar to that of physico-theologians of the seventeenth and eighteenth centuries, whose God worked like a craftsperson and designer, or like Newton's clockmaker, who from time to time had to set the works right.[4] What Theodosius Dobzhansky named the God of the gaps[5] and declared dead reappears in the writings of modern scientists. For most of them the central question seems to be about a beginning. The Big Bang, in 1952 prematurely claimed by Pius XII as a demonstration that the world is created by God, is nowadays, for many scientists, the point where they want to prove or disprove that God exists.

This discussion among scientists seems rather meaningless. Little is shown about God's existence or nonexistence if the Big Bang, which is situated in time, is proven to be the beginning of time as we know it. At least theoretically and speculatively, the Big Bang could have a "natural" explanation. For example, tapering off the time-space cone at a radius of 10^{-33} centimeters allows for a finite universe without a beginning. In human thought there is no possibility of ending the chain of causes without referring to an eternal existence. Every scientific, causal explanation of the beginning of the universe confronts us with the same problem that Thales of Miletus could not solve. When asked by a boy on what the earth rests, he told him: "On the back of a turtle." And on what does the turtle stand? On another turtle, and so on and on. Exasperated, Thales finally stated, "It's turtles all the way down."[6] Scholastic theology knew quite well that there is no proof for or against the eternity of the world, nor did it see in this lack of proof a reason to question the fact that God created the world. Thomas Aquinas considered it a question of faith, not a question of proof. This did not hinder him, as is well known, from offering five ways to demonstrate the existence of God. His demonstrations, however, never referred to *creatio ex nihilo* (creation out of nothing) or to a beginning of the world.[7]

A more central theological question to be asked concerning the scientifically known world and the cosmic process is, How in the eyes of faith[8] does the Creator become visible through creation? The theologian may try to answer the question *Does God exist?*[9] But this question belongs to the prolegomena of theology. For the theologian this question is already answered positively. The central theological question to be answered is, How does God appear in this world, God's creation? The point is not to prove God exists, but to see the Creator in what Teilhard de Chardin used to call *God's Diaphany*.

To try to see God through God's creation, we can look closer at the universe in which we live, not only with a few general statements, but in some general detail. For the scientist the facts are known, but for the majority of theologians concrete knowledge about them is limited. We find in newer manuals on the theology of creation[10] broad discussions about nature conceived as God's perfect creation disturbed by humanity. Some generalizations can be misunderstood, for example, an open universe (Moltmann) with little attention given to the concrete universe that science discovers in ever greater detail. Therefore, to discuss a theology of creation of the universe, we cannot escape the need to sketch at least some details about this universe in which we live.

A BRIEF VIEW OF THE UNIVERSE

There are many accessible descriptions of the universe. Although most scientists agree on the story after the first 10^{-33} seconds,[11] their difficulties are linked to understanding what happened before, especially when at the Planck-time of 10^{-43} seconds the laws of physics no longer apply. That is the status quo in physics. But at present there seems little doubt that after *The First Three Minutes*,[12] the history of the universe can be explained as a continuous expansion of matter, forming galaxies, stars, and finally planets.

Opinions diverge regarding the beginning of the universe itself and about the various ways to explain the whole process of expansion. It turns out to be more a question of personal convictions and often unsupported speculations than the result of verified data integrated into a general theory. Models differ depending on a commitment to strict determinism or to growing insight coming from chaos theory. This theory concludes that there is no possibility of seeing clearly into the future of the universe, since there is no way to gain perfect knowledge of the status in the beginning of a dynamic system such as the universe. The theory shows further that the slightest difference in the conditions at the beginning can make enormous differences in the future. Thus the background radiation in the universe, for many years measured at 2.73° K everywhere around us—a fact that made the understanding of galaxies difficult—has shown a very slight irregularity of about one-millionth of a degree as measured by COBE.[13] This slight irregularity may allow for the formation of galaxies.

Many points in the history of the universe are not fully understood, but there is little doubt left that the story is real. It started some ten to twenty billion years ago.[14] Its story includes narrow allowable limits for a number of important physical constants in the cosmos, which permit the world to be as we know it. Observations of these extremely sensitive values of physical constants have led to what is known today as the anthropic cosmological principle.[15] A slight deviation from one of these values—especially the Coulomb constant and the gravity constant—would have prevented formation and evolution of the universe as we know it and from which we have evolved. Since there is no known reason why these values are what they are, one might be inclined to invoke the argument from divine design. But this would once more introduce the God of the gaps: filling in our ignorance by introducing God into the world. The gaps may support one's faith. But that horizon of understanding belongs rather to the physico-theology of the eighteenth century, and this kind of natural theology carries within it, as Michael Buckley[16] has shown consistently, the germ of modern atheism.

The classical scholastic vision of order in the universe, found in texts of the Pentateuch as the work of six days, was based on the text from the Wisdom of Solomon 11:20: "You have arranged all things by measure and number and weight."[17] (See figure 6.) It explained the presence of order in nature and inspired the Scholastics to search for this order everywhere. They came up with an interpretation of the world in which everything except human free will was ruled by strict determinism. Modern science has no such text on which to build the continued widespread belief in complete predictability once all the data are known. As Ilya Prigogine has stated, predictability was never "more than a theoretical possibility. Yet in some sense this unlimited predictability was an essential element of the scientific picture of the physical world. We may perhaps even call it the *founding myth* of classical science."[18] The all-encompassing order commonly sought by the Scholastics and by modern science has vanished, and today our world is known to be chaotic with some order.

Order is still of high importance for everything we see in the universe, and certainly our own existence is linked to a highly ordered physical system comprising the body and the environment. But if we judge by quantitative parameters, it seems that, on the whole, order is rather an accident in the universe. The ordinary rule is chaos. Most of the original energy contained in the fireball of the Big Bang is stored in featureless background radiation. Only one part in a billion of the energy present in the original universe became matter as we encounter it, as particles having mass. True, it is still enough to form the impressive multitude of billions of galaxies. But overall it is actually just one part in a billion. Thus matter is rather exceptional in the universe, and it seems preposterous to build a theory of the universe on the knowledge of an exceptional part of it. On the other hand, to study the rest of the universe, that is, the background radiation, seems rather dull for the long run despite the interesting irregularities recently discovered by COBE.

The explosive beginning of the universe, although not an event in time, is by analogy looked on as an event creating time-space.[19] During the first

Figure 6   The Creator at work as seen by the Middle Ages: creating the Ptolemaic world, not the world of the Bible. The compass is a hint that everything is created according to number, measure, and weight. Miniature from the Bible moralise, thirteenth century. (Vienna: Nationalbibliothek, Cod. 2554, fol. 1). *Reprinted by permission of Deutsches Museum, München.*

period of about one hundred thousand years, one would have observed, if able to do so, a simple expansion of matter, primarily protons, alpha particles, and electrons, mixed with radiation. Not a very exciting universe, where not much really happened except expansion. After one hundred thousand years or so, radiation decouples from matter, the electrons find the protons and alpha particles to form the chemical elements hydrogen and helium (about 75 percent and 25 percent respectively of the mass of the universe),[20] although the background radiation continues to expand. After two billion years of expansion we observe a rather dull universe: nothing has happened, at least nothing causing any change in composition. The matter is still expanding hydrogen and helium. Thanks to infinitesimal deviations from homogeneity in the background radiation, expanded centers of accumulation of matter occur. These centers of mass and, consequently, of gravitational force act more and more as local centers of gravity. Within these clouds of matter (their formation is still not really understood) more local centers of gravity form, which eventually become stars.

A process of nuclear fusion within the stars brings forth new elements: first helium, then carbon, and finally iron. Having reached this last level, the fusion process ends, and the stars reach a final stage as white, or eventually brown, dwarfs. Fortunately, the young galaxies contained numerous giant stars, fast burning and imploding violently after expending their fuel. Heavier elements beyond iron in the periodic table of elements were created in the explosions, while the rest of the stars survived as neutron stars, in which electrons are absorbed into protons, or into a black hole by the force of gravitation. We can be grateful for the explosions, which appear in the sky as fireballs called supernovae, because without them a great number of elements necessary for life would not exist. The process is not very orderly, but out of the accumulated debris evolved more diversified systems such as our own solar system with its planets. The diversified composition of billions of these solar systems should not obscure the fact that less than 1 percent of the matter in the universe is other than helium or hydrogen. For the last fifteen or more billion years, except for less than 1 percent of one part in a billion of its original energy, the universe has been rather monotonous.

Before we consider the "quantitative" argument, we turn away from what might be described as macrophenomena, as described above, to microphenomena. These are relative notions depending on what is taken into consideration. On smaller scales we do not find the same monotony in time. We observe an accelerating sequence of events: the formation of the isotopes of the ninety-two elements, the formation of simple molecules and macromolecules, the appearance and evolution of life, and the appearance of thought in the universe. The story is marked by the emerging of points of order sustained by some structure.[21] Evolution can be seen as creating more and more order. Humans in every age have recognized this element of order, and more often than not they have declared order to be sacrosanct.[22] But this seems to be in contradiction with the very notion of evolution, as we shall see in more detail later.[23] An order established for all time would permit sure projection into the future, but that is not possible. The evolutionary events tell a long story, which unfolds in retrospect, but whose next chapter cannot be known in prospective, let alone the end of the story. We may state confidently only that by the known laws of thermodynamics, this universe with at least one living planet will not be functional forever.

Thus the evolutionary history of the universe is open-ended in its continuation: we do not know, at least not by studying the past, where it will go. But it appears in the long run to be the prisoner of entropy. At least this is the judgment of science, a judgment that some scientists try to escape by wild speculations.[24] Though evolution is real, it somehow seems to be in constant contradiction to the entropic universe. This dilemma between an order-creating ongoing evolution and an order-destroying entropy does not permit a clear answer to the meaning of the universe. Entropy points to a meaningless universe, while evolution—at least on the human level—has brought forth a quest for the meaning of human beings. One solution to this dilemma often advanced is based on what can be called the "quantitative" argument.

THE QUANTITATIVE ARGUMENT

Some people have been educated to consider the opinion of the majority as the valid law deciding between good and bad. Democracy is based, they think, on the belief that what the majority of the people do is the right thing. According to this stance, there are no respected values in anything but the ones accepted by the majority and that eventually must be respected by everyone. Every individual will not be limited to these values; individual value systems are allowed as long as one does not try to impose them on others. The greater number makes for law, but it leaves wide open the question of the validity of the voted value system. This is not the place to analyze any further the validity of the democratic system of imposing values on a society, but it certainly instills in us a high respect for the greater number, the greater quantity. This is not to say that we had to await democracy to be stunned when confronted with great numbers.

Ever since the discovery of the ever-growing vastness of the universe and the quantitative insignificance of the planet earth in the world of billions of galaxies, we have been confronted with the argument that in the universe life is like a mold on a grain of dust lost in space, and especially that humans are totally insignificant in this world. Similar statements are made on a purely biological level concerning the relative biomass of humans and bacteria, the latter being declared the really successful feature in the kingdom of life.[25] As a quantitative statement it is factually correct, but is it significant in the evolving world? The question to be answered is: In the evolution of the universe is quantity the most striking feature and most significant parameter? To answer this question, we need to have a closer look at the history of the universe, using the parameter of quantity, and to explore how it relates to the evolutionary process.

If we look at the early universe with its soup of equal amounts of matter and antimatter, which annihilate one another into energetic massless photons radiating into space[26]—that is at least the postulate of most theories—only one part in a billion of this original universe becomes matter. The bulk of the early universe becomes background radiation. If we draw a Gaussian curve, matter would hardly be visible. Its existence would need to be put many standard deviations[27] away from the mean. Statistically, the material universe of mass particles would be considered as not existing. If we look at the material universe itself, we see a similar type of distribution. More than 99 percent is composed of hydrogen and helium, and all the other more than ninety naturally occurring elements make up less than 1 percent of the matter of the universe. Statistically, all elements besides hydrogen and helium quantitatively are reduced to insignificance. Moreover, a very small percentage of atoms ever enter into molecular combination: the overwhelming mass never gets any farther than into a star, becoming part of a white or brown dwarf, a neutron star, or a black hole. Furthermore, molecules are not of quantitative significance in the universe of atoms. Among the molecules only very few ever enter a macromolecular structure. Thus from a quantitative perspective, macromolecules are not successful and therefore not significant. If we look into the world of macromolecules, a certain number enter into living structures, which represent a very small part of material reality, and we know about these structures only on this planet. Thus far no traces of life have been found in outer space, although amino acids[28] have been found in tectites. In the realm of life, the bulk of mass is represented by bacteria; the eukaryotic protozoa are comparatively negligible. But they in turn easily exceed the mass of metazoa. And so we can go on to vertebrates, mammals, and finally human beings. Wherever we see something new appear on the stage of evolution in the universe, it represents a statistically insignificant amount as compared to the realm out of which it arose. (See figure 7.)

If those who use a quantitative argument were serious, they would turn to the only really overwhelming quantity, namely, the cosmic background radiation. But evidently, nobody is interested in that, except in studies of quantitatively insignificant deviations from perfect homogeneity. In other words, a quantitative consideration tells us one of two things. Either all elements besides hydrogen and helium are negligible—and even these two elements are negligible compared to the background radiation—or quantity is not a feature that tells us much about what is relatively important in the universe. Hence a universe judged according to its quantitative aspects is dull. The above remark often heard, that life is just a mold on a grain of dust in a quasi-infinite universe, belongs to this quantitative kind of evaluation, which gives the highest rank to the dullest aspect of the universe.

We might state conclusively that the quantitative argument can be correct in its data. But to take it seriously as it pertains to the significance of reality leads to the absurd conclusion that evolution is an insignificant matter that should not arouse our interest. In such a universe where quantity is the

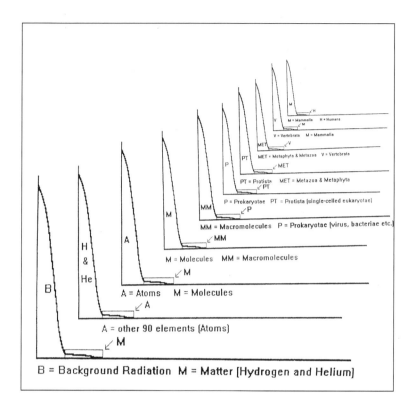

B = Background Radiation M = Matter [Hydrogen and Helium]

Figure 7   If quantity is accepted as the parameter to measure the orientation of evolution or its lack of orientation, one arrives at the paradoxical statement that evolution is a negligible phenomenon. Against the background of the environment, all evolutionary steps are quantitatively without any importance. As schematically shown, evolution is always taking place in the quantitatively negligible region of the general distribution of phenomena. Though some quantity is essential for all evolving realities, otherwise the realities would not be there, their quantity says nothing about their position in an evolutionary distribution that is marked by the appearance of new realities in regions of statistically highly improbable events. To make statements about the orientation of evolution based purely on quantity leads to an erroneous understanding of the evolving reality. It is the quantitative fallacy.

criterion, any research unsupported by the quantitative parameter becomes an anthropocentric enterprise. The selection of this parameter is evidently not necessary, and we feel free not to accept the quantitative argument as serious when value judgments about the orientation of evolution are discussed. We have to search for another key to understand the universe.

Having looked at the universe's history, we have no difficulty in distinguishing periods marked by the local appearance of new realities. As we go back in history, these realities are less and less understood. Methodologically, therefore, the quest for the beginnings as an explanatory basis is not particularly helpful for our understanding of the evolved world. The closer we get to cosmological singularity, when even all the laws of physics lose their meaning, the less we can predict about the future of the universe. The story from the beginning to the rise of the human species could not have been told beforehand; it can be reconstructed only in retrospect. To understand the importance of the physical constants in the universe, the so-called anthropic principle emphasizes that we must first have human existence. These constants, from the point of view of physics, cannot be said to be important, except that they made possible the appearance of life, especially human life.

We can conclude that the classical explanation of our world, starting with its beginnings, does not offer an adequate understanding of what is happening. The potential of the methodology is neither visible nor determinable except in retrospect. Instead of starting with the beginning and yearning for some indescribable wave function of the universe that explains it all, following Hawking and many contemporary cosmologists, we propose that a better methodology is to begin with the latest known product of the universe in evolution. This end product is accessible to us, and we know it in one case, at least from the inside, namely, ourselves, as well as from the outside in many cases, namely, in other human beings. It is more reasonable to start with the known than with the unknown.

THE HUMAN AS THE KEY TO UNDERSTANDING THE UNIVERSE

To start from the human being instead of the beginning—as the biblical text, the creation myths, and the scientific cosmologies do—is quite a different approach. It is justified only if the evolutionary process is real, if it brings forth newness in the sense that the new is not contained in the preceding realities. It is the practical consequence of the axiom that the later has more truth than the earlier, that *id verius quod posterius*.

To choose the human being as point of departure might provoke an allegation that this would be an anthropocentric approach.[29] It is, but it is also true that the mere allegation is not an argument against using the approach: it says nothing about the validity of using the human to understand the universe as an evolutionary process. Since this process is time-structured and follows the arrow of time and, according to Dollo's law,[30] excludes reversibility, there is no retrograde evolution from the elephant to the amoeba. There is good reason then to look at the latest product.

The question what is a human being has no easy answer. As far as we can look back in the history of philosophy, this question has always remained open. Nevertheless, we can state that, as far as we know, humans are the only beings in the universe able to ask such a question and to inquire about the universe. Humans alone are not limited by their senses in their perception of the world; they can supply instruments that go beyond their biological limits.[31] And humans can think beyond the limits of the universe, though they have their own physical limitations and are limited by the time cones of perception.[32] This seems to be the rule in physics as long as nonlocality has not been mastered as a carrier of information, a task of rather speculative character and impossible according to the known laws of physics. But within their own time cones, open to both past and future, there seems to be no limit to human exploration and projection. So we may state with confidence that the human being manifests properties that are not found elsewhere in the universe as far as the sciences have explored it.

All philosophies and religions have assumed the special role and place of the human. They often developed a dualistic view of the human being as a composite of body and soul.[33] The body submits to the temporality of decaying matter, but the soul is linked to the eternity of the heavenly and the divine. The rejection of death as final, expressed in these myths, seems to be one of the earliest manifestations of the emergence of the truly human. The funeral rites of Neanderthals document this belief in survival beyond the tomb for at least the last two hundred thousand years. This confidence in survival translated itself into soul stories that are still far from being understood from within our present experience.

Research on the brain has taught us much about deficiencies in mental activity caused by brain lesions. In a dualistic perspective some have proposed to understand the brain as the organ linking body and soul. Others have identified the soul with the mind, which is declared an epiphenomenon.[34] Another proposal sees the brain and the mind as a complementary unity, the one not existing without the other within our concrete human reality.[35] Contemporary science, fascinated with matter, hardly allows for a realistic dualism in the human being as it has been proposed by most religions and within the Christian tradition. The latter tradition has struggled for centuries to overcome the problem by making the soul the form or active principle of the body-soul dualism (*anima forma corporis*). But the Augustinian belief in a soul immediately created by God—a belief credited with *de fide* qualifications by Catholic theologians for many centuries[36]—has not been abandoned. It led to the concept of animals without rational souls being subordinated to strict natural laws guiding every step they made. This perception culminated in the concept of the animal-machine (Descartes), which influenced the sciences into our time. Since Darwin, and before him Linnaeus, had classified humans among the primates, the concept of animal-machine was extended to the human animal. This was, and still is, one of the barriers that impede theologians from accepting evolution's being extended to the human race.

On the other hand, evidence of the evolutionary origin of humans has become so overwhelming that the refusal to think of and to describe the human being within this evolving world seems unreasonable. The humans to whom God is speaking through revelation were created by evolution. This is true not only for the body, but also for the whole thinking, knowing, artistic, creative, believing, and adoring human being. The human is not a stranger to this earth, whose soul comes from another world. The human emerged as *homo sapiens*, and indeed *religiosus*, in the evolutionary process; we can search human history in order to understand the process and to investigate the creation aspect of this process.

The human self-experience of being integrated in self-consciousness permits the human being to experience herself or himself as a someone who is distinguished from and relates to the rest of the world. In experiencing this unity we know well our body parts. When speaking about ourselves, we know we are more than the sum of hands, feet, eyes, and brains. We know we are not just our parts. Losing a limb does not destroy our unity, though we may be diminished. I can hurt my finger, but if someone hits my finger, he or she hits me. We experience ourselves as a centered unity, which we usually identify as the person we are, and on the human level we are typically called by name. Calling someone by name does not address any of his or her parts but the whole person. At the same time we know we are a composite: our fingers can hurt us.

Thus we experience ourselves as unified centers composed of multiple parts that belong essentially to us. This polarity between parts and center seems to be one constituent of human beings brought about during the long process of evolution and whose past history may be explored. How did our experienced unity come to be? Was it created specifically as the human being from scratch, or were there preceding stages?

UNITY AND THE CREATION OF UNITY AS BASIC ASPECTS OF EVOLUTION

If we look back in history, we realize that species that have preceded ours are by no means totally distinct from us. They have features that we recognize in ourselves. The anatomy of the great apes, who like humans are classified today by taxonomists as primates, is very close to ours. In pre-Christian times, when investigation of the human corpse was taboo,[37] Galen learned and taught human anatomy by dissecting apes. Moreover, the similarity goes beyond anatomy: we recognize clear behavioral traits as our own. Respect for the property of others among chimpanzees,[38] sanctioning of asocial behavior,[39] the ability to learn to master complicated and abstract tasks,[40] and even to master simple concepts as symbols[41]—all these behavioral traits have been shown in the research of ethologists during recent decades. Accepting animals as instinct-guided machines had to be abandoned. They are different from us humans. They are not artists and they do not believe in life after death, but they act as unified beings. They relate the world to themselves, and they act with purpose. Certainly, their world is limited to what they perceive with their senses, and they are unable to overcome the limits of these senses. Nevertheless, we see in our biological ancestors the reality of unified, centered beings at their own level of life. One clear difference, besides the lack of abilities already mentioned, is the limit set in the radius of their field of action. This limitation is linked to their awareness and understanding of what they perceive. For example, the chimpanzee or any other animal sees the moon as a shining source of light up in the sky, not the mass of rocks we know it to be.

When we look into the past, we see centered living beings with a limited radius of perception. They share with us to a certain degree a perceived world, but not the totality of what we can see.[42] This statement is certainly true not only for our immediate relatives in the family of primates, but also for a great number of animals with which we are able to communicate. They behave as centers with a limited radius of perception, which might be overcome by our influence. For example, dogs seem very close to their owners, and there seems to be something more than pure instinct in their friendly behavior and playfulness. They are to some degree able to relate to the human person. Even lions, who consider humans in the wild as prey or enemies, are able to follow their trainers in a circus. The point to be made is that they behave not as automatons but as individuals who know the world within the radius of their perception and know what they want to do. Within the realm of mammals we have no difficulty seeing this centered unified behavior: obviously, they see their environment and situate themselves within it according to the radius of their perception.[43]

The farther we get back into the past, the more the radius of perception regresses. For example, blackbirds do not seem to be able to see worms and insects that are not moving. A similar example is found with snakes that can see only a moving target. We can follow that line of regression back to a very low level. Naturally, it would be an error to draw one unique straight line backward. It appears rather that on all levels we find a great number of realizations of similar radii of perception, some developing into a special direction that finally appears to be closed. On the level of mammals we find specializations into definite lines of no return. For example, among the family of horses, some become more and more specialized runners. In the line of birds, we find hummingbirds that are perfect nectar collectors but without any visible further evolution in that line. The realm of insects is filled with specialists, which are highly adapted to their niches, but which seem hardly able to evolve further. All of them, however, are unified entities within their world and have their defined radii of action.

If we go farther back in time, the mammals and vertebrates disappear and so do the insects some time earlier. In the very early stages we are confronted with sea anemones, sea lilies, and jellyfish: colonies of cells forming some kind of unity, without being as completely unified as a dog. The full unity is only in the cell, although the remainder is more or less united in a structure. If we go even farther back, we find only eukaryotic cells at the highest level of evolution. They behave as unities toward their outside and are able to respond to their environment by learning within the radius of their perception. Simple learning behavior at this level has been observed. If we go even farther back to the level of bacteria, behavior is like a living unity within its environment. Small as they are, bacteria still are clearly limited to their environment and act as a unity on that environment, though the radius of action is limited.

If we go back still farther, we find macromolecules that have their own structural unity and can act, for example, as enzymes do on their environment. They fold and unfold in adapting, but they do not reach out actively to their environment. Within an organism these macromolecules actively move and are moved in many different ways.[44] They are passive if left on their own, and if exposed to some heat may easily fall apart, losing their unity.

Scaling farther down to simple molecules, we find composites that may react as a unit with their environment in the right conditions. An example of this level occurs when an acid like HCl meets calcium carbonate and forms a series of other units (CO_2, H_2O, $CaCl_2$). On this level the radius of action on the environment is limited to a very short range. Each unit acts gravitationally as well as with the field around it. For any effective action on its environment, closeness by touch is the rule. Molecules need the closeness of touch to interact, and thus the radius of action is close to zero.

The same is valid for the still more elementary units we encounter from the beginning of the universe: atoms, which show a clearly differentiated behavior in their interaction with one another. Each atom is clearly distinguishable from any other. Today's tunneling microscopes[45] even make "visible" the singular atom so that it may be handled. For many years scientists believed there would be no further element to look for beyond atoms. But the atoms decayed, and only the simplest one, hydrogen, with its single-proton nucleus seems at present to be time-resistant to decomposition.

Neutrons, which are stabilized within the atoms, have a relatively short lifetime if left on their own as they decay into a proton and an electron, plus a number of particles such as the neutrino. Beyond the neutron, proton, and electron, which make up the bulk of the known mass of the universe, are a number of particles now grouped in three families.[46] The protons and neutrons are each composed of three smaller particles called quarks,[47] which for the proton are characterized as two up and one down, and for the neutron one up and two down.[48] Four other quarks are rare and not very stable. An extremely heavy top quark,[49] which may have been detected recently, with mass of approximately a gold atom or several billion electron volts, does not appear in ordinary matter.

Though numerous particles such as the muon and the tau particle play an important role in stellar processes and cosmic rays, they do not seem to have a role in atomic structures, but they may have a role as causes of chance mutations in living beings. Thus beyond atoms the unity of single particles becomes more elusive and difficult to grasp. For the present the question of the composition of particles making up quarks is open. Within the neutron and the proton, quarks cohere very strongly. So far it does not seem possible to separate them, and scientists anticipate that such an attempt could create another quark plus an antiquark, leaving the proton or neutron unchanged.[50] Therefore, it seems reasonable to stop our retrospective of the earliest unified realities at this point; we know quite well that the numerous particles beyond this limit play an important, though transient, role in the production of stellar energies. We are aware also that stellar energies are responsible for the appearance of the atomic elements and for the development we know as evolution. But only the relatively stabilized elements—protons, neutrons, and electrons—have a lifetime long enough to play any concrete role in the process of evolution beyond the creation of atomic elements.

Our retrospective analysis has found unity to be a feature ascribable to all realities we encounter in the history of evolution. Though this feature is a general mark of everything that has evolved,[51] there are qualitatively distinguishable levels of unity. We shall now try to find levels of unity that allow us to see commonalities in the general process of becoming and then to distinguish these levels of unity by the way they are realized in evolution.

UNION AS THE COMMON FEATURE
OF THE EVOLUTIONARY PROCESS

If we seek common features of evolution leading to new entities that are unified, we do not see the same process continuing over the total period of evolutionary history. Union continues, but the elements forming the union can change as evolution proceeds. Only in a general way, and always respecting changes in the mode of formations, can we speak about union of elements as the foundational process. At the very basic level of proton and neutron we see three quarks forming units, entities, whose properties and stability depend on their composition.[52] The union creates a new reality with properties not present in the earlier particles of the quark-gluon soup. Ever since Planck-time, neutrons and protons along with electrons have an essential part in the evolutionary process, although neutrinos and photons may be the most numerous particles in the universe.

In a next step two protons unite with two neutrons to form an alpha particle that, as in interstellar processes, may include an intermediary stage of deuterium and tritium, two isotopes of hydrogen. Historically, protons and alpha particles are the only[53] important particles with mass that dominate, not only during the early stages of the universe but even today. After the decoupling of radiation from matter about 10^5 years after the beginning of the expansion and the combining of electrons with protons and alpha particles, a second step of union can take place in which atoms are able to combine with other atoms to build higher structures, namely, molecules. In a stellar environment one stage of union takes place, in which protons and neutrons naturally form more and more complex nuclei containing up to ninety-two protons and about the same number of neutrons.[54] These same nuclei now combine with electrons to form atoms.

Whereas the union of protons and neutrons into atomic nuclei permits the formation of more or less stable atoms with their different properties, the union between atoms creates molecules with clearly new properties. For example, the union of two hydrogen atoms and one oxygen atom forms a molecule of water. At this level it becomes evident that the new entity does not arise from a cause containing the new in a hidden way, but the elements unite to form a unique new entity that was not contained in the elements. The elements are a condition for the new reality to emerge, but they do not contain it. The more comes forth from the less. At this level we can grasp the basic process of becoming as a process of union. Quarks unite to form protons and neutrons. Neutrons and protons unite to form nuclei, which can unite with electrons to form atoms. Atoms unite to form simple molecules, which are observed throughout the universe,[55] and which become the elements for macromolecules.

It might be thought that the union of elements into new unities is similar at different levels of becoming, but it turns out that the same type of coherence does not exist everywhere. Gluons, the force of coherence of quarks within the proton and neutron, are described differently from the electromagnetic forces that bind electrons to nuclei. Atoms are bound into new unities by forces generally described as ionic, covalent, or hydrogen bonding.

The scientific description of how these elements combine is not, however, an ultimate explanation of the inner unity they manifest. It explains the unity no more than the nuts and bolts in an engine explain its unity. Means of connection must exist as the necessary condition for union to occur; otherwise the new entity could be deemed a supernatural miracle. These elementary parts, however, do not explain the wholeness of the newly created unity. The whole is more than the sum of its parts. It displays new properties that may not be suspected when we study the parts. This phenomenon becomes even more evident when we observe the primal elements at a higher level of evolution. Nobody could suspect that a carbon atom could have the part it actually has in human thinking within the brain.

Closer to the present, the process of union goes beyond chemical reactions uniting elements into more complex structures such as amino acids, whose origin from an original atmosphere was first demonstrated by the Miller-Urey experiment.[56] There is still no clear understanding of the polymerization of proteins necessary for the origin of life. The most primitive living being we know today is so complex in its structures that we are still unable to reproduce it from its basic elements. But evidently these beings, viruses or similar structures, show a high degree of unity. For a period of time this unity may disappear as the virus integrates itself into a cell and manipulates the cell for its own purposes by transcribing its RNA into the DNA of the cell. Unity is more clearly visible in pre-eukaryotic organisms such as bacteria of all sorts and archaea (or archaebacteria). They all are clearly unified beings, differentiating themselves from and relating to the rest of the universe as unified entities. But we are hard put to indicate what accounts for the unity of a bacterium. The wall surely holds it together; the DNA stores its information; the multiple proteins present inside the wall interact in complex ways. All are necessary for the bacterium to exist, but we do not see the unifying factor, which we call life.

Since science is concerned with such distinguishable components as sugars, phospholipids, and proteins in the cell wall,[57] biologists generally are unable to answer the question What is life? Life exists only with the whole, not with the parts. Life is present through union of the parts that cooperate as if they were under a direction rather than merely reacting on one another. This direction may be seen at work when an organism ingests or eliminates food. And it becomes even more evident when by endosymbiosis of early elements of life, such as bacteria, flagellata, and archaea, the eukaryotic cell arises and exhibits multiple types of behavior, including some kind of learning. The unity created by integration of elements cannot be completely explained by referring to the laws of chemistry, though naturally these laws are still valid and actively adopted by the eukaryotic cell.

We can continue this description of the evolution of ever more highly unified wholes that show new properties not explained by the preexisting elements. Multicellular organisms together behave as a whole, as the organism itself displays a union of ever diversified and specialized cells from brain cells to skin cells. The organism visibly behaves as a whole formed by union of billions of diversified cells. Though we have learned how some of the cells, using certain molecular configurations, form a single organ,[58] the molecules are a means, not the cause, of the unity of the organism. In atoms and molecules we recognize this unity in relatively simple structures, but this is an illusion: we experience these simple realities as unities, but we cannot say what makes their unity. This gap between knowing the means by which the individual reality is held together and what makes its unity, somewhat blurred in the simple elements, becomes more and more evident in living beings. In living beings the principle of unity is called the soul, an entity unknown to science. The fact that most languages use this word expresses well the universal human experience of the unity of any entity as more than just the sum of its parts. This phenomenon is certainly not the only aspect of the evolved unity. As we shall see, life itself evolves into more and more clearly conscious and finally self-conscious, centered beings, which themselves may become elements of a higher structure. We shall return to such phenomena in the next chapter.

So far perhaps we have not insisted enough that union does not destroy the identity of the elements involved in the union. The carbon atom remains a carbon atom even as it is integrated into a neuron of the human brain. Union is not a kind of fusion that eliminates its identity. Rather, this union enhances the identity of the element. By being integrated into a higher unity, elements find a more open future for themselves: only a carbon atom integrated into an amino acid can become part of a protein and finally a part of life and thought. Thus union does not dissolve the elements. As Teilhard de Chardin stated early in this century, union differentiates the elements that are united.

An overview of the evolving process of the universe manifests a phenomenon that is not the only aspect of evolution. But the phenomenon can be followed from the beginning to a point where we find ourselves today as the most evolved creatures within our horizon of knowledge. The following sentence emphasizes this conclusion: *the evolutionary process proceeds by union of elements into higher unities in which something new comes into existence.*

This general statement has to be qualified. As we have seen, the process of unification of elements can differ. Just as "being," the central term of classical metaphysics in a static world, was used analogously, so in an evolving world "union" is again used analogously: means and degrees of unity reached obviously differ. The unity of an atom, to which we do not ascribe a soul, differs from the unity of something living. The universe appears as an evolutionary process of union that brings forth new realities at ever higher levels of being, of unity, starting with the most simple elements and reaching a highest level—at least within the limits of our experience—in humans. What are the implications of this process of union for theologians?

UNION, ONE ASPECT OF GOD'S WAY OF CREATION

If we look at the process of evolutionary becoming as Christian theologians, we perceive this process of evolution as one aspect of God's creation. If the analysis is correct that evolution proceeds by unification of elements into ever higher unities, then Teilhard de Chardin recognized correctly that God creates by unifying. This appears to be a basic aspect of the creation we know. Of course this conclusion cannot be proven by science. On the one hand, we can speak about creation and the Creator because Christians believe that God created this universe. The Creator cannot be proven, or disproven, by science. On the other hand, God's creation obviously has not been so badly done that it requires a visibly constant exterior interference. Either this would make God an object of science because God's constant interferences would need to become part of a competent scientific theory, or it would make science impossible because arbitrary interferences make the search for laws of nature impossible. The interest of theologians is not here: they look at the universe as God's evolving creation to learn from it about God. By reading the ongoing process as God's self-revelation, theologians can reach a deeper understanding of God's intention in creation. Through divine works God makes God and God's intentions known, as revealed in many psalms, for example, 104.

Creation has become visible to us under the basic aspect of union as an ongoing process of bringing forth new beings that emerge from, but are not identical with, the elements they unite. Therefore, we can say that more being comes into existence through union. The more united something is in itself, the more being it realizes. The Teilhardian statement that

$$esse = plus\ a\ pluribus\ uniri\ \text{(to be = to be more united out of many)}$$
$$\text{or}$$
$$esse = plus\ plura\ unire^{59}\ \text{(to be = to unite more the many)}$$

brings out the point. In this vision being is no longer the most general concept thinkable; rather, it has become definable. Being is realized and maintained union. This union is most evident in living beings. Their union, physically an open system in constant need of input of energy, decays easily. There is not a constant amount of being in the universe, like the constant amount of energy predicated by the first law of thermodynamics. In an evolutionary perspective being is created by union of elements.

The modes of union indicate levels of being, from the atomic level to the human or personal level. The material aspect in this story is secondary. The classical metaphysical principle of being representing matter can be reduced to *prime matter*, which is pure potency.[60] This passive principle in all material beings is opposed to the active principle, *substantial form*, and should not be confused with an erroneous notion of materialism in which being is identified with matter. In this materialist vision, being is reduced to the earliest elementary particles. In a strictly materialist world there would be no emergence of being through union, whereas in the metaphysics of union, the potency principle is concretized in the elements that are the condition for the formation of a higher unity. Here being is identified with union. We exclude from this reasoning a beginning of creation, or we would be forced either into a *regressio ad infinitum* to the point that questions cannot be answered within the radius of our experience, or into wild speculations about the cosmic singularity. Such speculations would not give us a clearer understanding of how God creates, though some might be impressed by a visualized Big Bang as an expression of the almighty God. The most interesting point for the future of the universe that might be said about these early moments, which in a very wasteful manner transformed the original energy into mass particles, is that somehow the process of union started producing the first simple elements. The way God creates the evolving world is less visible in the beginning than later, when creation through union brings forth ever new, higher levels of beings.

It might appear that this understanding of reality has a certain relation to the classical Platonic and Aristotelian philosophical perspective. This is true because Aristotle's metaphysics was built on his physics. Separated from the physics known to him, metaphysics becomes an abstract construct not related to the reality in which he lived. One might see here rather an Aristotelian or Thomasian[61] enterprise that tries to understand the known world. And we find at least one parallel statement in scholastic philosophy, which is rooted in the Platonic tradition: the statement that union creates being has its counterpart in one of the universals, namely, that *omne ens est unum* (every being is one). In the metaphysics of union this translates into *omne ens est unitum* (every being is united).

This statement applies to all beings that we know about in this world and that we believe to be God's creation. We can say that God's creatures come to be by becoming united out of elements. This enables us almost to see the Creator, the hidden Creator, at work. There is no interference from God's side in the process, at least no visible, measurable interference. God's ways are obviously more subtle than the story of Genesis 1:1–2:3.[62] God acts, as Teilhard would say, from the inside of things that cannot be reached by science. God acts immanently in the world. We shall return to this point.[63] We may here note that Christian faith sees God's immanence clearly counterbalanced by God's transcendence.

But God's transcendence does not make God totally distant from the universe. As Christians we traditionally confess God to be the Supreme Being. The fathers of the church and the medieval tradition taught that all perfections are realized and present in God. The very notion of God, expressed in the ontological proof of the existence of God, is associated with this totality of perfection in God. The notion led medieval thinkers to the conclusion that every existing being possesses its being insofar as it is similar to God. There cannot be anything whose level of being, of perfection, is totally alien to God, or God would lack some perfection. Everything must in some way be similar to God. This similarity may be the faintest imaginable, and the fainter it is, the lower the degree of being. Humans, according to the tradition, created in the image and likeness of God (Gen. 1:26), more closely resemble their Creator than other beings.

Comparisons on the ladder of being are known as the classical analogy of being. If it is applied to the metaphysics of union, we can ask if being united, and therefore existing in a state of union, can be related to God's own being. If being is defined by union, we shall have to accept this possibility as a necessary consequence of the definition of being in God's becoming, evolving creation. This will oblige us to rethink the meaning of the classical talk about God as pure act and absolute being. These statements about God were made in a time when the world was static, when nothing new under the sun[64] was thought possible, and God was imagined as the supreme and unchanging being resting in the divine self (Gen. 2:3). On the other hand, if God is revealed as creating by union, it seems inevitable to find in God the analogy to God's way of acting as Creator. If the similarity in being is to be upheld, it is reasonable to think of God not as the Supreme Being, but as the Supreme Being realized in a supreme union.

At this point we are plainly speculating without having any way to verify our statements by referring to any information that science could deliver. But here we speak as Christians believing in the Creator. If God reveals God through divine creation, then God is the Supreme Being realized and actualized in the supreme and continuous act of union.

This raises the question of the supreme level of this divine union. In our experience the highest level of union between elements is where human persons unite on a personal level with other persons, forming a unity that transcends the individual. In a certain way, the individual might even be said to become more a person by uniting with other persons.[65] If God exists in union as Trinity, the level of union cannot be below the level of a human person. This leaves the strict monotheist with the dilemma: either God lacks the quality of a person, or God needs to create other persons, humankind, to unite with God. The first answer would make God a nonperson, an answer not acceptable within the Judeo-Christian or Islamic tradition. The second answer would make God dependent on God's creation; the Creator would need to create. This notion is obviously not compatible with the traditional notion of the transcendent and free God, the Supreme Being, confessed by the three religions mentioned.

The God of the Christian tradition, the triune God, on the other hand, lives in the constant realization of the union of three persons. God is the *Urbild* (the original), in resemblance to which all creation comes into existence. Realizing for all eternity this act of highest union, God transcends the world, and to exist in perfect union God does not need the world.

The force that unites, especially the force that unites persons, is love. God exists in perfect union, we might say, because God is love (1 John 1:4). This biblical text has fuller meaning than before because love has been conceived heretofore primarily as a moral attitude. If this more existential understanding of God's creation and its revelatory dimension is accurate, love becomes the constitutive force in God's life. God is love in the pure act of uniting. This reflects into God's creation, love becoming the constitutive force, the driving force of the evolutionary process of progressing union.

What has been said theologically is not a scientific view of the world. It is rather what appears when we try to see this same world with the eyes of faith as God's creation. In this view the world of science is not strange to theologians; rather, it has become a source of theological insight. The theological perception of the world as creation is not in contradiction to the world seen by scientists, though some, as scientists, may abstain from accepting this or any other viewpoint of faith.

SUMMARY

Having seen that proofs of God as the Creator show at best that this universe is not self-explanatory, and having looked at the universe as the "book of nature," we first evaluated the often-heard quantitative argument in evolution, and we showed it to be self-defeating. Accepting human experience as a point of departure, we have discovered this evolving universe as a process of becoming through union. Union brings forth new realities, new levels of being, so that the classical notion of being as the basic description of realities had to give way to the notion that being is defined by union. By applying the principle of analogy, we arrived at the conclusion that the Supreme Being can be understood as the supreme union among persons. Thus analysis of the process of becoming raised the level of perception so that this world as God's creation points to the Trinity. The notion of personhood used in this chapter leads us to questions of how personhood evolved and whether there is theological significance in the evolution of human consciousness and personhood.

3 CONSCIOUSNESS IN THE UNIVERSE—OF THE UNIVERSE

In search of an orientation of the evolutionary process, which is often negated by use of the invalidated quantitative argument, we introduce the phenomenon of human consciousness as one aspect of the universe to be integrated into a coherent description of evolution. The retrospective description of the becoming of consciousness allows the adoption of consciousness as one parameter of the evolutionary process. Using this parameter, we perceive God's creation as a non-order-dominated process leading toward consciousness. By becoming conscious, the universe is on its way to encounter God, becoming in the human being *capax Dei*. Since human consciousness is time-bound, we raise the problem of time as related to the eternal God.

ORIENTATIONS OF BECOMING IN THE EVOLVING UNIVERSE

We have seen the universe as a process of becoming through union. This process started as far back as our knowledge can reach. Theologically, it matters not whether this process is given a quantum mechanical interpretation or whether it started with a pointlike singularity. Higher levels of being are not reached because of a greater quantity of matter. If that were so, then black holes would represent the highest level of being.[1] But in their structure black holes are not the product of the process of becoming through union. Rather, they are an accumulation of quarks that, having formed into the black hole, lose all possibilities of a future.[2]

The second law of thermodynamics predicts that the universe will end in a state where black holes and other dead stars, such as neutron stars and white and black dwarfs, will represent the largest part of the mass of the universe. If we judge the relative importance of the reality surrounding us by the quantity of energy involved, the background radiation would come first and black holes would be a distant second. The rest, representing just one hundred-billionth of the total energy in the universe, would not need to be considered.

As we showed in chapter 2, the quantitative approach is not significant. Values are not measured by the quantities of matter involved. The temptation might be great, since quantities are readily defined and could indicate the general orientation of the universe, and therefore clarify our place within it. But such a judgment is incompatible with the received values in philosophical and religious traditions, such as life and human dignity; values defined by quantity would be compatible only with a meaningless universe where ultimately nothing counts.[3]

Against the mass-valued universe we observe the reality of an evolution that has been going on against all seeming probabilities. We might understand the structure of atoms and molecules with regard to their forces. But in the overall composition of the universe their relative scarcity indicates that their existence is not self-evident. Despite spectral measurements[4] revealing their omnipresence, atoms are a curiosity when compared to the total energy of the universe. The really interesting matter in this universe that permits the evolution of life and thought comes from this scarce curiosity. This leads us back to seek a key to understanding the universe and creation. Looking for large quantities is simply an error of perspective. Materialism gives us access to an extremely dull universe with highly interesting curiosities that remain unexplained.

One of the curiosities is consciousness, which seems rare in the universe. Other planets around the sun have nothing like it on their surface. We may speculate on a possibility of thinking beings on planets belonging to other stars. It is unlikely close to us, but we cannot know today whether other planets are inhabited by conscious beings in the universe with its billions of galaxies. So far, the search for extraterrestrial intelligence has not been successful, and public funding of the program has been cut off.[5] But even if there are other planets with living creatures who think reflectively, they would still be rare phenomena.

Some persons like to object to the importance given to human consciousness as a key phenomenon in the universe. Their argument is based on relative quantities, which, as we have seen, is arbitrary and ultimately points to a most uninteresting aspect of the universe. But on all levels of becoming, we see activities that are linked to the capacities of the agent. In the human being these activities are controlled by consciousness. Though fortunately many of our life-sustaining activities, such as the beating of the heart, breathing, and digesting, normally are automatically controlled, we know them as our activities, especially when they do not function correctly. There is also a large field of consciously controlled activities, some of which may become semiautomatic, such as walking, car driving, and writing—all of these must be learned. Though the center of all these activities in space is the human body, the outreach seems limitless. In principle, the outreach of human consciousness goes as far as the limits of the visible universe. There are no borderlines in space and time for our ability to know and understand, even though there might be physical limits such as the speed of light and the limit of time at the generally accepted singularity at Planck-time. We are able to analyze the light coming from the farthest galaxies and to know their material composition. And we can at least speculate about the possibilities of a time before the Big Bang or about a quantum origination of the evolving universe.[6] The human mind can reach far beyond any physical limitations: this is true for those who believe in a Creator, and for all early forms of religious belief. But even those who deny a Creator and a transcendent reality claim to be able to make this judgment; evidently, they feel competent to make a judgment about the existence or nonexistence of God. The same is true of the agnostic who decides what we may know or may not know.

As the long philosophical discussion from early skeptics to modern theories of science has proven, there is no way in which the human mind can assure the exact limits of its ability to know. We experience boundaries and degrees of certitude, but they may be temporary. Definite boundaries exist for our sensual experience, and there may be absolute limits when we consider that the reality of God transcends the capacity of our minds. But in our consciousness we do not see a limit to understanding.

The small mass of the human brain, the visible infrastructure of the human mind,[7] can reach out farther than our whole universe. The human being is able to outdo in its spiritual dimension the quantitative reality of this universe. Therefore, it appears to be a purely subjective judgment to believe that the human mind is of no importance for understanding of the universe. We know of no other reality seeking to understand the universe. All the matter accumulated in black holes and in stars knows nothing about the universe. For the physicist as physicist, black holes might be the only interesting subject of interest. But for the physicist as human being, able to do physics, it would be a catastrophe if the matter described by physics were all there is in the universe.[8] Physics could not be done.

On the other hand, life on this earth and its latest outcome, the human being, have roots in the very beginning of the universe. Life in human beings has an age of more than three billion years: from the beginning the chain has never been interrupted. Every human being is alive with a life that started shortly after the formation of the earth. In a precise sense, every human being incorporates the condensed history of the universe from the beginning of the formation of protons to the formation of the brain. In the human being the universal process has reached a state where it becomes reflective. Quite meaningfully, we can state that the human being is at least potentially reflecting the totality of the universe. This becomes evident by the search for a theory of everything.[9]

The relegation of human beings to insignificance in the universe on the basis of their quantitative presence may thus be considered an ideological artifact: quantity does not say much about significance in the universe. Otherwise the only significant reality would be background radiation. This would leave even the physicists without a subject to study.

The topics worthy of scientific study are the exceptional: the table of atoms and their history, molecules and their history, life and its history, humankind and its history. Quantitatively, all these are negligible. The more they show interesting diversity, the more they become quantitatively marginal. Moreover, most scientific research and human interest are not directed at quantitative aspects of the universe.[10] Therefore, the human being rather than the quark is justifiably a key element to understand the universe.

Such a starting point might be considered by some as anthropocentric. But this is a purely ideological argument. The label "anthropocentric" is no argument against the position of the human being in the evolving world. Anthropocentrism must be accepted because the human being is central to the process in the universe: quantitative "insignificance" corresponds perfectly to the exceptional character of all evolving reality. The least we can say is that there is no good reason not to consider the human being in all its dimensions as essential to an understanding of the universe.

The hypothesis that the evolution of the universe has tended toward the emergence of the human is at least as well reasoned as the notion that evolution can be reduced without loss of meaning to its material aspects in their most primitive form, such as quarks, electrons, and electromagnetic radiation.[11] That there is no orientation to the evolutionary process is based on a quantitative argument: since we have invalidated this argument, the only way to prove that there is no orientation in evolution would be to refute any criteria that manifest such an orientation. The question concerning the hypothesis proposed here is whether it permits a more coherent understanding of the universe than a quantitative argument.[12] Coherence is a generally accepted sign of truth in a universe conceived as inherently one. All sciences presuppose this unity. For example, the search for extra particles attempts to fill the gaps in a system perceived as a coherent unity. Proof of this coherence by experiment in the case of evolution is not possible, because we cannot repeat the evolutionary process starting with the Big Bang.

Since quantity is relatively insignificant for understanding the universe unless linked to meaningful qualities, and since meaningfulness is not linked to pure quantity, there is no other criterion than coherence to test our hypothesis concerning the evolving universe. Any hypothesis that explains away a part of the universe as an epiphenomenon, as a negligible quantity, or as anthropocentric misses the point. Therefore, any theory that neglects the reality of the mind (the source of all hypotheses about the universe), while reconstructing the evolved reality, falls short of a coherent description of the universe in which we live.

HUMAN CONSCIOUSNESS AS THE HIGHEST POINT OF THE EVOLUTIONARY PROCESS

The human is the only being that everyone knows from one's own consciousness. As the word *conscire* indicates, we know about the motives of our doings. We can say why we have done certain things, though we do not always like to lay our innermost thinking open to others. Even the law respects this desire for privacy, and the right of accused persons to lie and to deny guilt. Without knowing about one's motives, about truths and lies, one would not be able to use these rights: they presuppose self-consciousness. Philosophers and psychologists are uneasy when asked to define consciousness. Society recognizes by law its existence, and all persons in contact with other persons know about the consciousness of the other persons: wife and husband, parents and their children, experience it in their relations, and they know what it means to lie.

Though the mind-body problem[13] has not been solved in a generally accepted way, we can certainly say that the mind is highly effective by being reflectively conscious. As Teilhard stated correctly, one important aspect of the human mind is that it knows what it does and what it knows. This awareness makes possible the development and use of abstract concepts that can be handled while the concrete reality is absent. Modern physics has not developed merely by making experiments, but also by constructing theories and models that can be exposed to falsification by experiments created to fit the theories. Modern machinery, from harvesters to airplanes, has been designed by the human mind before being realized. The environment of human beings is to a large extent formed by human design. The surface of the earth is covered with products of minds. What humans build and breed and what they eventually decide not to submit to agricultural use—for example, conserving the rain forests—is the largest portion of all land.

The survival of the planet, as a living planet, depends on human decisions. Indeed, life will not subsist on earth for all eternity, since the earth's lifetime is limited by the lifetime of the sun. There could also be an accident from space, such as a large asteroid, that might hit the earth and destroy all forms of life. But even without any cosmological interference the human race could well make this planet unlivable. No other living species in our experience could take a similar responsibility, and none has had a stronger influence on the whole biosphere.[14] Humans know about the world around them, and they use this knowledge effectively to change the environment.[15]

Consciousness is thus not only knowing about oneself; it is understanding the world around us. Human consciousness is always identified with a worldview that can be grasped and described in abstract concepts. It experiences itself as the center of the perceived and conceived world, which it relates to itself.

Without pretending this to be an exhaustive description of human consciousness, it is one that can be verified through introspection by all humans, even though some might need help in language skills to express themselves about their consciousness. Moreover, we can verify it negatively when we lose consciousness, which happily is not our normal state of existence. But we know afterward what was missing during that period. And we are able to distinguish between persons who are conscious and those who are not. Thus even though our description of consciousness is quite rudimentary and by no means exhaustive, we know what we mean. Our inability to give a full description of consciousness does not lessen our awareness that we are conscious. We are in a situation similar to that of biologists, who are unable to give a clear definition of life, although their descriptive efforts offer a good picture of its reality. Though experts are unable to agree on a definition, even a child knows the difference between a dead dog and a living dog. More abstractly, insufficient definitions do not negate the existence of genuine knowledge about realities such as life and consciousness.

If we look around, we quickly realize that humans are not alone in showing some kind of conscious behavior. The classical Cartesian concept, largely based on medieval ideas about natural laws of behavior of animals governed strictly by deterministic laws, has during the last century been replaced by a more open view. Research into the behavior of many species of animals has shown that all vertebrates have learning abilities. Chimpanzees, genetically the species closest to the human, have been shown to learn the use of symbols to express their wishes and to solve highly complicated tasks.[16] Dogs are visibly not machines, and they are able to show their owners what they like and dislike. They act as centers of their world.

Though there is no identity between human and animal consciousness—humans being capable of reflection—there is more than a faint resemblance between them. Before humans emerged from the long history of evolution, some animals acted as centers of their world and communicated with one another by some symbolic means. The most unexpected and therefore famous example of such use of symbolic communication is the way bees inform their mates[17] about where they found food. There cannot be any doubt: animals and all living beings act as a unity, unlike the rest of the world. Their perception of the world may be limited; some birds do not see a nonmoving prey,[18] but at least they have a limited view of the world around them. They orient themselves in their environment, which for migrating birds ranges over thousands of miles. And many animals actively alter the world around them to make it more viable: birds build nests and foxes build burrows. Behavioral scientists typically have performed learning experiments with many species of animals in order to develop theories about learning that can be applied to humans.

To consider consciousness as exclusively a human reality would be difficult. There is no doubt that we find in the animal world a great range of phenomena analogous to consciousness. But we would hardly expect the degree of consciousness to be everywhere the same. Though we may have difficulty in making the fine distinctions between different mammals or different birds, there is little doubt that differences exist between one family and another. Classical theology tried to find the differences between lower and higher animals in families from fish to mammals, as was described in the sequential creation in Genesis 1. Roughly speaking, levels of classification are confirmed when we consider the learning abilities of different species. The range of learning possibilities widens with the emergence of higher species.

On the other hand, the farther we go back in evolution, the more simple the most evolved species and the more limited the range of learning capacities and perception of environment. Potter wasps, for example, which otherwise display a highly complex behavior, are unable to change their breeding behavior.[19] Insects can learn, but some parts of their behavior seem to be unchangeable. They do have a wide range of perception of their environment and reaction to it. Even small creatures such as nematodes, worms one millimeter long, have an astonishing range of perceptions. *Caenorhabditis elegans* with just 302 neurons is able to distinguish about sixty volatile odorants and to learn to store information in its memory for more than twenty-four hours.[20] With only a few neurons, learning and memory are possible.[21] Even amoebae and other protozoans have been shown to have some learning abilities.

Animals adapt actively to their environment and use past experiences. In one way or another, information about the environment is stored internally. The range of this information—in content and in outreach into the environment—diminishes the farther we go back in evolutionary history. The smallest protozoan is still able to react actively to the information it gets from the outside. We might hesitate to call this ability consciousness, and there is only a faint resemblance to human consciousness. But something common is there: information from the outside is internalized and reacted to in order to maintain one's own existence. We see all signs of consciousness gradually vanishing, the farther back we go in the history of the universe.

We have not mentioned plants, which are more different from us than animals. They have their own manner of reacting and of seeking their way, for example, by tropism and by their roots' searching for water. We might imagine here some kind of reaction to the environment that is internally directed. But our understanding of the inside of plants is hampered by a lack of analogical relations.

In view of a commonly held reductionistic approach to behavior—such as the chemistry and physiology involved, which are the needed infrastructure—we insist on a holistic aspect. This is necessary even though some behavior, especially in animals of lower developmental status, seems to be purely mechanical responses. Nevertheless these are responses of the whole animal and not of only one or two neurons.[22] It is always the whole animal or plant that reacts and is concerned, and not just this or that part. At least in animals we find traces of consciousness in that activity. Therefore, the farther we look into the past of evolving life, we see ever more vanishing traces of consciousness, which may be characterized by ever-diminishing ranges of activity within their environment. And consciousness seems to disappear completely below the biosphere. Some phenomena remind us of activities of living beings, such as autocatalysis, which seems to be an essential step toward the appearance of life.[23] But there is no active exploration of the environment at this level. The activity range of molecules and atoms seems to be limited to their physical size, though even here higher molecules such as proteins show different configurations that change their shape and their reactivity. However, it is difficult to find more than a holistic aspect in this behavior of molecules and atoms. Consciousness is no longer detectable. Yet out of this matter, life arises, and with it consciousness: atoms and molecules are the condition for consciousness to appear in this universe.

Thus consciousness appears as a reality in humans and diminishes the farther we go back in the history of evolution. In an approximate way consciousness is even measurable by using the range of knowledge and activity as a parameter, since this parameter diminishes the farther we go back into the past.[24] In the beginning consciousness seems to disappear; the early universe of particles seems unaware of outreaching activities.

In retrospect we see the universe begin with relatively simple structures. To a great extent these cosmological structures seem to be understood; at least physicists are confident of reaching a fuller understanding of their history. As P. J. E. Peebles states, "We are seeing in cosmology a developing network of interconnected results. This network suggests that we really are on the path to a believable approximation to reality."[25] As we have seen, the most simple structures such as the particles that make up all matter with mass are exceptional in the universe, as compared to the background radiation. Understanding the universe with quantity as the decisive parameter opens the view to a meaningless universe, as we have noted. In such a universe no orientation can be discovered in the natural process of universal evolution. Everything of evolutionary significance is a negligible quantity.

On the other hand, if we look at the emerging realities in the universe that represent only minimal quantities, we can see some general direction. Certainly, the emergence is not predetermined by some known natural law. We are unable to predict the future of a carbon atom. But in principle we can write the story of a carbon atom that becomes integrated into a human brain or into an enzyme. The atoms we find in living beings have their own long story. But this story is only one of the less important aspects of the evolutionary epic. The main plot of the story informs us how the universe, in special places like our earth, which may even be unique, has brought forth more and more complex molecules, which at some moment formed cooperating units with an outer shell.

Theories about the concrete details of the beginning of life are still uncertain. Practically, science has not gone much farther than to establish that some of the necessary elements of life may have been created spontaneously within the original atmosphere of the young earth.[26] The phenomenon of life, as a new reality that emerged out of the molecular evolution, is not contained in the description of the molecules. It is a new property. But of what? This seems to be a wrong statement: life is not a property of something that acquires this property. Rather, it is a new reality in an already highly complex infrastructure that emerges out of the complexifying and simultaneously unifying process of evolution.

Today it is common knowledge that the process of evolution at all stages is a process of complexification.[27] At a certain point this process emerges into life. Consequently, as we have seen, the earliest traces of consciousness become describable as a whole that internalizes the experience of its environment (learning) and reacts actively as a whole to that environment.

Evolution is not a linear process starting with the appearance of the first particles, which merely change into more complex particles. We must insist that evolution is not a determined process that can be deduced from the existence of the first particles. As explained by the anthropic principle, on a slight difference in the Coulomb constant—there is no known physical necessity for it to have the specific value it has—the whole evolutionary process would have never gone beyond the stage of the proton. But even with the Coulomb constant as it is, most of the universe's matter never goes beyond the stage of protons or alpha particles before being absorbed into some black hole. And the most significant evolution has taken place within a statistically improbable range. The statistical average does not inform us about the orientation of evolution. Evolution follows the path of the improbable, and it is reasonable to consider the story of emerging consciousness as the significant story of the universe within this context. The parameters of evolution are concerned not with quantity, but with quality. And at least one quality to be considered to understand this universe is the evolution of consciousness, which in our experience starts with the beginning of life.

Having established a reasonable alternative to a purely quantitative argument with a recognizable orientation of the evolutionary process toward consciousness, we must caution against the often-heard identification of this approach with classical, deterministic orthogenesis. Orthogenesis is a linear process, deducible and predictable. Evolution brings forth probabilities that allow at their extremes the emergence of higher forms of consciousness: there is no built-in necessity that this process took the direction it did. But in retrospect we cannot fail to see that it has happened. In writing the story of evolution, we recognize one important continuous direction of emergent consciousness, quantitatively insignificant, but most important in its effects. Without it there would be no science.

Evolution goes in the direction of consciousness toward its qualitatively highest level, which is probably very rare. And in a precise sense we can state that in the human race, the evolving universe becomes conscious and can reflect on itself.

GOD'S CREATION:
EVOLUTION TOWARD CONSCIOUSNESS

It is possible to deny the importance of the previous statement and to declare it an epiphenomenon. Nevertheless the effects and the historical background of this so-called epiphenomenon better support our statement. In any case, we make here a value judgment. Ours is surely not unreasonable, though we can argue for it only without definite proof. Proof is not possible where values are concerned. If we presupposed a meaningless universe, any value judgment would be purely subjective. But the presupposition itself is subjective in that we cannot present irrefutable arguments for it, and so ultimately we rely on relatively reasonable judgments.

The universe has effectively produced beings, humans, who ask for meaning. And evolution made its way, despite a quantitative improbability. Thus pointing to the finality of the quantitatively understood universe does not make this a meaningless universe. Instead, the history of evolution supports a meaningful universe with a parameter of evolving consciousness. We believe such a judgment is well supported within a universe that is meaningful. Personal experience reveals that the universe has produced beings that seek meaning. Could this quest for meaning be an error in evolution? Or is it that God's creation has become aware of a trend toward consciousness and meaning? Neither the time involved nor the scarcity of human consciousness, compared to the universe's total mass, is an argument against this perception of reality.

At this point we recall that we have no intent to prove the existence of a Creator by arguments drawn from science. Science cannot tell us why there is a universe rather than nothing. Science-based arguments from design may seem helpful, but they open the door for the "God of the gaps." God appears as a part of the universe with a scientifically necessary function to explain what for the moment escapes scientific explanation. God in this understanding becomes a part of the universe, which may be explained away by science in the future. But God is not a part of the reality explained by science. Science cannot answer the question Is there a creation or an eternal self-subsistent universe? Science cannot stand outside the universe in order to view it objectively. There are even limits to our perception of reality, like the cone defined by the speed of light. And even if we were to discover a nonlocal means of communication and perception, making the speed of light an obsolete limit, science could speculate only on a preexisting quantum vacuum out of which the universe would have evolved. But where did the quantum vacuum come from? If we call upon God to create the quantum vacuum, we invoke a *deus ex machina* to help scientists solve a scientific problem. Ultimately, therefore, what science shows us is the contingency of the universe. Nothing is the way it is by absolute necessity. That is why science is more descriptive than explanatory. Science cannot make a clear case for or against a Creator.

In any case, we do not intend to demonstrate that this universe has been created. As we stated in the first chapter, Christians believe in God the Creator. There are good reasons to believe that the universe is itself fundamentally contingent and not fully intelligible in all its aspects, physical as well as spiritual. But this cannot be exploited to prove in a conclusive way the fact of creation and a Creator. And to adduce this proof would be the primary task not of the theologian, but of the philosopher. The philosopher tries to understand by starting only with the immanent reality of the universe. Plato and Aristotle sought a natural theology. Modern philosophy has withdrawn into a skepticism of delimiting the knowable, leaving the task of philosophy to physicists, who often raise questions about God. Some questions like those of Einstein showed deep insights, while others like those of Stephen Hawking show theological naïveté. Thus modern philosophy leaves a void. But it should not be the task of the theologian to fill this gap.

Theology begins with faith as its precondition. Therefore, its task is not to demonstrate creation, but to understand the universal process of evolution as creation. Can we find anything about the Creator's intention from the story of creation as we read it today?

The classical understanding of creation, based on the first chapter of Genesis, described a world dominated by an all-powerful God, who created a habitat for humankind. The actions of God, reported by the priestly record, overcame chaos and assigned places to created realities. Everything, especially every living creature, was put into place and had its function within God's creation. As the Wisdom of Solomon (11:20) records, "You have arranged all things by measure and number." The story in Genesis was viable for a static universe.

Christian cosmologists from the early centuries to modern times had little difficulty in describing the universe and its history in accord with the biblical story of creation. Basil in his *Hexaemeron* elaborated the order followed in God's acts of creation. Such interpretations of God's work of the six days offered for centuries a full understanding of the order inscribed in the universe. That was not done by relying only on the biblical text. Actual knowledge about the universe was integrated into a theological understanding of creation. Therefore, all theologians had to study the universe before they could be admitted to theological studies. Naturally, it took some time for theologians to become aware of the importance of what we call today the natural sciences, which for many centuries were taught as the *quadrivium*. In the fully developed scholastic theology the order of the universe was of primordial importance. Order, observed especially in the seven planets, was seen everywhere. The macrocosmos became the rule for the microcosmos and was superimposed on all human order, whether spiritual or social. The notion of order and of natural laws appeared to scholastic theologians as an expression of God's creative will, to be imitated. That was the generally accepted theological view in the thirteenth century.

The interpretation was by no means particularly close to the biblical text. The two great luminaries in the biblical text were supplemented by the five "other" planets. The seven planets demonstrated the perfect heavenly order, which was to be realized on earth: the praying order in the monasteries followed the order of the heavens. Everything was dominated by the number seven, taken from the seven planets: seven sacraments, seven virtues, seven capital sins, seven ranks of chivalry, seven ages of the universe, seven steps to priesthood that, as sacrament, were named *ordo*. Cathedrals had seven chapels around the choir, and the human body, a microcosm, had seven parts: four elements and three souls. This list could be prolonged. Traditional theology was centered on the notion of order. In the *Weltchronik* by Schedel in the early sixteenth century, we still find the tendency to see the order of the Ptolemaic world when reading the biblical text.

Modern science is still looking for order, oblivious of the origin of this search in a deeply rooted belief in determinism. This confidence in strict determinism and an eternal natural law goes back to the old idea of ἀνάγκη, which in the Middle Ages became the notion of eternal law, rooted in the belief that it had its reality and force as God's unshakable will.[28] Modern science has maintained the notion of laws of nature as eternal laws, which are taken for granted. Their contingency has not been considered in science: the existence of nature's eternal laws has been a foundational belief of science. This belief, though shaken by quantum mechanics and chaos theories, is witnessed by the search for a theory of everything that would explain the whole universe deterministically. Steven Weinberg speaks correctly of dreams of a final theory.[29]

On the other hand, the universe does not seem to be dominated by determinisms that create a strict order, but by various entropic phenomena that reveal less and less order. Wherever order appears, it is only marginal as compared to the general process. Whatever our interpretation of God's creation, it appears that God's primary intent was not to create a well-ordered universe. The universe is neither a perfectly running machine nor an economical, orderly structured whole. Taking into account the featureless background radiation and futureless black holes, most of the energy invested in the universe seems to be junk without recognizable order.

Considering the traditional scholastic understanding of creation as a well-ordered reality, we are confronted with a difficulty. If order is a criterion, this world is certainly far from perfect. And the traditional interpretation of disorder in the universe, which was attributed to the effects of sin in general, or more specifically to original sin, is no longer helpful. Most of the disordered energy is the result of the Big Bang, as background radiation. Order in the universe is only an exceptional status in what is called evolution.

Some rudimentary levels of order can be seen in gravitation-dominated structures such as stars and galaxies that are clearly recognizable and develop forms of gravitational ordering. They do not reach levels of complexity, having no definite structures that coordinate their parts. These heavenly bodies are rather accumulations of matter, with structures and activities dependent on gravitational forces. It would be difficult today to ask the scientists who know about the distribution of stars and galaxies to recognize there the hand of an order-creating God. When in the Ptolemaic vision of the universe the heavens displayed order, it was reasonable to ask people to look at the sky to see the heavenly order that should be the model for the order to be realized on earth.[30] Today the skies have obviously ceased to give a good example to be followed.

When we look at the night sky, we may admire its beauty, and we may feel awe in looking at the vastness of the heavens in which we cannot make out our place: there seems to be no center point in space. Pictures of stars and galaxies through modern telescopes fill us with admiration.[31] But we would hardly find any exemplary order in the distribution of the billions of galaxies scattered over the sky. Even poorly understood structures such as the Great Wall[32] do not bring order into the skies. The evolutionary story of the universe requires some kind of scattered accumulations, but they have not organized in a recognizable way. Order in the skies is minimal. But this minimal order from the accumulation of matter is a necessary condition for evolution to proceed at the atomic level. The process that makes the stars shine is rather violent. All our sunshine, therefore, is the result of the heating of the sun by its internal nuclear reactions, by the fusion of protons via deuterium and tritium into alpha particles, helium nuclei. As in the hydrogen bomb, the process is explosive, but it is contained by the gravitational attraction of the mass of the sun.

As noted in chapter 2, the nuclear process itself first generates helium, then in a later stage carbon, and finally iron. The process may also bring forth the first twenty-six elements of the periodic table;[33] all the other elements have been formed by supernova explosions.[34] The process at the macroscopic level is noteworthy not for its order, but for its violence. The outcome of the process at the microlevel, on the other hand, shows clear signs of order: atoms of each element have a definite structure and specific properties that make them distinguishable. And although they differ from one another, atoms follow a common structural plan: nuclei composed of protons and neutrons and surrounded by electrons, whose atomic number is defined for each atom by the number of protons in the nucleus. Heavenly bodies have many sizes—size defines the violence of nuclear fusion reactions and therewith the "lifetime" of the stars—without clear distinctions. Elements are clearly distinguished from one another by the structure of their atoms, which suggests order as a necessary condition of their existence.

Though this condition of order is important for the evolving universe, quantitatively in relation to the total mass in the universe, atoms represent less than one part in a billion, or for the elements beyond hydrogen and helium barely one part in a hundred billion. Most of the matter in the universe does not last further than the first two steps of nucleosynthesis. If quantity were the correct parameter to evaluate the place of anything in the universe, we need not ask more questions. But on the other hand, nobody is willing to limit questions to quantitative criteria. Rather, most persons are interested in the world of the exceptional: the becoming of higher, more complex structures by chemical evolution, and finally through autocatalysis, production of primitive forms of life and even higher complexes.

As far as we know, all this does not happen to quantitatively relevant parts of the universe. Moreover, a universe structured by the principle of order would proceed in an orderly way to produce more order. This would be visible through the use of quantitatively adequate and economically available means. We conclude from our analysis that some order appears, but in a disorderly way. The story of the evolving universe that brings forth new realities is told in this way: order appearing out of disorder. All living beings evolved from those simplest particles that appeared first, and a theory that they could eventually be described by a wave function may be true.[35] For the reality of the story of evolution such mathematical reductionism is irrelevant: it confirms that the story begins with the origin of the universe; it says nothing about the evolved reality, which by its newness transcends the past. Higher complexes are not only quantitatively more; they are different because they show new qualities:[36] the story of biological evolution is not just some mutations in DNA structures, but is a constant rise in the quality and range of life, which becomes more and more conscious. Human consciousness is the highest stage reached in this evolutionary movement with an open future, a stage in which the universe has begun to reflect on itself.[37]

THE UNIVERSE: CREATION ON ITS WAY TO ENCOUNTER GOD

Qualitatively, God's creation tends toward consciousness. It has become evident that this tendency does not follow a blueprint; the universe is neither orderly nor economically conceived. Consciousness did not arise by the shortest conceivable path. All the steps leading toward it were taken without massive movements and were exceptional, at least quantitatively. Life itself, the biosphere, forms only a thin coating around the earth and is rare compared to the rest of the stuff of the universe.[38] But there is no doubt, at this final stage of the evolutionary process, God's ongoing creation, that we find human beings with reflective consciousness linked to the most complex physical structures known.

Thus from a technological and materialistic viewpoint, the universe is not a masterpiece, and so we might offer two reflections: first, it is not economically constructed with the least amount of material available, if bringing forth the human mind is the goal; second, the general path of evolution is not dominated by order. We need to keep these facts in mind, and we shall return to them.[39] But the last point reached by this process brings forth new qualities—not merely modifications of properties, like the annoying mutations of the influenza virus—that transcend all other qualities of life, such as self-reflective consciousness, creative abstract thinking including mathematics, artistic creativity, and symbolic language able to express realities that escape sensual perception. In humans the universe not only is engaged in its evolution, but also starts to seek its meaning. As humans reflect on themselves and their universe and are aware of the dimension of the future, they cannot avoid looking for the meaning of their engagement with this universe within the evolutionary process. Having recognized this latest and exceptional level reached by evolution, they know that in a precise, quantitatively negligible but qualitatively highly significant way, the whole story of the universe is present in them.[40] Their quest for meaning is also the quest of the universe.

The human quest for meaning is part of God's creation, and it seems evident that the contingent universe in itself does not hold an answer. The universe as a whole in its material structure follows the second law of thermodynamics, which states that the entropy of any system with a limited amount of matter cannot function forever in a life-sustaining way. If the universe is a system—the hypothesis most supported by data[41]—it will end cold and uninhabitable. Moreover, if there is to be a big crunch to follow the expansive phase of the universe, there will be no place for reflective human consciousness. As Steven Weinberg has pointed out, the universe, and therefore life, can be considered utterly pointless. Only qualitative parameters offer meaning and orientation. Humanity has not an unlimited future open to it within the framework of this universe. Its contingency becomes obvious within this perspective. God did not create a universe that is self-sufficient in being able to give satisfaction to the quest it has brought forth. In human consciousness the universe becomes aware of its limitations and of its need to be related to God if its quest for meaning is to be satisfied.

This is not a proof of God's existence, but we may state that faith in the Creator is not contradicted by the evolution of the universe: the process may be read with a materialistic faith that denies all definite meaning to the process, or it may be read as the ongoing work of the Creator. The Christian theologian obviously takes the latter position. As stated in the beginning of this text, we start with the first article of the Christian creed, which confesses faith in the Creator.

Our task is not to demonstrate the Creator, but to ask what the Creator intended in creating the evolving universe that becomes reflectively conscious in humankind. Very early human beings became aware of their limitations, most evident in the fact that they must die. But absolute death was not accepted, as witnessed by burial rites of Neanderthals, which reveal belief in some kind of life after death. Humans became aware of their uniqueness and recognized one another as persons as they began to perceive the unfathomable depth of the other.

We do not know exactly how humankind became religious and how the notion of God entered the human mind. Experience of the numinous[42] is one way that is proposed; experience of natural forces in tempests and thunderstorms is another. There is more speculation than knowledge about the real process by which God entered the human mind. The psychological approach of Feuerbach might well be the path by which the notion of God became part of the human heritage. The rationalist error is to believe that Feuerbach succeeded in reducing God to a mere projection. Projecting is a normal application of the potential of the human mind to explain the experience of the numinous. But no matter how humankind learned to speak about God and to have faith in God, faith in God is a fact. In faith humankind encounters God, and the universe has become *capax Dei*. Reflective consciousness is the point at which the universe can address itself to God, its Creator.

The long history of the universe starting with the Big Bang—or however the evolutionary process began—thus shows contrasts with the biblical story in Genesis 1. The chaos of the origin is at least overcome locally in the process of becoming, but in the totality of the universe, we do not see an almighty Creator at work making order out of chaos. Rather, God seems to let the universe explore all its exceptional possibilities and waits with infinite patience for the appearance of reflective consciousness, the human mind. For the first time in the history of the universe, at least as far as we know and can experience it, there is a being able to receive the revelation of God. For about fifteen billion years there was no mental reality to address in God's creation. We shall have to go deeper into the question about why God created with this extreme patience and not as earlier ages believed God to have done it: with immediate effect, creating a perfect world.[43] The remark sometimes heard that Genesis gives us the right order, at least vaguely, of the evolutionary succession of plants and animals is without significance for understanding God's evolving creation. Genesis attests that the writer was aware of physical necessities: animals must be able to feed before they can live. Thus the creation of plants logically precedes the creation of land-bound animals.

It would not only be difficult to harmonize the biblical story with the historical evolutionary process, but it would be superfluous. As Bonaventure insisted:

> Scripture normally narrates what is sufficient for doctrine, though it does not so explicitly describe the distinction of the spheres whether of the heavenly bodies or of the elements, and it says little or nothing about the movements and the forces of the superior bodies and about the mixture of elements and elementata.[44]

To try to harmonize evolution with the biblical account would be to misunderstand the biblical text, which is to be read in the context of its time. It proclaims the Creator as the only source of being, against widespread dualistic concepts among peoples living around Israel. This revealed total dependency of all being on the Creator must be understood as related to the evolving universe. We shall say more about this, once we have examined some more aspects of the universe itself.[45]

But at this point we can recognize that the special status of humanity as expressed by the notion of *imago Dei* is by no means lost in an evolutionary context. The biblical text gives to humankind this special status by an arbitrary divine decision. In the evolutionary context we learn from our position in the general process and our function as a reflective consciousness of the universe that God wants to encounter the world through us. We have evolved close enough to God that our resemblance to God makes contact possible. This is evidently linked with the danger that humans may think themselves godlike and independent. To sever the links of dependency may make humans feel free, but as far as we can see today, the old story of the biblical Fall, though not historical but metaphorical, still contains the basic teaching that humans revolt against God by using magical means to become like God, whether it be an apple or a mathematical formula.[46] This aspect of reality is not changed by the transition in the universal mind-set from static to evolutionary. Human beings can know about God and can refuse to accept God.

By humans being reflectively conscious, the possibility of a conscious relation of the universe to God has become possible. The evolving universe, so far phenomenologically struggling to reach some level—at least when we observe its historical path—has finally reached a level where it no longer blindly follows its inner drives, whatever they are, but sees a guiding light coming from the experience of its Creator in the conscious human mind. With the human mind the universe finally transcends itself.

Such transcendence is definitely found only in the believers, those who know by faith that they are related to the Creator, whereas others can take an agnostic stance by denying any knowledge about a transcending reality. But God's reality does not depend on the agnostics' approval or disapproval. In faith we know that this whole universe depends in all its existence on the Creator, and having followed the story of this evolving universe, we may say that God wanted to be known and to be encountered by this universe's becoming conscious.

By going back to the classical idea of the analogy of being, we might go a step farther. This analogy begins by seeing God as the fullness of all being. Every being exists only because it is in some faint and limited way similar to God.[47] Seeing conscious human beings within the vision of the analogy of being, we may state that God is not a blind force, not a sort of fate as conceived by the Greek notion of ἀνάγκη (necessity), or the sum of natural laws, but a knowing God, who is conscious not only as we humans are, but, as we may state by projecting our abilities on God, conscious by knowing the divine self completely and knowing the whole of reality to the least detail. Theologians have always named this God's omniscience, which is the necessary condition for human consciousness to evolve within God's creation. Having evolved to become the image of God, humans know by personal experience of consciousness, even though deficiently, about the knowing God, who creates the evolving universe. But we are aware that God's knowledge of reality goes infinitely farther than our own.

Classical theology speculated about the knowledge of God as related to the reality of the universe. As Plato showed in the parable of the sun,[48] God by divine knowledge makes things knowable and gives them being. The Scholastics translated that to the statement *omne ens est verum*. Everything is real and therefore true as it is known by God. Humankind, having attained the ability to know to some extent the world around it, being able to search for the essence of things, and for the laws of nature that have emerged in history, imitates God, and is imaging God in the attempt to apprehend and to understand what God knows.

TIME, CONSCIOUSNESS, AND GOD'S ETERNITY

Here we might be tempted to fadd "what God knows from all eternity." This would lure us into a discussion about what it means if we call God eternal. That would require another book.[49]

Human thinking finds it hard to liberate itself from time-inspired concepts, though we hardly know what time is. As Augustine asked: "What, then, is time? I know well enough what it is, provided nobody asks me."[50] The notion of time has been the subject of endless discussion for eons. Aristotle reduced time to movement in space. With relativity, time has been geometrized; it is handled as just another dimension of space. It is measured by cycles and at least in principle is reversible. On the other hand, the arrow of time as found in the second law of thermodynamics describes a nonreversible direction.[51] Time for us humans is also experienced as strictly irreversible: no one can return to the mother's womb. And even though in a mathematical description we may think of time as negative,[52] a time machine is a dream of science fiction. What Kant in his *Critique of Pure Reason* calls "forms of perception" delimit human ability to think about reality. We cannot conceive a timeless horizon. Therefore, whenever we try to speak about God's eternity, our language is tinged with time. We seem unable to imagine a timeless eternity of a living God.

Even more difficult is the problem of how to relate the time-structured universe to the eternal God. On the one hand, we know by faith that God acts in this universe that is dominated by time, and on the other hand, we confess God to be eternal. Whitehead tried to separate time from eternity by speaking of the *eternal nature* of God, in which all potentialities of the universe (like Platonic ideas) are contained, and of the *consequent nature* of God remembering the potentialities realized in the course of the evolutionary history of the universe. But Whitehead considered the consequent nature of God also as eternal, God being somehow part of the universe. In our opinion Whitehead's God loses the transcendence needed to see God as Creator, though Whitehead throws a sharp light on our inability to understand eternity and its relation to temporality.

These problems have been recognized among Christian theologians[53] of all times. Eternity is one of the more important issues of what is known as *theologia negativa* since the time of the church fathers, in which the central premise is that we cannot know God directly, but only through metaphors. The notion of eternity is accessible to us only in this negative way, by denying the properties of time we experience in its transience. To us, God becomes present in time. It is in the relation of this universe to its Creator, our Creator, on whom the whole universe relies and in whom we trust, to whom we pray for help, and whom we adore in time, and it is in time that we know about God and that we confess God in our worship. Thus we can apprehend but not comprehend the eternal God. We believe that the God who created space and time and everything in them in God's own way, by letting them evolve, transcends space and time in a way beyond our time-bound understanding.

But we might see in time not merely limits set for us. Time also offers the potential to evolve. If modern physics measures time by the distance covered by light (electromagnetic waves)—they travel roughly 186,000 miles in one second—or by frequencies as in atomic clocks, it is related to the time of classical Aristotelian physics with its regular and most often cyclical movements. For "exact" time, regular movements are useful: sunrise and sunset in ancient times, the rotation of the earth today, and older measurements of time by distance covered in heavenly cycles. But such regular movements do not measure the world of becoming, which rightfully is considered as important if not a more important parameter for measuring time. By physical standards, these are enormous lengths of time that are rather empty in regard to becoming.

If the appearance of a new reality in the universe is measured by the parameter of time, a variable that would not be useful for physical measurements because the unity would not allow its use in algorithms, it will appear that time has a tendency to become more and more dense: the scale of physical time needed to bring forth something new has shortened greatly over the history of the universe. Thus time need not be seen as the isotropic reality that physics uses in its calculations. Evolutionary time is measured primarily not by cyclic movements or by the movement of a photon, but by the becoming of new realities. Within this perspective time is the essential dimension of God's creation. By creating time, God created the dimension of becoming, which seems to be the only meaningful dimension of the universe: through time, humankind evolves in the universe and becomes able to encounter its Creator. This seems to be the important aspect of time in its relation to the Creator.[54] Understanding time and eternity is not within our grasp; we can only speak negatively about eternity. But the time we experience is the condition without which nothing, including ourselves, could have evolved.

By becoming conscious, we became aware of the time dimension and its limitations, especially death. Whereas past centuries saw time only as a measurement limited arbitrarily by the Creator (just enough to rebuild the original order of the universe) we have learned to understand time as necessary for becoming in an evolving creation. But this temporality also gives us a glimpse of eternity. As Goethe's Faust says in the last scene: "Stay on, moment, you are so beautiful," we all know this deep desire to stop time from running.[55] For God, time does not run away. The Creator, in an incomprehensible way, transcends time and is fully involved in time: God is transcendent and immanent. Though we do not know how to solve such paradoxical statements, in God according to Nicolaus of Cusa the "complex of opposites" is the answer to which our consciousness might at some moment open.

SUMMARY

Having shown the inadequacy of the quantitative argument, we have begun to look for parameters that would allow a coherent description of the evolutionary process, that is, of creation. Consciousness, known to us by internal experience, has been followed backward in its history. It appears to have started early, becoming visible in its most reduced forms with the earliest forms of life. Consciousness becomes measurable by the range of its effects and the range of its perceptions and projections, though these measures reveal only some aspects, not the core of the reality of consciousness.[56] Using these measures permits description of creation as the ascent of consciousness, which in humans reaches the point where it opens to the awareness of the divine. Theologically, this is significant for understanding God's creative intention: human creation means humans become able to encounter God, to become *capax Dei*. Because evolution is a time-dominated process, this encounter unavoidably raises the question of how time and humans in time relate to the eternal God. Human consciousness, being time-bound, can offer only negative language to answer the problem, as given by a *theologia negativa*. Even though there is no solution to the time-eternity paradox, the parameter of consciousness remains valid for the description of evolution, of creation, and hence for understanding the intention of the Creator. But this is not the only possible parameter, as we shall see in the next chapter.

4 THE EVOLUTION OF INFORMATION: A HALLMARK OF GOD'S CREATION

A third parameter, after union and consciousness, that we propose is information. In information we distinguish meaning and carrier. Information is present and is used in different ways on all levels of being. New aspects of information become evident on levels of being, and wholeness of living creatures becomes constitutive. Information in its essence appears essentially immaterial. But throughout evolution it is extremely effective, taking new aspects and opening new possibilities as evolution goes on. The evolution of information reveals new qualitative levels, but so far we cannot say what are the creative forces that bring forth these new levels of information, which becomes more and more effective. A more manageable aspect of levels of information is the way information is stored. And storage is complemented by the ways information is communicated. Using insights into the evolution of the parameter of information, we see creation as a universal process on the way from materiality to spirituality.

BITS AND MEANING

The universe as God's creation is not perfectly ordered, but as we have seen, the evolutionary process brings forth highly complex forms of order that are necessary for life and thought to function. In the human world, structures are created that inform the surroundings. This is recognized early in Aristotelian and Platonic philosophy. Aristotle especially uses current images of artisans to show how things become what they are: an artisan, who has conceived the form of a table, gives this form to the material he uses. Information as a concept is related to this Aristotelian hylomorphism, though modern thinkers may have forgotten about it. In our world, the newly created information of science and technology brings about changes: inventing machines, finding new medical treatments, obtaining more refined knowledge about the structure of the universe—all this creates information. To possess information may give one power, and often information protected by patents leads to high income.

Information theory has been widely discussed in recent years. Interest centered on the possibility of storing information, especially in a form that could be fed into a computer system. Consequently, information has been measured by counting the bits needed to store certain information. Artificial intelligence imitating and even surpassing human intelligence was, and sometimes still is, thought possible. The power of modern computers is without doubt astonishing, and to those who do not understand their internal structure, computers seem to be able to calculate at a rate humans are unable to follow. In regard to results, this is certainly true, especially if the same algorithm is employed many times. But there are always two points to consider:

First, the computer is only as good as the combination of its electronics with the program. Human beings made both. The program instructs the computer to memorize data in binary code and, when computing, to add or to subtract, following a code based on the same basic instruction.[1] Though the versatility of the computer is remarkable because of the ingenuity of the programmers, at its basic level it only registers and adds and subtracts binary numbers.

Second, the computer never knows what it is doing. The meaning of the bits is not recognizable by the computer. To the question Is the human brain a computer? John Searle, using the convincing Chinese-room argument, answers with a clear "No. A program merely manipulates symbols, whereas a brain attaches meaning to them."[2] The essential point is that computers cannot handle meaning. That is why translating machines are best for technical languages, whereas with poetry they are lost. Even though one may write a program eliminating most errors in translating, the essential point is that the computer never knows it: the output has no meaning for it, since it handles only bits, never content. Bits can mean anything.

Though computers are very helpful in the workplace because they eliminate much tedious rewriting in revising a text, they do not handle meaning, and the manuscript collages of the 1960s and 1970s belong to an age that is past. Theorizing about the use of bits and measuring information by bits, information theory has lost much of its appeal because it did not come to grips with meaning. Information has value only in its meaning. Information is not measurable in bits; we can measure only the bits needed to store information in a meaningful context. In a program we need one bit to distinguish between male and female, war and peace, dead and alive, guilty and not guilty, but the computer handles only one bit, without ever knowing its meaning. We shall therefore not ask for the number of bits needed for information: beyond the technological handling of information within an informed context, this number does not contain any information. To understand the role of information within the evolutionary context, we ask where information occurs and is valued.

INFORMATION AS AN ESSENTIAL PART OF EXISTENCE

Information in its valued form is meaningful as related to the real world: technological, agricultural, environmental, spiritual. Information that is not related to anything is worthless and meaningless. What the computer churns out is meaningful only if there are human beings to read and/or to use the output, be it a bill or a car.

We find meaningful information on the levels of evolution. On the human level there is no doubt about the enormous amount of information created and exchanged. Teaching in schools, colleges, universities, and similar establishments is an institutionalized way of transmitting information created by others. We consider that in modern societies, the first twenty years of life are needed to give the next generation the information to survive in our world.

Nobody today can use all the information available in the human world. To make the necessary information accessible has become a major problem. Publications in all fields of knowledge—certainly a mixture of new knowledge with large amounts of redundancy and pseudoknowledge—are so numerous that no one is able to read it all. The total information contained in the knowledge of the human population of the earth is not in the hands of an individual, but is a communal possession. To participate actively in the use of this information, we have to become specialized, at least to a certain extent. The role we may play in the society is defined by the information at our disposal.

Obviously, information is not limited to scientific information. Poetry, music, the arts in general, news, and mystical experiences are informing us in their way, defining our actions and our attitudes. Information is not limited to the libraries, the data banks, though they contain very impressive and useful accumulations of data. Whoever has studied and thus acquired information knows that one cannot do this without books. Fortunately, acquired information is handed down from one generation to the next; we do not need to invent it all anew.

If we took away the accumulated information of humankind, we would find it difficult to make even the most simple stone tool. As humans we have enormous amounts of information at our disposal. Though this is not our only aspect, it is an important one. For the last fifty years we have become increasingly aware of information as a widely presented constituent, not only of human reality, but of the whole biosphere. Ever since breaking the DNA code, ever since we learned to read the four-letter alphabet in its triplet wordings, we know the means by which genetic information is stored. We can read the protein that is to be produced if a certain sequence of DNA is translated via the RNA replica and the functioning of the ribosomes. But we are far from understanding the code in its complete meaning for the living being.

Some correlations between specific genes and their expression in individuals are known. For example, we know for certain whether certain hereditary illnesses, such as Down syndrome and Tay-Sachs disease,[3] are present by looking at the genes. But for most other diseases there is no one-to-one correlation, which makes genetic counseling difficult. "Everybody is genetically defective,"[4] carrying "at least five to ten genes that could make him or her sick under the wrong circumstances."[5] Genes have not a one-to-one relation to the phenotype; rather, they cooperate to produce a single effect. To define the parts of the genome that produce hair color, fingerprints, or intelligence is a task far from being mastered. Writing out the human genome will give the total sequence that is not the same for all humans. But we are still unable to read the material meaningfully, with a few exceptions. We know about some of the splicing mechanisms. And we have learned that some DNA sequences may be read differently according to where one starts reading. The enormous amounts of so-called junk DNA, parts that seem to be unused in the hereditary process, are not well understood. As has been shown recently by Werner Arber and his team in Basel, what has been labeled junk can play a decisive role in establishing drug resistance of bacteria. We may safely state that, even though some progress has been made since the discovery of the DNA structure and the genetic code-letters, we are not able to interpret all meaning in the code, and beyond the first line of proteins produced, we are far from having unraveled it.

But for all the large gaps in our knowledge, which may eventually be filled, there is no doubt today that all living beings carry with them the information that constantly replenishes used cells. Folklore has it that the body cells of a human being are renewed completely every seven years.[6] Actually, the time is variable: blood cells last a much shorter time, but neurons of the brain and the heart muscle cells last for a lifetime. For all these renewable cells, the correct information has to be sorted out from the total program stored in the nucleus of each cell. However this is realized, there cannot be any doubt that all living beings continue to exist by continued processing of information.

We can be assured that information is of crucial importance not only in the human world, but also in the whole biosphere. If we go one step farther back in evolution, it is more difficult to see information as an essential part of reality. But there are at least a few hints that some kind of information is at work even on the level of chemistry. Autocatalysis, perhaps the last step in building molecules before life originated,[7] uses information contained in molecular structures. The molecule itself with its structure is its information. This is recognized especially in the generation of levogyric or dextrogyric molecules,[8] when both forms energetically are equally probable. In macromolecules, without changing the composition, the left or right configuration of a molecule changes its activity, most visibly within living cells. To be active, enzymes must have the correct sequence of amino acids and need to be folded in the correct way. Even on the level of atoms we see some information present as memory. When the inner structure of simple atoms is deformed, it is remembered and regained.[9]

The simpler the structure we encounter, the less visible is the information it contains. In the simplest atoms it might even become difficult to postulate the presence of information, which can be more clearly distinguished in more complex entities. This would correspond to the evolutionary structure of the universe if information is a relevant parameter of the process. Like consciousness, information fades away the closer we get to the earlier states of the universe. All the hydrogen atoms in the universe date from the time of the Big Bang. Their nuclei, the protons, have a lifetime more than many billion times the age of the universe, though theory postulates their eventual decay.[10] This decay would indicate that they contain some information, which might be seen in the inner structure of the proton with its nucleus "composed" of three quarks.

The farther the evolutionary process advances, the more visible information becomes as a constituent of reality. But as we have already seen, information is not present in the same way at all levels of evolution. Information itself has its story of evolution.

ASPECTS OF THE EVOLUTION OF INFORMATION

At the atomic level, we cannot differentiate information from structure. Though more complex nuclei can assume many shapes, some kind of memory appears to allow the atoms to regain their original shape, and information does not seem to be distinguishable from structure. In the atomic world, we might say that each atom is its information for itself and for its environment. But in this world we do not see information at work that could be distinguished from the atoms themselves. The most visible information at this level might be crystals such as diamonds, in which the lattices show clearly ordered structures informed by the atoms. The carbon atom is interesting in that it forms multiple crystalline structures: diamond, graphite, and the fullerenes. The same phenomenon of ordered, informed structures is found on the level of molecules. Crystals like salts of organic molecules, and sugars are part of everyday life. Though it seems to be justifiable to state that these highly ordered structures are informed, we are unable to find any other information than the structure of the atom or the molecule itself.[11] They are their information; they do not, at this level, carry information distinguishable from their structure.

This situation changes fundamentally with the appearance of life. In appearance molecules are the same as on the prelife scene, but they have changed their function. They have now become carriers of information. We can clearly distinguish between the molecular structure and the information contained in this structure. There is still a largely unclear process leading from DNA to the phenotype, say to blond hair and blue eyes. But there is no evidence of identity between the blue eyes and the DNA structure. The latter contains the information that must be read and transferred. The DNA in itself does not produce the living being; it is the library, which needs to be read by a living organism. The human genome is not a human being; it is not even part of life outside a human cell.

The expression of the DNA of a genome in its full meaning, say in the blue eyes and blond hair, needs multiple intermediate steps that at present are not well understood. We have learned to read the first expression of DNA in peptides (protein molecules) and to make use of this knowledge. In recent years we have induced bacteria to produce human insulin by splicing the necessary DNA into plasmids that can be introduced into the bacterium, which multiplies this information and starts to produce the desired enzyme. Such an accomplishment is still relatively easy on the level of bacterial evolution. If one tries this procedure with eukaryotic cells, the new information must be spliced into the DNA in the nucleus to become effective. In principle a cell recognizes its own chromosomes. If one introduces foreign chromosomes, they may be effective for a few cell divisions, but the cell will eliminate them quickly.[12]

Even on the immediate DNA level the information is not strictly defined. In fact, the DNA language is not univocal. There are at least two DNA languages: the one used by the chromosomes in the nucleus of the cell, the other by DNA in mitochondria, which seem to be related to the archaea.[13] Evidently, meaning in the DNA sequences is identified not only by the sequence of triplets, but also by the locality where it is read: the nucleus or the mitochondria. Meaning is not knowable from the structure of the molecules alone, even if we were able to read it completely. To identify the meaning of two identical sequences, we need to know where the sequences are read.

At this point of evolution the information is no longer completely identical with the atomic or molecular structure, as we might suppose it to be on the preliving level. The material structure becomes rather the carrier of information whose meaning depends as much on the reader as on the DNA sequence. We find an analogical situation in human languages, which may understand the same sequence of letters in quite different ways, for example, *belle* in German and French: the Germans ask a dog to bark, and the French think of a beautiful woman. In other words, the infrastructure or the material carrier of information can no longer be identified with the information. The exchange of messages uses some kind of material carrier, but the carrier is not the message.

DNA is by no means the only form of information we encounter on the level of living creatures. In living beings we can observe several communication systems. Cells can receive and release messages[14] via hormones. The result is not immediately recognizable in the structure of the hormone; the structure is a signal understood by the specific cells, which in turn go through a cascade of internal signaling before the information contained in the message is transformed into results. Here again we see information carried by a molecular structure, but not identical with that carrier.

Similarly the neural system, the other important communication system within living creatures, uses various means to communicate messages from one part of the body to another, from sensors of all kinds to the brain, where the input is transformed into a symbolic representation of the sensed reality. Neural signaling, though using transmitter substances, the number of which is not yet definitely known (at least there has been a slow but constant increase, starting with the first few molecules such as serotonin and norephedrine identified as transmitter substances),[15] transmits information that cannot be read from the transmitter substance. The information might rather be contained in places like synapses where the transmitters are released, whereas the molecules used seem at best to contain only some of the message. Today we can follow in some detail the combination of transmitter substances with electrical impulses running through the nerves, but we recognize here that all our research into the fine structures of the brain has not shown how we know consciously what we know: brain structures have not elucidated how we recognize meaning.

We know that the unity of a living organism depends on this internal communication system, be it hormonal or neural, or some other yet unexplored system. If one or other system fails, the organism may fall apart or lose control over its parts, as in paralysis. If the propriosensors of an organism fail, the individual can no longer control its movements because the necessary feedback information is no longer communicated to its central nervous system. When the sensors to the outer world are no longer usable, as in blindness or deafness, orientation in the environment and viability of an organism are reduced. The viability depends directly on the organism's ability to gather inner and outer information and to relate it to the organism as a whole. An enormous part of this information is used subconsciously, as when the movement of the muscles is coordinated in walking or running. Fortunately, we normally need not move muscles or the digestive system consciously. The lower and early evolved parts of the brain handle these matters. Thus the coordination of muscle tension in movement is assured by the cerebellum, which leaves the forebrain free for more conscious, nonautomated actions.

No higher organism is viable without a highly developed communication system by which its parts are held together. The unity is realized not through mechanical means, but through appropriate signals containing information.[16] There are mechanical junctions as well. But these junctions are still present when the organism is dead, even though they will then start to fall apart. The reality of life exists in a system not only because of information transmitted to it by DNA, but also because the system is continually processing information. Living organisms maintain their reality, their wholeness, through information. What was once called the soul may be identified today as the totality of information at work in the organism. This understanding could open a new realization of the soul, *anima forma corporis*, as the informing reality of the organism. This could help to avoid the dualistic misinterpretation of the soul overcome by scholastic philosophers but dominant in European philosophy since Descartes.

One might have some hesitation about using the concept of soul in this context because it seems dualistically laden. But recall that the unity of a living being is assured because of information constantly transmitted by a communication system using carriers not identical with the information. And information is essentially immaterial. This is evident if we consider the phenomenon of communication among animals. The language of the honeybee is clearly symbolic: the message transmitted uses the orientation of the honeycomb with reference to the gravitational field to direct to a food source by giving orientation with reference to the sun's polarized light.

Regarding communication of living organisms with the environment, there is a symbolic interpretation of what an eye receives as input. We normally take too quickly for granted that we see directly the outside world. The colorful picture we see is a symbolic representation of the interpreted input from electromagnetic waves of the small portion that the eye can register of a much wider spectrum. We know what the world looks like. But this does not mean that the world is like that. On the other hand, all animals seem to be successful in orienting themselves within this world. Thus we may at least postulate a correspondence between the world out there and its perception by animals. This correspondence is mediated by symbolic means, which are typical for the brain's representations of the environment.

Symbolic preponderance is most evident in languages: the song of birds and warning shrieks are signals well understood, though regionally different; a Canadian crow must learn the language of French crows before it can successfully participate in the life of a French flock. Among insects we find chemical signals, pheromones, attracting males.[17] By taking the exterior appearance of poisonous or aggressive insects, some try to induce their aggressors to avoid them.[18] Mimicry, used by animals and plants, deceives predators and prey. Cuckoos lay eggs that resemble the eggs of their hosts. Male fireflies of one species are tricked by females of other species, using the firing code of the male's species; if the male goes for it, he becomes prey to be eaten. In the biosphere a wide range of information and disinformation is going on.[19]

There is even a wide range of sign language among mammal vertebrates. Dogs raising a foot show playful expectation, a sign often misunderstood by cats. Among chimpanzees social behavior has clear signs. A successful hunting chimpanzee, whose property rights are respected, will be asked for parts of the prey by outstretched hands. To pass the alpha animal, a lower-ranked animal puts its hand on its forehead,[20] a sign still in use among most military establishments.

The influence and the use of information in the biosphere are visible everywhere. The ability to use information is gained by observing the environment, by heredity, by watching other animals (e.g., mothering among chimpanzees), by learning new ways of acting (e.g., titmice in the English Midlands learned to pick the covers off the milk bottles delivered to houses, knowledge that spread within a short time over most of England and even to the Netherlands). Informed behavior is by no means purely instinctive, though among insects and mollusks instinctive behavior seems to be preponderant. Thus one may study the mechanized behavior caused by stimulation of a single neuron on this evolutionary level.[21] On a more advanced evolutionary level the information is no longer codified in such a strict way. Animals show flexible behavior and sometimes clear use of past experiences. Baboons trust the experience of a weak older animal rather than the fighting powers of the younger males to avoid the menace of deadly danger from lions.[22]

The closer we look at the biosphere, the more it becomes evident that use of information is quite diversified, and it appears that, even without taking into account the human species, we can distinguish clearly recognizable levels in the quality and flexibility of information. With the appearance of humankind the qualitative jump in using and in producing new information is evident. Humans started to make tools on a large scale, and traded them over enormous distances, in Paleolithic times. They developed highly sophisticated hunting weapons that enabled them to kill prey many times their own size. They domesticated animals and bred them into quasi-new species, and selected otherwise unviable grain for farming.[23]

They discovered human personhood in its individuality and uniqueness; they discovered their openness to the divine. They began to pray and to worship gods. Humans desired information and asked questions about the heavens and about the earth; they wanted to know whence they came and whither they were going. Religious experiences were translated into myths of origins and destiny that gave information about the unknowable. Science as the enterprise to explore knowable reality has created an enormous amount of information that enables humans to go to the moon, to build instruments of extreme destruction, to grow food in amounts sufficient for a larger population than has ever lived on the earth, and to plan for the future in respecting the conditions of the earthly environment. There is no doubt that in humankind information has reached a peak of essential importance within the evolutionary process. So the question arises: If we can scale this process, which aspects could be used for such a scaling?

SCALING THE EVOLUTION OF INFORMATION

We have claimed that we can see qualitative jumps or innovation in the evolution of information. To use information as a parameter, we shall have to get some kind of scaling. The scale will not be numerical, since bits do not provide a scale for meaningful information. To find a useful scaling, we shall require a closer look at and clarification of aspects of information, as it evolves. Three principal questions concerning information need to be answered: (1) How is information created? (2) How is information stored? and (3) How is information communicated?

Creation of Information

We know very little about the process of creating information. The informed structures of atoms and molecules are explained by the existence of natural laws, which themselves are taken for granted. They are found, but we have no explanation why they exist. Some laws of physics can be reduced to more basic laws, but ultimately, we have to accept the laws. The very concept of law demands a lawgiver, though some modern scientists have tried to make this an abstract issue. Instead, they refer to a body of laws, which presumably exist in themselves, and they claim that the very notion of a "body of laws that would precisely regulate *all* nature" was unknown "until Galileo, Kepler, and Descartes."[24] Such ignorance can be called science hagiography or mythology. In reality this concept of universal law, governing all of nature, is science's heritage from the Middle Ages. Knowledge about the existence of universal law directed all research and was based on a theological argument. Aquinas states, in justifying the term "law,"

> The very notion of the government of things in God, the ruler of the universe, has the nature of a law. And since the divine reason's conception of things is not subject to time, but is eternal, according to *Prov.* 8:23, therefore it is that this kind of law must be called eternal.[25]

Since all things subject to divine providence are ruled and measured by the eternal law, as was stated above, it is evident that all things partake in some way in the eternal law, in so far as, namely, from its being imprinted on them, they derive their respective inclinations to their proper acts and ends.[26]

Modern science has certainly made an abstraction of the lawgiver, but the concept of eternal natural law is inherited from what some persons call the Dark Ages. If the theory of everything is not just a dream, but would give the secret of understanding of all natural processes, it would to Aquinas mean to read the mind of God. Stephen Hawking, in his claim that by knowing the theory of everything "we would truly know the mind of God,"[27] probably did not realize that he argued like a Thomist. In any case, we are unable to explain or understand the origin of the laws of nature. We may discover them and understand their interrelations, but we take them as given information instructing the whole of reality.

Natural law as a simple all-encompassing law is probably a dream. The laws of physics, though they govern the physical aspects of matter, have so far failed to explain the laws of living creatures. Physical laws are naturally at work in living beings, but do not explain their living reality and the laws by which they are governed. We are ignorant of how the laws of physics came into being and of how the laws governing life arose. Matter obeys the laws of physics, but we do not know where these laws come from. As Einstein stated, science is based on "faith in the possibility that the regulations valid for the world of existence are rational, that is, comprehensible to reason. I cannot conceive of a genuine scientist without that profound faith."[28] He often repeated his deep conviction "that a persuasion, akin to religious feeling, concerning the rationality or comprehensibility of the world is at the basis of any finer scientific work."[29] The most fundamental information found in the universe, such as the laws of physics, as laws of nature, escapes reasoning.

We must accept that the universe is informed by laws; we do not know how they have come to exist. Einstein answered his own question "Why is the world comprehensible?" with the statement: "The fact that it is comprehensible is a miracle."[30] Einstein is by no means the exception in acknowledging this reality. Eugene Wigner speaks of "the miracle of the appropriateness of the language of mathematics for the formulation of the laws of physics" as "a wonderful gift which we neither understand nor deserve."[31] Steven Weinberg finds "the ability of mathematicians to anticipate the mathematics needed in the theories of physicists quite uncanny. It is as if Neil Armstrong in 1969 when he first set foot on the surface of the moon had found in the lunar dust the footsteps of Jules Verne."[32]

Physicists obviously accept the universe as informed by laws, even though they have no theory explaining the origin of these laws. We might doubt that, without the deep conviction expressed in the quotes just cited from Aquinas, modern science might ever have come into existence. Einstein asked in this sense: "What a deep faith in the rationality of the world structure and what a desire to understand if only a small reflection of this reason revealed in this world must have been alive in Newton and Kepler that they were able to unravel the mechanism of the mechanics of heaven in working solitarily for many years."[33]

The origin of biological information is no better known. According to Neo-Darwinist or synthetic theories, the origin of any information is due to chance. Darwinist dogmatists constantly refuse to look at the deficiencies of this theory. As any second-term student in statistics knows, chance is defined as the unexplained variance in a distribution. How the unexplained is to serve as explanation is barely understandable. The statistical probability of chance mutations making possible the concrete historical evolution has never been shown to be viable with real evolution. Some dogmas of Neo-Darwinism have been shaken in recent times, and their defense is weakening today.[34]

In biology we know no more than in physics how the rules of life were established and why they are what they are. Nor do we understand how the biological code was fixed. For the time being we have no clear understanding of how the DNA code was written out. We speak about change and selection, but we do not understand how these progressive changes from archaea to human beings can be explained. In Darwin's time it was a courageous step to postulate mutations: the majority of biologists still believed in the immutability of species.

Carolus Linnaeus (1707–78) published the first comprehensive classification of flora and fauna since Aristotle. He introduced the binomial classification, which allowed him to classify every living being according to its genus and species: the classification system still in use with some refinements. Linnaeus classified humans among the primates as *Homo sapiens*, later refined to *Homo sapiens sapiens* to distinguish today's humanity from earlier human forms. Linnaeus's classification became in the nineteenth century, and is still today, one of the principal arguments in favor of evolution. Linnaeus rejected such an idea: he meant to describe species as they sprang forth in the creation story from the hand of God. When on June 30, 1860, at Oxford, Bishop Samuel Wilberforce, in a debate about evolution with Thomas Huxley, discussed Darwin's ideas, he could refer to opinions of the most renowned scientists of the day. Despite the myth, believed by many scientists, that Huxley overcame the bishop in their debate, the bishop was in the eyes of the public more convincing by pointing out the weaknesses of Darwin's arguments.[35] Understandably, mutation became a kind of battle cry for the defenders of evolution.

Having in the meantime made the point that evolution is a reality, one should now explain, within the statistical framework of the DNA structure, what specifications are required for mutations in order to bring about the evolution that has led from primitive forms of life to ever more complex and conscious forms. Though it is clear that mutations occurred, creating new information that was selected on, and though we understand fairly well the process of selection, we still have no explanation for the appearance of selectable information. The evolution of highly complex information is still unexplained. We know the general story, as in physics, but we cannot explain the laws creatively at work in this story.

If we leave the purely biological level to enter the human world, we seem to have clear experiences of how new information arises, and we seem to have a good understanding of the laws governing human existence. But on closer look, we are again in difficulty. We can learn mathematics, but why are humans the only ones we know about who are able to discover the laws of geometry and arithmetic? Why can humans argue logically? Why have some persons new insights or ideas in science, in mathematics, in politics, in architecture, in music? Who invented the wheel, agriculture, schools, writing? Who thought first of burying the dead, of praying to God?

We are more or less able to tell the story and even to date these events. But the information going into the creation of human abilities is still unexplained. We know the story, but its creative aspect transcends our understanding. We can say: "It just happened,"[36] but there is no good theory to explain why in the thirteenth century Europeans were able to build Gothic cathedrals, and why in the Middle Ages weavers began to use pedals on looms. Invention on all levels is not fully explained merely by reasoning. Afterward we see that anyone could have had the idea. In hindsight, the egg of Columbus is an easy solution to a problem. But how we get ideas escapes comprehension. We need insight before we begin to prove something in science. A new hypothesis is not deduced, but intuitively grasped and proven or disproven. Thus on the human level as well, new information arises unpredictably.

The creative process of the universe seems to be little understood. But we should not call for a god to fill gaps in our knowledge. Even though we do not understand it, we can read the story of the creation of information, from the laws of physics, through the development of life, to the insights of humans. If we look at this story without prejudice, we can discern three basic levels: matter, life, and mind, which may be structured into sublevels such as prokaryote and eukaryote, protozoan and metazoan. As is evident, the later always build on the earlier. But beyond serious doubt the story of the evolution of information is marked qualitatively, not quantitatively, by these three levels.

Having been unable to grasp the process of creation of new information while recognizing qualitative levels in the evolution of information, we shall try to verify these levels by looking for their specific features.

Features of Storage of Information

We can follow the story of creation of information under another aspect, namely, its storage. This is not a question of megabyte hard disks or a question of the number of bits involved. The question is how informational content is stored.

On the lowest level of matter we do not clearly see where the laws of nature are localized. The atoms follow laws; they do not store them for further reading. With some exceptions such as autocatalysis and perhaps crystallization, matter does not present information to the outside and is not active in using information. One may say that matter has its information in its structure, but it does not actively reach out to communicate it. Hydrogen atoms are not actively in search for oxygen atoms in order to form water, though their structure is informed to do so when conditions are right. Information is used in chance encounters. Only organisms and chemists bring together the right elements under the right conditions to make use of the information contained in the structure of atoms. In the universe these encounters are chance events: the enormous mass of the universe, compared to our living planet earth (plus possibly other living planets), makes the probability of the evolution of matter not totally zero, even though more than 99 percent of the matter of the universe is only hydrogen or helium. The transformation of matter according to the laws of physics into structures may be seen as a path to fix information and to make present in the universe a series of some ninety-two[37] informed elements, which are able to form molecules if chance does allow for this or if an organism or a chemist uses them.

The storage of information exhibits another quality on the level of life. DNA contains the information; it is not the information. The structure of the DNA sequence has little in common with the realized, the informed structure, which is the realization of the information stored in the DNA. We can differentiate between the molecular structure of the stuff of the genes and the meaning. Elaborating the human genome eventually will produce a kind of cryptogram that seems more difficult to decipher than cryptograms created by human beings: there is visibly no code breaking for the sequence in general; the meaning of every bit will require identification. The progress in the field, for example, knowing start and stop sequences, is helpful, but since most genetic information needs splicing after having been read into RNA, we are at a disadvantage at the start when reading DNA information.[38] Our knowledge of how this cryptic information is used to make blue eyes or a highly gifted mathematician is at present quite limited, although it is an active field of research. Knowing exactly the DNA sequences of a newborn baby does not allow us to make predictions about the future adult's intelligence. Knowing about the parents would allow better predictions.

DNA is clearly the carrier of codified information. Its function in the cell is that of a deposit of information to be tapped when needed. In nonliving matter the molecular structure is all the information to be found, but within the living organism the molecule is used to store information that in itself has nothing in common with the DNA. There is a natural process, by use of the information stored in the DNA, to go from the fertilized egg to the fully developed mature organism. This phenomenon of information storage is something absolutely new: no other matter is known to store information whose content is not essential to this matter as such. There is even something immaterial about this information: though matter is used to store the information, the order, something nonmaterial imposed on matter, contains the information.

Thus life is not only living matter, but it shows features of information storage that are unknown in nonliving matter. From this perspective genetic information transcends the qualities of nonliving matter. To serve as information, DNA must be contained in a living organism. Left to itself, DNA does not produce an organism. The information must be read by an adequate living cell.

The information carried by DNA is central to life. But DNA does not contain all the information we find in the animal kingdom: animals have genetically fixed instinctive knowledge and the ability to learn by experience. A blue jay, having once eaten a butterfly that fed on a poisonous plant, will regurgitate it and will in the future avoid those butterflies.[39] We have already mentioned the language of the honeybee, which is able to store information about the place where it collected food. Birds learn new melodies by imitation. Chimpanzees learn their mothering behavior in this way. Past experiences are stored in memory. Birds learn routes to their winter quarters by following older birds. We still do not understand how homing pigeons learn their landing place and how they find their way home more than a thousand miles away. Squirrels learn to adapt to their dangerous environment by using electric cables to cross busy roads. Chimpanzees learn to make primitive tools like sticks to collect termites, and they learn to use branches as weapons to defend themselves against predators. At least among vertebrates we have clear evidence that information is stored not only in DNA, but in the brain as well.

The memory, where information is stored, is made possible by the structure of the brain. But the content of the information stored in the memory cannot be studied by looking at the brain. The physical structure does not tell us anything about the experience of the animal, though somehow this information is stored there. The quality of the storage is not the same, in that we can find some graduation: nematodes[40] may remember for a day or two, but elephants are said to never forget. The range of memory grows as evolution of higher animals proceeds. As the brain becomes more complex, it becomes the organ of central organization, which coordinates the functioning of the parts, and it becomes an organ of information storage. This organ enables animals, depending on their evolutionary status, to have an ever more complex informational representation of the world around them stored in their brains.

We may distinguish two systems of information storage in living creatures that are unknown in the world of pure matter. One is DNA, which is basic to life and its continuity, and carries the information to build the second storage system. In some animals, especially insects, DNA contains as well the information for specialized informed neurons, which we know as fixed instincts that always follow the same routine. Some kind of genetic transmission of information may be found even in higher animals such as the Galapagos finches, which after more than a million years still recognize instinctively the shape of predator birds not present on the Galapagos Islands. Human fear of snakes may be transmitted this way as well. But in general, the brain and its information storage are too complex to be transmitted genetically.[41] DNA contains guidelines to build the brain, but these guidelines become functional only by exercise. To a large extent this exercise results in a selective elimination of a large number of neurons, which in humans occurs primarily during the first ten years of life. This process of selective elimination of neurons over a long period has been observed in all higher mammals.[42]

The second system of storage of information in the brain differs from storage in DNA in a number of essential features. DNA information is relatively stable; the information stored in a brain is rather flexible. The range of information collected and processed is extremely wide. Higher mammals can remember visual impressions and relate them to their present perception.[43] And they learn by experience: the information can be rectified, complemented, or replaced. Thus the information system linked with the brain evolves faster than any DNA could permit. Stereotyped behavior, as in insects, is rare in higher mammals. Conditioned reflexes like those of Pavlov's dogs work best if one removes a large part of the forebrain, but when the intact brain is functioning, the conditioned reflexes fade rather quickly.

Although there is a possibility to correct transcription errors in DNA during a short interval before methylization of the newly formed DNA molecule, the only way to handle established errors is to eliminate them; to live with them might cause an illness such as cancer or enzymatic defects. But storage of information in the brain is at least in principle always accessible to correction. This informational flexibility, open to new experiences and doing away with older ones, is naturally not without some costs, and requires effort to adapt to conditions other than those familiar to the individual. It is therefore not astonishing that there will be individuals with fixed ideas, dogmatists in science, in religion, in politics, and in economics. This is understandable, because correcting information is not merely a question of exchanging some bits; it means carrying the consequences of these changes. To follow a routine is always easier than to blaze a new trail.

On the human level the storage of information gets quite a new dimension. Animals store information in the soma, in the brain and in the DNA. Humans not only possess an enormous storage reservoir in their brains with theoretical capacity probably greater than the accessible knowledge, but they have begun to store their information outside their somatic system. The only approximation to this way of information storage in the animal world may be the marking of territory, as we observe in the habits of rabbits, dogs, and cats. These are signals to the outside world, like those still in use by humans who put up signs like POSTED or NO TRESPASSING or build fences or walls. Such behavior belongs to a world of primitive signaling of territorial behavior. Still, there is some difference between humans and animals. Animals use pheromones, but humans use sign language.

Besides this borderline case, there seems to be no extrasomatical information storage before humankind appeared in the course of evolution. The earliest form of extrasomatically stored information can be found in the cave paintings of Paleolithic times; the next step was the invention of writing, which for the storage of information can hardly be overestimated. In fact, the invention of writing was an evolutionary step comparable to the invention of DNA as storage for genetic information. The invention of writing liberated the evolutionary process from the limitations of the generational process: suddenly ideas could be handed down over centuries without the intervention of a biological ancestor.

As long as oral tradition was the only way to hand down information between generations, some biological connection seems to be of primordial importance. With written texts this is fundamentally changed: we can read Aristotle and Confucius, the letters of Paul and the five books of Moses without ancestral relations with those men. Information storage and transmission were liberated from biological constraints. The invention of printing made the storage of information more reliable. Accidents like the destruction by fire of the library of Alexandria, which resulted in the loss of many handwritten books forever, are today more unlikely to be such a profound loss: the accumulated information will be preserved in copies in other libraries.

Recently electronic storage of information has been added to printing. The advantage of this new storage system is most evident in its condensing and retrieval power, plus the capacity for voice and picture storage. Past events can be stored as they were seen by persons with cameras: filming, videotaping, or just taking photos. Historical information concerning passing events, and not only signed treaties, can be stored in a density unprecedented in evolution.

All three systems—writing (including painting), printing (including photography), and electronic storage—have one thing in common: the information stored cannot be deduced from the material used for storage. The information does not change with the medium or with the ink used by the writer or printer. The kind of lettering used does not influence the informational content. Though extrasomatic information needs a medium to be accessible, it is essentially independent of the medium. Humans can make use of information independently of whether it is stored in print or on some hard disk. Clearly, information is here an immaterial and causally effective factor.

We have thus found clearly differentiated ways of information storage, corresponding roughly to the levels of the evolving reality: matter-life-mind. But information is not only stored; it is communicated as well. This leads us to the third aspect of information, which enhances a clearer distinction of the evolutionary levels of becoming information.

Communication of Information

Information is communicated in many ways. But if we try to differentiate these ways, we find a pattern similar to the different ways of information storage.

At the lowest level of purely material structures, exchanges of information are not known. Atoms and molecules, when energetically excited, may emit photons of specific wavelength, and they absorb only photons of specific wavelengths that create the spectral lines, which signal the presence of the specific elements or molecules. These signals, though readable by spectrometers and giving valuable information to scientists, are not addressed to anyone in particular. The emitting or absorbing atoms or molecules do not communicate with the scientist; the spectral lines, which identify their presence, are indicators of the structural properties. The spectra are not coded information. They are not addressed to anybody or anything.

On the level of life the situation is different. As with the storage of information, we distinguish two levels: genetic information transmitted only by molecular communication, and symbolic information transmitted by sounds, smells, and signs.

Genetic information is transmitted from generation to generation by DNA, which assures the stability of a species and a limited evolutionary flexibility. The transcription of DNA into a living creature, starting from a fertilized egg, follows a long cascade of molecular transcriptions and influences. From the DNA, with the help of various enzymes, specific information is transcribed into an RNA strand that, after being spliced into a definite useful sequence, serves as the matrix of the amino acid chain that is the desired polypeptide or protein. These may need to be spliced with other polypeptides to form an active enzyme. This is the case with insulin. Or the protein needs to be folded with specific matrix molecules into a special conformation to become activated: the cell has to add further information, which is not transcribed directly from the DNA. The presence of this protein within the cell, together with other proteins, may indicate this cell has some specific function, like a nerve cell or a liver cell.[44]

Some molecules guide a cell to find its place, for example, in the liver or within the neural system. The molecular signals are probably complemented by electrical signals. The plasticity of the embryonic cells varies over time; cells cease to be able to become any part of the body. How the one original cell develops eyes, fingers, lungs, and brain is only poorly understood, though it happens without doubt. Not only must the original information contained in the DNA be communicated from one cell to the next two in mitosis, but the cells must communicate with one another in order to create a whole organism.[45]

The communication necessary for development of an organism, starting with an egg cell, if not dominated, at least in a large part depends on molecular signals. On the other hand, the sensory input and motor output of the neural system seem to be dominated by electric signaling, combined with multiple transmitter substances at the synapses, which combine neurons with one another—one neuron receiving signals from as many as ten thousand synapses. The organism, becoming more and more a centralized system as evolution progresses, handles inside communication—a task complemented by hormonal signaling—by which animals know, as humans do, what is the position of the foot or body in relation to the gravitational field of the earth. The system also handles signals it receives from the outer world: images, sounds, smells, tastes, and tactile impressions. Information received as waves, as molecules, or as sensory pressure is transformed into knowledge that relates the organism to the outside world by means of a symbolic representation.

But living beings not only receive signals emitted by radiation or vibrations, or hard and soft bodies, they also communicate among themselves by means of chemicals, movements, and sounds.[46] The complex mating behavior of birds and mammals may be mentioned in this context, as may the warning cries of many species of birds and small mammals. These cries are by no means genetically fixed, but differ from one population of crows to another.

Communication on the human level has become multidimensional, and is flexible in the means employed. Information can reach an addressee today by phone, by letter, by E-mail, by messenger (animals do not send other animals a message to be transmitted to a third animal) in many types and languages. We are living in a time in which communication networks are playing an ever more important role. The medium used for communication is irrelevant to the content of the message, to the meaning of the information. Information can be transmitted by written or spoken words, by pictures, and by films. Even music can be transmitted, either recorded or written. Here as well the meaning is not changed by the carrier of the message, though the quality of the transmission may depend on the carrier.

On the human level, communication of information has become virtually independent of specific material carriers, though some carrier is necessary. But the information is not changed by changing the carrier. We have no difficulty in distinguishing the message from the carrier. The ink on the paper is not the message, nor are the sounds of the words: one might say *tree*, *arbre*, *Baum*, or *arbor*, and the meaning is the same.

Thus in the communication of information as well as in its storage, we find a continuing evolutionary process, which establishes a more and more important causal factor that is not materially fixed. Information uses a carrier and therefore some energy, but this usually small amount of energy has no relation to the consequences of information, which may be enormous.[47] Information, like the world of mathematics and the laws of physics, cannot be identified with any material substrate. The more the evolutionary process advances, the more information becomes visible as a matter-independent entity.

This short analysis of creating, storing, and communicating information clarifies distinguishable levels of evolution: the levels of atoms and molecules, of life, and of mind. The orientation of the evolutionary process, though not explained, is evidently going into the direction of a reality marked by more information. Evolution itself takes place more and more on a level that transcends the materiality of the world. Information used as a parameter of evolution thus confirms the orientation of the process we have already found with the parameter of consciousness. But our task is not to discuss evolution; the consequences of the stated orientation for a theory of evolution must be elaborated by science. Our task is rather to understand the evolving reality as God's creation. Does the evolution of information assist us to understand the work of the Creator?

INFORMATION, AN ASPECT OF CREATION

So far we have tried to see the reality of information within the evolutionary universe we live in. And we believe this world to be God's creation. The science-based description of the levels of information, its storage, and its communication does not contain immediate references to the Creator. But if we adopt the basic relations of the analogy of being, we can have a second look at the evolution of information as it becomes less matter-bound and causally more effective. God's evolving creation is gradually bringing forth more effective and less materially bound information. Within this perspective, information shows a certain degree of similitude with the Creator, whom we believe to transcend all materiality. By evolving to a higher informational level the universe reaches a closer resemblance to its Creator. Regarding immateriality, we are reminded that in our normal language matter is opposed to spirit. Information is certainly more closely related to spirit than to matter. The story of information's evolving traces concretely the path from matter to spirit. Is that too dualistic a description? There is no totally unspiritual, uninformed reality. Pure matter without some information does not exist.[48] Matter is thus a relative concept, defining a minimal presence of information, of spirit. Therefore, it might be better to say that the evolution of information traces the way from materiality to spirituality.

With humankind this evolution has reached a level where the evolution of information becomes knowable and is pushed forward by consciously searching for and creating new information. We experience this as a spiritual activity, essentially not bound by matter. We experience consciousness as transcending the brain structures it requires to function. Though the materiality of the human mind's brain is not to be denied, this recognition of its material infrastructure is no reason to deny the spiritual aspect of the human mind. This transcending reality is experienced with any sentence or prayer we say. The wholeness of the human being does not allow for a separation of these two aspects; we are material and spiritual at the same time. But there cannot be any doubt that the mind produces information that is basically immaterial in its effectiveness. The matter involved in transmitting or storing information is irrelevant to the content. The human, by being not only body but spirit as well, has reached a new level of likeness to the Creator, whose creation reveals an evolution of information.

Humankind, by becoming heavily engaged in this information-creating process in a conscious way, becomes what Philip Hefner has named, mostly in its societal aspects, the cocreator.[49] By creating new information, humankind changes the surface of the earth and changes itself: humans no longer evolve by storing information in genes, but by creating new information and storing it by various means inside and especially outside the body.

Humans have thus a growing body of immaterial, but very effective, newly created reality. Humankind surrounds itself with a spiritual, bodyless aura of effective information transmitted by material means. It is also able to receive information of a purely spiritual kind, even though typically it needs to be transmitted by material means from one person to another. The human communication closest to this purely spiritual kind of information transmission is found in the arts: in music and poetry, in painting and architecture, for example, in the Gothic cathedrals with their awe-inspiring atmosphere. And even though there is no scientific verification for it, knowing about the immateriality makes mystical experience of the divine compatible with the evolving creation.

In an information-dominated universe an evolved mind able to create new immaterial information should be able to enter into some kind of communion with pure spirit, which the mind can recognize as the Creator, who contains all possible information. As Whitehead's eternal nature of God contains all potentialities, as Plato's[50] and the Scholastics' God knows everything and thereby gives knowability to it, we may add that the Creator of the evolving universe, which is on its way to a growing likeness to the Creator, holds in the divine self all possible information. We might even go further. If the Creator is the fullness of all being, then all being exists because in some way it resembles the Creator. The information-dominated universe thus points to the God in whom all information is contained. We might then say that all evolved reality exists insofar as by being informed it has some resemblance to God.

The biblical teaching that humankind has been created in the image of God may be newly interpreted: humans are, among all creatures we know in this universe, the species most able to handle immaterial information and to communicate it through arbitrary codes, without intermingling code and meaning. With this ability to differentiate between code and meaning humankind is, at least in principle, able to receive divine revelations without confounding the signs with the information. Even more, understanding the creation itself as revelation, humankind has manifested the talent to recognize the hand of God in the evolving universe. Obviously, we do not speak here of scientific proof. Science has no way to prove or disprove a transcendent God. It may show the contingency of this universe. But this is no proof that God exists or creates; it is only a demonstration of our limited knowledge.

God becomes visible in creation if one looks at the world with the eyes of faith. Those who look for only scientific evidence do not see beauty. Whoever asserts that science is the only valid approach to reality cuts himself or herself off from the divine. Faith transcends science, without negating it, but even positively integrating it. Whoever is not willing to worship and pray must first be converted to be able to see God at work in the world. One needs the eyes of faith.[51] For the Christian at least, it should not be difficult to see in this information-oriented and information-dominated evolution the work of the Creator, who lets creatures become more and more similar to God and thus to participate in God's spiritual fullness.

SUMMARY

Analysis of the evolution of information beyond the technological question of bits confirms the orientation of the evolutionary process from atoms to mind, from materiality to spirituality. Information has become more accessible as a parameter using the criteria of storage, coding, and communicating information, which point in the direction of a growing independence from specific material carriers. Information transcends its material aspects and manifests the spiritual dimension of the universe as most important, bringing about evolutionary changes that lead to higher levels of being. Creation thus appears on its way to becoming spiritual, and more similar to the transcendent God, who is the fullness of the spiritual creative power. This ascent of evolution to higher levels of spiritual reality does involve a small part of the universe; most of it has reached the final status of background radiation, and most of the rest is on its way to becoming dead stars. We therefore ask if there is any recognizable purpose in what in human terms would be considered a terrifying waste of energy.

5 EVOLUTION OF FREEDOM IN GOD'S CREATION

The question why the Creator accepted such a wasteful way of creation seems to be related to the phenomenon of freedom, which we consider as another parameter of evolution. We know from our own inner experience that freedom exists. So we ask, How did freedom evolve?[1] The Cartesian distinction between free humans and machinelike animals is replaced by a gradual process, from early stages of freedom in animals to human freedom. Evolving freedom in the animal kingdom makes us aware that deterministic causality is to be replaced by a statistical model. The statistical description of the universe offers indications of a partially free universe, where higher degrees of freedom appear. Structures that support freedom assure stability in this universe. Religion has its own role to play in the balance between freedom and structure. Being present in the universe, freedom brings with it evil as a statistically unavoidable possibility. Evil is the price to be paid for freedom, but freedom is the necessary condition that makes love possible: love of neighbor and love of God.

FREEDOM, A BASIC HUMAN EXPERIENCE

During the last two centuries and especially during this century, scientists have tried to convince us that there is only determinism and no room for human freedom. In this they are to a large extent victim to their heritage of the notion of the all-encompassing eternal law taught by medieval Scholastics. In their time this notion led to endless controversies between defenders of God's providence determining everything and defenders of human freedom and moral responsibility. The Middle Ages had no solution to this dilemma. The notion of an unchanging eternal God, who guaranteed eternal laws governing everything, and human freedom, on the other hand, seemed to contradict each other. Naturally, moral theologians and preachers such as Berthold von Regensburg insisted on human freedom, not by proving it, but by proclaiming it to be there because of God's free decision. In the deterministic medieval world humans were deemed to be free because God does not want to exercise power over human decisions; human freedom in this view exists without being submitted to any force or to any person.[2]

Scientists cannot appeal to God in order to explain the existence of human freedom. The notion of eternal unchanging natural laws governing everything in the universe, which is not modified by the belief that God is the master of these laws, stimulates a tendency to believe in strict determinism.

Fortunately, deterministic-minded scientists do not represent the majority of humankind. If they were correct, education and especially moral education would be meaningless, since all persons would be determined in their activities. Moral responsibility would not be possible. Any crime would be condemned or not condemned, based on the determination of jurors and judges. Lawyers would fake disputes, and proofs would be meaningless. In a thoroughly determined world no one would be responsible for what one did or failed to do. The reality of our courts is obviously not based on the acceptance of such a deterministic world. Jurors as well as judges are convinced that criminals are responsible for what they do, as those who judge them are conscious of their own responsibility.

Though we all know that there are more or less deterministic necessities, such as eating, drinking, breathing, and sleeping, we also know of times when we can refuse to bow to them, as in a hunger strike, which might end in death. And in general we all know from our inner experience that we are responsible for what we do, that we can decide about our actions, and that nothing can force us to consent to anything we do not want to do. Of course, under torture we may be forced to do things to which we do not freely consent. And in this case nobody would excuse torturers: they are held responsible for what they do. Human freedom, though not to be proven within a scientific framework of all-encompassing eternal laws that represents a belief system excluding freedom, is held to be real by various freedom movements. Organizations such as Amnesty International would not make any sense in a fully deterministic world. For good or evil we cannot escape the individual experience, reconfirmed by moral claims made by others on us, that we can decide freely what we do or fail to do.

This is not to say that we always know what we are doing. We may be in error as to the value of what we decide to do. Even in following the conscience, the bystanding inner supervisor of our doings that makes sense only as controlling a free will, we might be in error. We may not be free to do the right thing because we are ignorant. As Thomas Aquinas stated, doing evil always involves some kind of ignorance.[3] Nobody does evil because it is evil, but in aiming at some good in an inordinate way. The decision is always ours.

All the attempts of various psychological schools to show that human action is determined by genes or past experiences, despite in some cases a propensity toward certain ways of acting, have never been able to show that persons must follow compulsive propensities. Kleptomania has always been considered a psychiatric disorder or illness, not a normal case of deterministic human behavior; but it cannot be aligned with the acts for which we are responsible because we have freely decided to act that way. The fact that we accept as a case for the doctor some persons, like alcoholics, who have a diminished ability to decide freely about their behavior, shows that there is commonsense agreement that normally we are able to decide freely about what we want to do and what we want to refuse to do.

To prove the existence of freedom is not possible within the scientific framework, which is looking for deterministic causes that exclude freedom. Since by definition freedom is a question not of deterministic natural laws, but of undetermined behavior, it escapes the scientific model. The human experience of freedom, though clearly supposed in judging everyday behavior, cannot be communicated in a stringent way, but it is there.

The burden of proof that the existence of human freedom is an illusion is thus laid upon those who deny it. As long as human responsibility is accepted as a given reality, and education in morals is not considered a vain enterprise, we know that human freedom is a generally accepted reality, a reality for the defense of which some are ready to fight and to die.

HOW DID FREEDOM ARISE?

We can be assured that freedom is essential to human beings, and that it can never be taken away from them. Outwardly, they may be enslaved, they may be made prisoners, but they can resist in never consenting, in never changing their value judgment,[4] ready to die for their convictions. The history of the church has seen many martyrs, not only in ancient times, but in our days as well, for example, in the Gulags and concentration camps, to name only the most obvious.

But though we encounter freedom as essential to humans, little has been thought about how human freedom came into existence. This is not astonishing. Philosophers and theologians have always been more concerned to show how the human being is different than to understand how humans stand in continuity with the rest of the universe. Science has shown no interest in human freedom: it is a reality disturbing to scientific search for all-encompassing universal natural laws. Freedom escapes the scientific approach in that it is by its very essence unpredictable in its outcome. Psychology itself, though by name it claims to be the science of the soul and tries to become an honest science able to predict future outcomes, has shown relatively little interest in the reality of human freedom. In modern times freedom has prospered in ideologies and politics, but has not aroused scientific attention. This is astonishing, since scientists often claim for themselves the freedom of research and teaching.[5] Thus we have little input from science when we try to understand how freedom arose and became possible in humankind.

HUMANS AND ANIMALS

Traditionally, philosophers and scientists have taught that animals are strictly governed by instincts. In the heyday of mechanism in the seventeenth century, Descartes could conceive animals as machines that function mechanistically. To some degree, this idea was a special expression of ideas handed down from the Middle Ages. Then it was believed that everything with the exception of the human free will was ruled by universal eternal laws, which made things happen by necessity. Motivation based on mechanism is clearly described by Buridan's donkey: Buridan argued that if one places a hungry donkey between two exactly equal heaps of hay at exactly the same distance, the donkey will not be able to make up its mind and will starve because the motivation from both sides is the same. Modern psychologists might expect the donkey to become neurotic. But in the real situation there cannot be any doubt that the donkey is not mechanically minded: it will go to the one or the other side and eat, without considering theories about its inability to do so.[6]

The idea that all animals are strictly following their fixed instincts is certainly as old as the scholastic school. It believed that "animals, which respond to their environment by natural instinct, are not spoken of as being moved by choice."[7] But the Scholastics knew well that humans and animals are not totally different. Aquinas stated: "So what is said, that man and the other animals have the same kind of origin, is true of the body,"[8] but he had an easier task with the soul. Since the soul was believed to be immediately "produced by God,"[9] the essential difference between humans and brute animals was ascertained. Having made this distinction, Aquinas recognized the different possibilities for animals to act. Life itself was defined as "self-movement," a definition closely related to the observed reality.

It was generally accepted that life knows lower and higher degrees. Some creatures move only according to their nature: "Such things are plants, which move themselves by growth and decrease according to the form with which nature endows them."[10] Other living creatures orient their movements according to their sensory input: "Creatures which have only the sense of touch, their self-movement consists merely in dilatation and contraction, like oysters—scarcely more than the movements of plants."[11] Other animals can sense objects apart from them, as hunting predators, and therefore are able to make more informed movements. But according to the Scholastics, this movement of a higher degree is nevertheless directed "by an instinct of nature which moves them to a particular activity by means of the form apprehended by the senses."[12]

This strictly instinct-directed behavior, though believed by the Scholastics to be informed by the senses, and thus a sort of reflex, dominated the scientific understanding of animals and their behavior until the middle of this century. Some even attempted to squeeze the understanding of human behavior into such a scheme, as Freudian mechanistic psychology did by knowing all the causes of behavior, the outcome, and how to repair bad behavior by using the correct mechanics. This scheme never really worked. Freud's most famous case, the Wolfman, when revisited in the 1970s in Vienna shortly before his death, still had his neurosis.[13]

This rather mechanistic understanding of animals (and humans) changed slowly in the middle of this century when ethology first became the science of instincts,[14] which had been considered to be fixed behavior. It eventually became clear that even instincts have to be learned. The notion of imprinting (Prägung) was developed by Konrad Lorenz, who was followed everywhere by the goslings that saw him as the first moving creature after they hatched. The releaser stimulus,[15] originally seen as perfectly inborn, has to be learned in an adequate way before becoming fully effective. Seagull chicks have to learn to hit the red point of their parent's beak to receive their food.[16] The notion of instinct as strictly fixed innate behavior has thus been softened.

Some behaviors, such as the coordination of members for walking and flying, are not all fixed from the beginning. Birds have to learn to fly and to see prey, and many animals have a more or less long period of learning to run. Such instinctive behavior is not fundamentally different in humans; they, too, must learn what they have been given by genes: they learn to walk, to recognize faces, and to speak. There are even clearly marked times during which these abilities must be mastered. Children who have not learned to speak by age six, because of deafness, will never perfectly master a language.[17] But the language spoken is not important for the ability to speak, though with each language specific ways of pronouncing, thinking, and arguing are acquired.[18]

Even inborn behavior such as the use of language is quite flexible and not fixed. This kind of flexibility is found in practically all mammals. Rats are able to avoid poisoned food by having seen other rats die from it, which has made it necessary to develop late-acting poisons to eliminate some rats. The instinctive fugitive behavior of most animals when confronted with humans can be overcome with relative ease. Animals considered to be wild can be "tamed." They may become accustomed to humans by more or less friendly approach and feeding. The whole range of domestic animals contradicts the theory of a strictly fixed instinct describing the total range of animal behavior. Most evident is the behavior of higher primates, which have a broad range of acting that is not instinctive. As the Middle Ages knew, the ape imitates human behavior. Thus one did not hesitate to include the ape in the hierarchy of humans, from pope and emperor down to the *homo silvanus*—humans supposed to be raised by animals in the forests[19]—and so the apes were inserted into the line of humans just above *homo silvanus*.[20]

During recent decades observers like Jane Goodall and Arndt Kortlandt have offered new insights into the complex behavior of chimpanzees.[21] We know with certainty that their behavior is far from being strictly governed by instincts. They have an aptitude to learn, such as making simple tools: they use sticks to get hold of termites, which they relish. They show simple moral behavior. It is good morals among chimpanzees to let others participate in one's find of a food treasure. But some cheaters among them try to have all the food for themselves, especially if it is something special. When this is discovered, the rest of the group sanctions this misbehavior: the cheater is excluded from sharing future finds of food. This is certainly not instinct. Nor is the consoling behavior observed among young chimpanzees who in friendliness bring back into the playing group a young one that has been offended and sits apart. Their capacity to learn, especially at a relatively young age, and to handle symbols seems to belong to this same potential beyond instinct. Chimpanzees exhibit a wide range of willful behavior that is not determined by their genes. They know how to imitate and to show among themselves friendshiplike preferences. There are more or less friendly animals among them. Kortlandt found respect for age, and even for disabled animals.

Everyone who owns a dog is more or less sure that the dog understands what one says to it. This is certainly true for some words, like those that indicate that its food is ready. A dog usually learns what it is allowed and not allowed to do in a house. And whoever has seen a dog getting off a chair that it should not have used can have little doubt that it knows that it did not behave correctly. In any case, behavior is not limited by ritualized instinctive behavior. The dog knows how to express its desires and to show what it dislikes.

What is said about dogs is found with most pets. They have a much wider range of behavioral possibilities than purely instinctive behavior, which is bound to follow a certain sequence of steps, and to start them again when they are interrupted. Higher mammals are not strictly determined in what they do. They follow cues from their sensory input, as the Middle Ages believed, and they have moods that change over time.

The point is that there is no abrupt gap between free humans and a mechanically determined animal kingdom. There is a rather smooth passage from human freedom to the kind of free behavior found in animals. Some instinctive habits are found in humans, and in a certain way we need such habits in the form of reflexes: fortunately, we can learn quasi-automated reactions, for example, when writing or when driving a car. One could argue that these are acquired instincts, as is our walking. We usually decide where we go, as most animals do, especially mammals and birds. Once we have learned to walk, or animals have learned to run or fly, there is no need any longer to think about how to walk, to run, or to fly: this has become an instinctive behavior.

Human behavior in its totality is not totally free; we are subject to the conditions of our existence. We are able to decide on a large range of activities for ourselves; in the extreme we can even put ourselves to death, though some psychologists may insist that this is no longer the behavior of a free person. No animal has such a wide range of possibilities upon which to decide. But there is little doubt that living creatures do have some choices and do choose. Moreover, in the animal kingdom we see the range of choices narrowing, the farther we go back in the history of evolution. Rhizopoda move around, and their movement is not strictly predictable; they have a certain vector of freedom, but this is far from human freedom.

Within biological evolution we observe an ever larger vector of possibilities to move and to act. There is no single line of evolving freedom, or of evolving complexity or centreity.[22] This is especially so when we observe a short range of evolution within a family of species. In the long range of evolution, however, a general trend toward more freedom can hardly be denied. Naturally, we avoid the fascination of quantity. If that were to be the parameter of value to judge the success of a group of animals, ants might seem to be the most successful. But as has been seen, we cannot reintroduce quantity as the decisive parameter, once we have decided to consider background radiation of no central interest for understanding the story of the evolution of the universe. And though ants in their biomass are a very successful group, which show a high degree of diversification in their species, there is no sign that any single ant species would have a radius of action and a vector of freedom comparable with those of a chimpanzee that eats the ants. An individual ant is limited in its possibilities, and in spite of their number, ants form no coherent network around the earth, as humans do in an increasingly more effective way.

FROM DETERMINISTIC CAUSALISM TO STATISTICAL CONDITIONALISM

By looking at animals and humans, we perceive different degrees of freedom incompatible with strict determinism. Though neither have absolute freedom, we can make predictions about their behavior. The behavior is limited in its possibilities. Statistical predictions become more reliable as the range of possibilities, that is, the degrees of freedom, decreases. Thus predictions about elections that involve a small number of parties are possible. Freedom of behavior is concretely linked to the possibilities open to the acting entity.

The more possibilities are open, the less the concrete behavior can be predicted. Statistical description, becoming highly unreliable with large degrees of freedom, is the best science can do. It may predict how an animal will probably behave under defined conditions. When conditions are right and degrees of freedom small in number, predictions become more reliable. Normally, deterministic activities described by science are statistical effects of the activities of many entities like molecules and atoms within a limited range of possibilities.

Even before life appears there is no strict determinism in the evolution of molecules. For example, amino acids form statistically at the same rate within the range of a standard deviation into one of two mirror-image molecules, enantiomers, according to chance. So far these relatively simple molecules have withstood attempts to synthesize them into only one of the single forms.[23] Generally, atoms have no immediate range of action beyond the electric and magnetic fields they exhibit, and the gravity they exercise because of their mass. Still, atoms have in their structure a vector of possibilities for combining with other atoms. This vector might be quasi-zero for the elements with filled electron orbits, like neon, argon, or helium, whereas for an element like carbon there is a quasi-infinite possibility of molecules in which it may be a part.

In the same way protons and neutrons can become part of any of the many chemical elements that occur in nature, plus a few very rare possibilities, which today scientists can synthesize.[24] Protons and neutrons in the universe do not search actively to form higher entities, but when conditions are right, as in stars, and especially during a supernova explosion, they may combine into chemical elements. Freedom in its negative form of not being determined to become one element or another—this is rather like a game of chance—can be seen even at this fundamental level.

On the basis of quantum physics with its essential indeterminacy within the range of the Heisenberg uncertainty principle, the proposal has been made that here the Creator had room to act. This seems an unfortunate idea, because it reintroduces the God of the gaps, which had been expelled by Dobzhansky.[25] God is not to be introduced to fill the gaps in a deterministic understanding of the physical world. The gaps in scientific knowledge are not there because God's action escapes the grasp of physicists. Physicists try to understand the reality of the universe, which only theologically is perceived as creation. In the world of physics there is no room for acts of God that physicists might discover, though one may find the whole universe a miracle that cannot be understood in its raison d'être if it is not related to God.

God's activity in creation cannot be proven by the uncertainty principle. This principle is, however, an indication that a strictly deterministic universe is no longer thinkable.[26] Moreover, chaos theory shows that even a small difference in the beginning of a process can lead to unforeseeable divergences, even if only one algorithm is applied. Actually, we do not have an algorithm that describes the behavior of an atom for any length of time. The often-invoked imaginary wave function of the universe has no more been written out than the wave function of an amino acid. Beyond the proton, the solution to the wave function equation becomes too complicated to be applicable, even when supercomputers are used.

FREEDOM AND STATISTICAL DESCRIPTION

It only appears that there is a strict determinism in the universe. Heisenberg uncertainty at the micro level and chaos theory at the macro level, along with the improbability of a wave function that explains everything, a theory of everything (TOE), prevent us from speaking concretely, with proof, of a deterministic universe.[27] Rather, all descriptions known are statistical ones. The chance of a possible event occurring may be approximately known. But it will always be impossible to absolutely predict the future of an individual proton, electron, carbon or oxygen atom.

Of course, a statistical description[28] is quite helpful for indicating a basic orientation of the vector of possibilities open to elements. Since on the level of atoms and simple molecules the distribution of possibilities is quite narrow, with a small standard deviation, the statistical outcome of reactions mimics deterministic behavior. The small number of events at the outer range of the statistical distribution is normally not taken into account. But as already noted, the interesting events in evolution always happen within the highly improbable range, at the limits of a statistical distribution. The median of the statistical distribution of events at a certain level may mimic determinism, whereas important events in evolution occur at the limits of the Gaussian distribution and thus are typically not determined in a describable way. They need some other explanation than the basic probability within a bell-shaped distribution.

No special reason is known why anything evolves and does not remain within the center range of the distribution. This raises the question of evolutionary theory, which is not our subject. The task of scientists is to find a satisfactory answer to this question. But the very fact that here we must use a statistical distribution exempts evolution from strict determinism. Statistical distributions like the Gaussian bell curve appear only when there are degrees of freedom, which permit the data to scatter around a mean. In evolution, the degrees of freedom allow probability distributions of elements around a mean that has established itself at a certain evolutionary level. If there were no mean in the distributions, nothing would be stabilized; the scattering would be totally unpredictable, and evolution would not take place. No species would be stabilized.

Scattering around the mean in our everyday experience is always rather narrow. At the lowest evolutionary level of background radiation, there is no recognizable mean: the universe appears isotropic. There is no center of the universe. Galaxies already reveal a mean; the distribution of mass in developed galaxies reveals a bell-shaped distribution from the center to the outside regions of the galaxy. In living creatures the scattering is around a type of a species representing the mean, which shows a high stability. This caused Aristotle and scientists of all times into the late nineteenth century to believe in a rather strict determinism ruling over the animal kingdom.

Escape from this apparent determinism is relatively rare. In our everyday experience evolution does not happen, at least not on the biological level. As already mentioned, only at the extremes of the distribution does something new emerge, which represents the widest escape from the expected, and which shows the greatest degree of freedom as compared to the mean of the distribution. The new entity normally introduces a new degree of freedom, a possibility of relations, actions, and existence that did not exist before.

Once a new reality appears at the extremes of the probability distribution, it establishes some kind of new mean and starts its own distribution. This becomes clearly visible in the kingdom of life, where new species must show enough stability within the environment to survive and procreate. The highly complex structure of life realized this by using DNA as the carrier of information about its own structure.[29] There is never a whole species that changes en bloc; new features arise only within relatively small groups at the outer edges of the distribution, but the bulk may survive unchanged for billions of years, as some bacteria of ancient times have survived.

FREEDOM AND STRUCTURES

New ranges of freedom appear therefore only within an environment that appears to be determined by the statistical mean. The mean gives stability to the environment and has a vector of freedom to be viable. Whether on the level of chemistry or on the level of life, if change in evolution were in the behavior of the bulk of the elements concerned, there would be no possibility for any form of life to evolve: adaptation in a quickly changing environment would be extremely costly, and no forms of life could persist. In order for freedom to exist in this world, structures are required to support it.

Freedom in the evolving universe is not an ideal reality. In the experimental world it does not appear as absolute freedom without restrictions. Such freedom cannot exist in this evolving reality. Rather, we see it evolve slowly with a growing vector of possibilities. The higher an element has evolved, the wider the range of its possibilities. However, a delicate balance exists between the supporting structures themselves and the vector of freedom supported by these structures. In evolution quite often the structures have a tendency to dominate by limiting the opening of possibilities. Horses, which started their history with the small hipparion, have become monoungulate quality runners and jumpers. They have become bigger with time, but their only future will be as horses. Their structure limits their range of choice and of action. They may survive as a stabilized species for a long time, but they are not likely to change dramatically in the future.

The history of evolution is full of such cases: species evolved to a certain level of specialization and were caught in a stabilized structure that was not open to any but this specialized future. Many mollusks that survived unchanged for the last six hundred million years can be classified as stabilized. The first way in which structures limit the future can be described as cladogenesis,[30] in which a branch forms with a closed future. The second way, more definitely closing the future and new possibilities, has been named stasigenesis: the level reached is definitely fixed or at least so it appears. Stasigenesis can easily lead to extinction: animals highly specialized for a very specific environment are unable to adapt to any serious changes. The history of evolution known through paleontology reveals a large number of animals that were unable to adapt to sudden changes because they were fixed in their structures. We need not invoke dinosaurs, whose disappearance has become a fashionable point of modern interest. Coral reefs have died because of relatively slight changes in temperature of the sea, long before humans made their entrance into this world. Stasigenesis can thus become thanatogenesis. (See figure 8.)

These structures can be seen on all levels of evolution. The noble gases are barely able to have any future outside nuclear processes within stars. Many stable substances in the earth's crust will probably change only by undergoing metamorphosis as they slowly slide into the depth of the earth's mantle by the process of plate tectonics. Elements in the core of the earth will probably not change until the sun becomes a red giant and churns the earth. Stability seems to dominate because evolution is a very exceptional process. Structures supporting freedom tend to stabilize, and if they become dominant, they have the tendency to last. Only when structures are strangled or become obsolete in the environment do they disappear, along with the species they represent.

There can be as well an overload of freedom in structures that can no longer support it. Examples of this kind of failure to survive in evolution are more difficult to find because the structures do not persist long enough to be registered in the fossil record. We may find examples in pathology: cells that

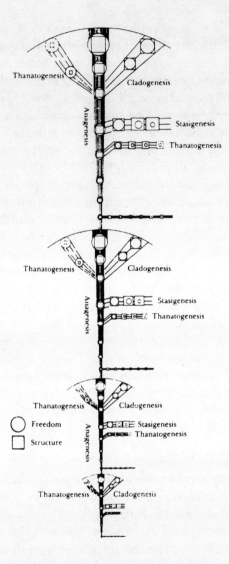

Figure 8 The schema tries to represent the evolution of freedom and structures in their indissoluble linkage: the circles represent the freedom supported by the structures represented by squares. The structures have a constant tendency to take over and to determine the evolutionary future by restricting the open possibilities, leading to cladogenesis, stasigenesis, and thanatogenesis. At all stages freedom too can become overly dominant, destroying the structures needed to carry it. This is the anarchical type of thanatogenesis. The evolution of freedom seems to depend on a very delicate balance between freedom and supporting structures. *Proposed to Karl Schmitz-Moormann by Professor Miguel Crusafont-Pairo, University of Barcelona.*

free themselves from their structural restrictions become cancers, deadly to the organism and deadly to the cell itself. In the real world this overload of freedom becomes thanatogenetic, death producing.

This relation between structures and freedom is most easily observed where we have the most experience of freedom, on the level of human evolution. Physically, humans are, like other vertebrates, restricted in movement by the structures of bones, joints, and especially the backbone. If freedom from restrictions were the ideal structure, then the amoeba with its numerous pseudopods would be the freest living creature, at least in freedom of movement. But the creature pays for this freedom of movement with the impossibility of any real speed or of any higher organization, and thus finally, its radius of action is limited. Any dog or horse, though limited to running with four legs, does better than the amoeba, which is highly adapted to the environment and seems not to evolve farther. Wherever we see a wider radius of action, we find the movements supported by structures that set certain limits, either in the movements themselves or in other capacities. Whereas most rodents can use their forelegs to grip nuts or other food, neither a horse nor a cow can do that anymore: their forelegs have become specialized into running structures that no longer allow another use of these legs.

Humans no longer develop their body parts for special purposes: bodily evolution has largely come to an end. No small populations would offer a chance for serious mutation:[31] the genes would quickly be taken up again in the common gene pool. But humans can develop special skills. Information and radii of action, and the freedom linked with both of them, are transmitted by extrasomatic means, for example, by teaching, reading, and television. The skill acquired offers an opportunity to exercise specialties, such as becoming an engineer or a doctor. As with all evolutionary specializations, this one may become obsolete. Many known professions are no longer exercised in the developed countries, but still have their place in developing countries, such as public writers. Blacksmiths, once among the most respected people in town, are a disappearing species. People who learned a now obsolete profession and did not adapt to a changing, evolving human world have lost their acquired range of freedom.

At this point in time humans show great differences from animals. Animals, outside the possibility of being trained by humans, cannot change their specialization, but human beings can. They can learn something new and exercise another trade from what they had before. With the general knowledge available in a society growing very quickly, and the consequent changes in the production of goods in all areas, most people recognize today that there is no guarantee of permanent employment in a specific job. But humans can begin something new. They are not captives of their specialties, of their structures. They can shed their structures and acquire new ones. Thus humans have acquired a new range of evolutionary freedom. Everyone is free to develop new ideas and new techniques, but no one is definitely bound by the knowledge of the past.

Genes may fix structures in a definite way, but knowledge and inventiveness set humans free to go new ways on which the genes have no information. Humans are free to transmit knowledge and ideas. Genes may give the basic structures of human beings from one generation to another, but the genes of an individual dissolve rapidly in the general gene pool, especially where intermarriage within a family is prohibited, as in most societies. Persons can be much more successful in handing on information to the future with innovative thoughts, ideals, and values. Probably very little is left of the genes of Augustine, Plato, or Aristotle that could be identified in anyone's genes. But the ideas and values they taught are still very much alive in our day. Humans have become able to break the boundaries of their genetic structures and to have access to a whole new horizon of innovations, some of which will survive, while others will not reach the marketplace of products, of ideas, of arts, of values. Some will live for a certain time, but others will surface only slowly, to remain longer and to influence the future much more profoundly.[32]

Obviously, this openness for innovation is finite. On the personal level, there are evident limits to what can be learned. No one could claim today the potential to acquire all available knowledge. Even if there were no need to make a living, learning takes time. To develop new inventions, ideas, and insights in science, philosophy, or theology takes even more time. And everyone has only limited time. Nobody can do it all. Whoever wants to know everything ends by knowing nothing about everything. Individual freedom does not permit an endless series of career choices. Persons are not confined in a kind of single-mindedness, since there is room for a number of genuine interests to develop. But human freedom is limited even under the best conditions. More often than not, these conditions are far from ideal; they force persons to make do with what they believe not to be their best choice. People are limited in their choices by their environment and by their abilities.

FREEDOM, STRUCTURE, AND RELIGION

Even the most innovative may encounter difficulties. The society into which new information, innovation, and new values are to be integrated is not waiting for such innovations. Like species, all societies need a certain stability, a structure supporting life, a constitution defining the central values of the society and the rules it has agreed to live by. If we are to believe Aristotle, the core of these structures is handed down as the religion of the particular society. The secularized societies of the modern world lack this basic stabilizer.

Most democracies live on the heritage of values that has come down to them from the religious traditions whence they started, especially from Christianity.[33] Once they have lost all relation to these transcendental values, they replace them with ideologies such as egalitarianism, which has its integrist dogmatists in the defenders of political correctness.

As we may observe in modern societies, the more religion has been relegated to the domain of privacy, the less reliable and more insecure the societies become. They need, like any society, the ability to pass traditional values and knowledge to the next generation. In times when anybody can proclaim a new value system, a new religion, societies begin to dissolve by overdoses of freedom. If everybody with a new idea were accepted as a great innovator to be followed, society would quickly turn into chaos with no basis known to be accepted as the rule for all members of the society. Too great an individualistic freedom turns into a form of limitless pluralism that makes the society unviable. The end will be the breakup of the society by a revolution that destroys the existing structures and makes life impossible. The society seeks a painful restructuring of itself or allows for the rise of a dictatorship that will impose structures.

Since humans are concerned, and not lemmings, they can in principle turn around at any time and reestablish lost values and have them respected. But the difficulties appear to be extensive. Sometimes outer constraints help to restore a more value-oriented society. This seems to happen especially when people are exposed to natural or human-made cataclysms: those in real need are more ready to help and to give than those with all the possibilities at their disposal. But in principle societies and individuals have at all times the potential freedom to search for values that give meaning to their existence and that structure the life of the society and of the individual.

As an overdose of individualistic freedom, with its loss of accepted common values, can be destructive for the society and for the survival of the individual, so can structures that are too rigid. They lead to a rapid loss of contact with the evolutionary movement of humankind. Evolution is manifest on the human level as rapid innovative movement. Strict structures inhibit innovation. Wherever a system is based on a conviction that centrally specifies the corpus of all essential knowledge, wisdom, and values, evolution will halt. Such societies stop participating in the evolutionary process and start to fall behind. An example is the Soviet Union, which could not keep up because of its rigid structures, and which finally broke up and destroyed itself in chaos, while the remainder of the society struggled to establish a commonly accepted value system.

If this description of the evolutionary process, especially on the human level, is correct, then the process itself, entrusted to some extent to humanity, naturally has a theological dimension. As we have often stated, the evolutionary process is the way God creates this world, and there is no other temporal world to look for. Humans have become at least partly responsible for the future of God's evolving creation, of which they are themselves a part. Churches, which are organisms that keep values alive within societies (one of their tasks, not their only function), have their role in this process. They must be stabilizing, but as churches want to proclaim the Creator of the evolving universe and be God's representative among humans, they must adapt their structures to this evolving reality. Any fundamentalism that claims to know precisely God's will is not a viable church structure within God's evolving creation, which brings forth ever greater freedom.

Bringing about and maintaining balance between the freedom necessary for creative innovations and structures that give security to the faithful are more difficult in the church than in other forms of community. People need to listen to the values upon which they may build their lives and to what they should believe. In a static universe there was relatively little difficulty since, in general, it was clear that "there is nothing new under the sun."[34] Religions had to be conservative, as the various forms of Christianity are. In the world of evolving freedom this mind-set is fundamentally changed. The one secure ground to build on is no longer stable. Churches resemble ships that had been tied to a mooring, but that have now been sent out on the ocean. New ways to find orientation are required. Some structures of the ship will be maintained, and they may even need strengthening, while others, like the moorings, have been given up. Since all of humanity has left the secure harbor of stability, no church can stay ashore and yet fulfill its mission of preaching the gospel in God's creation. Therefore, churches will have to give more room to freedom, permitting ideas and behavior to be tested before proclaiming an anathema.

FREEDOM AND EVIL

Any evolutionary development is painful. Mutations can be negative, creating defective, suffering creatures. But even when a mutation has a positive effect, it creates a painful situation for many individuals who lose their place: in biology their species might disappear, in humankind a learned trade is no more valued,[35] in science a theory is falsified and replaced, and in theology a cherished doctrine does not make sense anymore. As is evident from the development of Christian doctrine, the truth of tomorrow can make its appearance as today's heresy. But as is likewise evident, not all heresies of today will become tomorrow's doctrine. Some are just heresies. As evolution in general is not producing only the good, so new ideas can develop as aberrations, creating insecurity and destroying the basis of trust, if accepted uncritically.

There is a basic difference between establishing the truth by arguments in a static world and in an evolving universe. In the static world arguments could be linked to an unchanging reality, whereas in an evolving world this is no longer possible. In an evolutionary world truth cannot be definitively and absolutely argued. Rather, we are aware that truth is always surrounded by a halo of error. We do not know the future, which is an essential part of evolutionary reality. We are bound to be ignorant, at least to some extent.

Ambiguity may be considered the inescapable impediment for the human mind in an evolving world. But we must always make decisions about what to do and what not to do, as if we were really knowledgeable. Whatever we do or do not do involves infinitesimally the whole universe. Chaos theory reminds us that ultimately, each act is significant in this world. So we are taking risks all the time, whether consciously or unconsciously.

Unavoidably, we are constantly involved in doing things in an imperfect way. Whatever we do contains some error and can have some evil effect. Even the best-intentioned efforts, such as feeding people who are poor in developing countries, may have the undesirable side effect of inducing people to have more children, which enlarges the problem. Such dilemmas appear in different ways, and they have no simple answers. Whenever humans make decisions, the decisions will contain some error. Even more, since all decisions concern some structural change, and since there are no perfect structures, all decisions will hurt somewhere.

Human decisions and human actions are no exception to the general law of evolution. There is no perfect state ever reached that would allow a perfect human action. Evolution as a process is marked by errors. If we look at the long story that started with the Big Bang (or at Planck-time with the first laws of nature) and continues with humankind, we do not always have a pleasant sight. Many ways of life were explored and painfully abandoned. The story of evolution is not the glorious tale of ever better, ever higher forms of life. We must be blind not to see that any success of evolution was paid for by death and painful forms of dying. We see in television films big cats such as lions and tigers hunt deer, gnus, and other animals. Typically, we see the kill with some rather aesthetic remarks of the commentator, but we do not hear the desperate cries of the dying animals. The story of evolution is marked with long lines of extinct species, and there are more of them in the paleontological record than in today's living world. On the individual level, evolution is paid for with endless numbers of deformations and sick animals. Evolutionary dead ends are common. Nature is not good in the sense that it always produces the best forms. On the contrary, every step forward in evolution has been paid for with numerous painful events. Natural evil is quite common in the story of evolution.

Within the classical framework of a static world these phenomena might seem to indicate that there is no good God: this problem of theodicy has no possible answer within a static world, where the almighty God created a perfect world in the beginning. As Epicurus, quoted by Lactantius, stated: "If God cannot eliminate evil, then he is powerless; if he does not want to do it, he is envious; that he wants to do it and can do it is contradicted by common experience."[36] Luther's answer, that God need not be justified before the court of reason,[37] is hardly accepted by our contemporaries. The story of Adam and Eve and their Fall, which made sin responsible for all the misery, did not offer a convincing argument against the doubts of Voltaire, who was confronted with the earthquake at Lisbon. How could an almighty God permit thousands of innocent persons to be suddenly killed? In our day we may ask the same question with even greater urgency when we look at the Holocaust, the Gulags, the killing fields, or even Rwanda, where one out of eight humans was senselessly killed. Earthquakes in recent years with thousands of victims leave Voltaire's question still without an answer. This is true within the static universe we believed for millennia that we lived in. At least our understanding of the universe, derived from this faith, saw it as static.

In an evolving universe there is one essential difference: no definite perfection is ever reached. The evolving world is always imperfect. Some deficiency is normal in this world. There is always an openness to more perfection.

This difference still leaves open the possibility of attaining perfection step-by-step, following a rigidly fixed blueprint. God could certainly have created such a world. Every step in evolution would be clearly defined and consequently would lead to the next level. This would have meant creating a mechanistically determined world, in which humans would be the outcome of a rigorously determined process. But it would hardly be conceivable that humans would be free at the end of this process. Rather, they would have been utterly determined in their behavior. They would be unable to encounter God, and more specifically, they would be unable to love God and neighbor, since love is possible only if given freely. A deterministically created world might have been perfect in that no evil occurred, but it would have been a kind of mechanical toy for God to enjoy, not the object of God's love.

The story of evolution does not correspond to this deterministic process. We see that necessary conditions for a further step in evolution must be realized, but that the next step is not determined by these conditions. Evolution makes progress at the outer edges of the statistical distribution, and we see ever greater ranges of freedom evolve until in humankind freedom becomes one of the most essential features. Such progress at the edges of the statistical distribution necessarily implies that most of the distribution is not included and is left behind. Historically, the evolution of freedom is paid for with the nonarrival of the great mass of evolving species and individuals. The massive death of species documented by the paleontological record is the necessary price for freedom to evolve. Because nothing is strictly determined in evolution, anything can go wrong. In an evolutionary process that is not determined, in which freedom can appear, there are unavoidable evil and suffering. Therefore, there is a history of evil in the universe.

On the level of preliving matter we have difficulty distinguishing any form of suffering, but we see decay and enormous amounts of the original energy input cut off from a future: the background radiation, the black holes, the neutron stars, the white dwarfs. They all are, as far as we can observe, cut off from all evolutionary processes. Though they may last for billions of years, they have no history of qualitative evolution. Their existence seems to be utterly pointless. They seem to have no open future. From a physicist's point of view this is a consequence of the second law of thermodynamics, and there is no further question.[38] This does not make this enormous *loss* reasonable, at least not within a well-ordered and deterministic world.

But if we look into the universe, we find only a few indications that other planets might offer similar conditions to the earth that would permit the existence of living creatures. There are so many serendipitous conditions to be fulfilled that the chances for other living planets are not very high: the planet must have the right distance to its star, its sun not too hot or too cold. It must have a magnetic field strong enough to be shielded against most of the solar wind. It must have enough gravity to hold its atmosphere and its water. It must turn fast enough not to be overheated on one side by its sun while undercooled on the other side. The earth is believed by some to have gained its rather high momentum, making its revolution in one day, by the impact of an asteroid, which made the early earth at the same time lose matter that formed the moon. Venus, which C. S. Lewis saw in his *Perelandra* as a living star, turns once a year. It has become a very hot planet (about 600 degrees Celsius) with a cloud cover of sulfuric acid that makes for a strong greenhouse effect. The universe is not teeming with life, at least not according to our present state of knowledge. If qualitative parameters of evolution are applicable to the universe, then to a very large extent it is a waste.

In the realm of life, only an infinitesimal fraction of the evolutionary universe, but its significant part, we find a no less wasteful story. Enormous layers of chalk, dead coral banks, and other geological data tell the story of billions of deaths. Death has been a condition of evolution. And death is not simply dying; more often than not, it is a painful process. Physical pain, coming with death, is not limited to this final experience of living creatures. Suffering can last for long periods, even in animals. The living reality is in no way a perfected structure that runs smoothly at all times. Illness is not a phenomenon limited to human beings. Pain and suffering were a reality long before humans made their appearance. And they did not go away when humans emerged.

We do not really know if before humans, animals experienced some kind of psychic pain. What does the cheetah feel when it helplessly sees a lion kill its offspring, not as food, but just to kill? What do chimpanzee mothers feel who carry a dead child for days before finally giving it up? What do young animals feel when left on their own? What do animals feel that are sanctioned by their group because they are feeble, or because of misbehavior, as it has been observed in chimpanzees? We can only draw parallels to our own feelings. What appears evident is that animals already know a wider scope of suffering than bodily pain. Among humans, psychic pains are probably more important than bodily pain. The latter is certainly devastating, but psychic suffering goes deeper: it hurts in the core of the person.

Pain and suffering are clearly present at all levels of the realm of life; the higher the level, the greater the pain and suffering. And there is not only passive submission to them. The causes of these experienced evils are not only uncontrolled actions of the elements such as wind, rain, earthquakes, and volcanoes, but living creatures are the most widespread cause of pain and suffering. Life seems to be a constant battle against invading bacteria, viruses, and other infectious creatures. Animals fight for living space. What we call, euphemistically though correctly, the food chain is the reality of eating and being eaten. Within species the competition for domination and sexual priority is cause of endless fighting. The dream of good-natured animals, where killing within the species would not happen, is an illusion. One has to belong to the tribe to be accepted. For foreigners it is better to stay outside. This is very clear with ants and with rats. But even chimpanzees have been observed to kill other chimpanzees in order to conquer territory.

Finally, humans have proven to be even more dangerous to other humans than any animal or even microbe. They are able to kill one another for minor reasons like jealousy. Though it would be wrong to say humans do this normally, they do it, and sometimes they seem to lose all inhibitions in killing other humans.

Evolution has brought forth not only life and a living mind, able to decide freely and to reflect on its own decision, but the ability to do evil and do it by one's own decision. We do not know if animals really have a choice between right and wrong. They know what the alpha animal does not allow in a group, and they want to cover up when they overstep the rules. But this is far from distinguishing wrong and right. Humans—and this is an enormous step forward in evolution—not only have learned to transcend their immediate tribal context in accepting general rules and internalizing them, but also have developed the notion of a humanity in which all human life and human dignity is to be respected.

A presupposition of this latter step in evolution is that humans are free to obey or disobey such a rule. Humans, because they are able to decide for themselves freely, are thus responsible for what they do or do not. Humans are the first species that shows this clearly distinguishable dimension of morality. Though animals sometimes may suggest that they approach such a dimension, it is undoubtedly present among humans. Humans suffer evil, and they do evil consciously. Evil, as pain, suffering, and death, as decay and regression, as illness and defects, has been present at every moment and on all levels of evolution. Humans have added the new dimension of moral evil.

As humans became conscious of their responsibility to one another, and before they first dimly and later more clearly perceived the reality of God, they became able not only to pray, but to sin as well. Some disobeyed moral obligations that they experienced as laid on humankind by God. These phenomena are documented by many myths, including the human failure.[39] Sin in the strict sense is evident where God's commandments are clearly stated, as within the biblical covenant. Taboos and other restrictions of behavior are no longer important: sin is acting clearly and consciously against the known will of God.

This is the negative aspect of the human being's having become *capax Dei*. It seems to be a necessary condition of this human capacity. Only a being able to sin can obey God's commandments; only a free being who may refuse is able to love God and to be loved as a person, as a *thou*, by God.

In a world free of evil, freedom could never arise: everything would have to be ordered and strictly determined. In such a world any evil would be the fault of God, who could have prevented it. But apparently, God did not intend to create such a deterministic world. God did not follow a definite blueprint that would have brought forth a perfectly working world with no suffering and no evil. In that world, humans would be like puppets on strings manipulated by God. They would not be able to do evil. But they would not be able to encounter God or to love God. They would not be free.

There is no possibility for freedom to evolve in a perfectly predetermined world. The nondetermined world that we experience and see evolving cannot be perfect. Some waste, some pain, some suffering, some evil, are always present. In creating a universe that was to bring forth humans with free will, God accepted the inevitable consequence of concomitant evil.

Thus suffering, pain, and death are the price for freedom. The Creator evidently did not intend a world of perfection; God highly prized freedom as the outcome of evolution and accepted the inevitable consequence of deficiencies on all levels. Only if we recognize this rich intent can we begin to understand that the quantitatively enormous waste in the universe is not an argument against the Creator. The world is good not because it was created perfect in the beginning, but because it was created able to bring forth freedom, to bring forth free persons able to love God and neighbor. The price for the ability to love God in freedom, the only way love is possible, is the enormous amount of suffering we find in creation. It might be forever difficult to understand that a loving God would allow all this suffering, all this evil. Such difficulty is less a sign of human compassion than a sign that we humans underestimate how highly God prizes humans and their freedom to love. Without it, humans would not be able to encounter God, to find real happiness in loving God and being loved by God. It may for all time be beyond our comprehension that God could accept such a price for the exchange of love with humans. But for the Christian this mystery has its counterpart in the fact that God did not exempt the divine self from this suffering, from this imperfection of God's creation. By becoming human in the incarnation, by life, passion, and death on the cross, God paid the utmost price for the freedom of human beings to love.

SUMMARY

The evolving universe brings forth, in a nondeterministic and therefore wasteful way, freedom, which we experience as real, though limited, in our human existence. Abandoning the classical Cartesian distinction between strictly determined creatures and free humans, we have learned to see earlier stages of evolving freedom in the animal kingdom. The farther we go back in the history of evolution, the less freedom we perceive. Freedom appears to be possible only in a nondeterministic universe that can be the object of statistical description. Structures appear in this universe as support and menace to freedom, as freedom can be a menace to its own support and so to itself. The balancing role of religion in this interplay is important and needs to be rooted in a transcendent reality. For Christians this transcendent reality is a personal God. Since freedom can always lead to destruction of others and of itself, the appearance of evil in the world is concomitant with the evolution of freedom. This world is not free from evil. The Creator obviously did not intend to create a perfect universe that could not produce evil: a perfectly functioning universe would be strictly determined, and there would be no room for freedom. The intent of the Creator seems to be to create free beings able to love, even if it was unavoidable that the price for the possibility of freedom and love, the appearance of evil, had to be paid.

6 GOD, CREATOR OF THE EVOLVING UNIVERSE

So far we have had a close look at the reality of the universe and have tried to discern features helpful for understanding the process that, for our experience, began shortly after the Big Bang (or whatever happened before the Planck-time). We have done this not as a scientist would, but with a mindset for our theological task: that is, to understand this process we call evolution of the universe as the work of God, as creation. We have discerned features of this process, namely, that new realities appear in this world through union of elements in ever higher forms of complex unity; that this process leads to the appearance of ever more explicit forms of consciousness, levels of information and of freedom. Each of these features points to a special aspect of the intention of the Creator in this universe, and we have briefly described these aspects. We have now reached a point where it seems possible to attempt a first summary of a particular insight in an effort to acquire a more holistic view of the relation between the Creator and creation.

Since theology is taught in many places by many theologians, we shall first ask how far theology has become aware of the need to take into account the evolutionary structure of God's creation and how far it has responded to this need. Based on the structures recognized in this creation, a basic change in the God-creation relation is proposed, the *creatio appellata*. The new metaphysics of union calls for a change in our understanding of God, leading to the notion of creation as evolving by union as the *vestigium trinitatis*, and to a revision of the traditional teaching on the Trinity.

The parameters of evolution, especially that of information, reveal the universe as structured by spiritual forces, which in some cases can be understood as top-down causation. Hence this understanding seems useful: a highly important aspect of the significance of information in the universe seems to be that by evolution the universe is becoming more and more spiritual, and thus more similar to God. True similarity to God can be found only in free beings. Freedom, as another recognized parameter of evolution, indicates a Creator who wants divine love to be answered by the creation and who is ready to pay for it with the unavoidable price of evil. The basic force driving the evolving universe appears thus to be divine love, grace.

The universe, as it has become visible to us through science, but looked at with the understanding of a Christian who knows by faith that God created this world, reveals God to the eyes of faith in a new light. As children who grow up perceive their parents differently without the parents changing their identity, so humankind, having grown to a deeper understanding of the reality of the universe, of the creation, will relate in a new way to the Creator, who is perceived with the eyes of faith in new ways.

DOES THEOLOGY GO NEW WAYS?

When during the sixth and the seventh decades of this century the philosophical and theological writings of Pierre Teilhard de Chardin were first published, the fossilized structures of traditional Catholic theology began to show serious cracks. Evolution, admitted by the encyclical *Humani generis* of Pope Pius XII (1950) only as a possibility for the evolution of the human body, suddenly was no longer considered a serious objection to theologians' teaching on creation. This is not to say that all theologians were ready to draw the consequences of this basic change in worldview. The latest large textbook on Catholic dogmatics, *Mysterium Salutis*, still has a chapter on the original state of human beings, gifted with the *dona praeternaturalia*, and even in our day the *Catechism of the Catholic Church* proposes such a state.[1] Karl Rahner in *Sacramentum Mundi*[2] touches only lightly on the subject and links it loosely with a Christological perspective. The latest textbook on Catholic dogmatics available[3] does not mention this historically impossible state. In 1978, Rahner indicated that the Roman Curia still did not understand that the history of dogmas implies that old dogmatic concepts may become obsolete and wrong. How else could it have happened, asks Rahner, that the official commission wrote sentences

> in the schemata prepared by the commission of the Second Vatican Council before the latter's opening, to put forward as definable truths propositions which twenty years later can scarcely count on a majority among the theologians in the world or among the ordinary believers: propositions, for instance, like those on monogenism or on the limbo of infants?[4]

Today theologians seem to admit the notion of evolution, even in the sense of universal evolution, but only to say that it does not interfere with faith in creation. Using classical notions such as *creatio continua*, Theodor Schneider[5] tries to show that evolution corresponds to this idea. His main interest is to avoid any kind of Deism, by having God in the beginning create a world fully equipped with possibilities to evolve according to a certain plan or using *rationes seminales*. But in his treatment of creation we find scarcely any reference to the known world revealed by scientific observation, to the known creation.

Reference to Rahner's notion of "self-transcendence" is widely made today, and we find it here in Schneider's text. This notion is rooted in traditional ontological metaphysics with its concept of causality; it is not derived from analysis of the process of becoming as it appears in evolution. It states that something new comes out of its precedents, but we cannot explain it by its precedents. Jürgen Moltmann tries to link this creating of new possibilities to the Holy Spirit: "The Spirit is the *principle of creativity* on all levels of matter and life. He creates new possibilities and in these anticipates the new designs and '*blueprints*' for material and living organisms.[6] In this sense the Spirit is the principle of evolution."[7]

Unfortunately, Moltmann does not tell us how he reached this conclusion. It reminds one of old theories of natural theology. The Holy Spirit is used here to complement the theory of evolution by filling gaps in scientific understanding of evolution. The Holy Spirit is integrated into the chain of secondary causes and becomes part of the world, which needs an active designer. That the Holy Spirit, if acting as a planning demiurge, would have done a very bad job has been shown already, if we consider the enormous waste in the universe. Moltmann does not go beyond the traditional notion of God as creating a well-ordered world by following a clear design. As we have shown extensively, this is not the evolving creation.

The difficulty with Moltmann's understanding of creation is primarily linked to his use of the classical theological terms "original creation" and "continued creation." They belong to a static universe: the former establishes the creation in its perfection; the latter assures its maintenance. This separation of the act of creation is no longer applicable to the evolving universe. There is no first moment in creating matter, which is then modified. The Big Bang concept has certainly induced theologians and church authorities like Pius XII to identify the Big Bang with the moment of creation, but this is looking at creation from the temporal perspective of human minds.

Time is not before creation; this *before* is only an extrapolation from the temporal perspective that is ours. The differentiation into a time before and after creation is meaningless: there is no meaningful way to speak of the *before* because there was no time. In the same way as the notion of a *creatio ex nihilo* is beyond our understanding, the notion of the beginning of time cannot be grasped by our time-spelled thinking. By our tendency to read reality within a time continuum, we fall into the trap of differentiating God's act of creation basically into a constituting one and a sustaining one. The latter is then understood by Moltmann and other theologians as God's acting in evolution. This vision has the Creator first create matter and then work on this matter. The decisive point, how we are to understand God's action in evolution while respecting what we know about evolution, is not clarified.[8]

The fixation on the origin as the decisive act of creation is based on the old and obsolete idea that identifies the fullness of reality with the beginnings. Our knowledge about how the world originated is, despite the theory about the Big Bang, rather dim. We do not know if an unstable quantum vacuum preceded the Big Bang, or if our universe was spawned by a black hole. Physicists giving a data-based proof probably cannot answer these questions. But even if they could be so answered, this would not be a proof either of creation or against it. As Thomas Aquinas stated, this world could be eternal: "That the world [has] not always existed cannot be demonstratively proved but is held by faith alone. . . . The reason is this: the world considered in itself offers no grounds for demonstrating that it was once all new."[9]

This insight prevails as well in an evolving universe. We may reach a point where our ability to collect data comes to an end. That does not tell us anything about an absolute beginning: this is a question of faith, not of science. If we believe that God created this universe, then we are not contradicted by scientific analysis of the data we may collect about the universe and its history. But we should abstain from identifying the moment of creation: it does not make sense. There may have been endless times about which we are ignorant because they have their existence outside our time-space continuum. Within a static worldview, a world imagined to have entered into existence fully and perfectly realized, it might make sense to speak of the beginning as a decisive moment and to separate the act of initial creation from the consequent act of maintaining the world in existence.

Arthur Peacocke clearly sees that this is part of yesterday's theology:

> The philosophers of religion and the religious believer have now to reckon with their one God's relation to a continuously developing world—and this implies at least a continuously changing relation of God to the world, including persons, and so the further possibility that God is not unchanging in certain respects. So the question of the nature and attributes of God cannot in the end be separated neatly and clearly from the vital question of how God's interaction with a world described by the natural sciences is to be conceived.[10]

Here the theological awareness of a change in perspective is clearly evident. Peacocke's question about the interaction of the Creator with the creation is at the center of a theology of creation. Are there possible answers based on an understanding of the concrete process of creation, that is, of evolution? In what way does God act in the creation?

CREATIO APPELLATA

In an evolving universe, the beginning of creation is not the outstanding act that brings forth the whole universe that afterward has only to be sustained for the time of its existence. As we have seen, the start of our known universe is neither very exciting nor very fast. If we take the standard model as a valid description of the beginning universe—it may not be correct—then the universe started with a size that could not be made visible with the best and most exotic microscope and that lasted for a time so short, any clock available today could not measure it. After this first perhaps somewhat explosive moment nothing new appeared for billions of years, or at least a billion years. If we envision a Creator actively at work in making things happen after creating matter in the first step of creation, it appears to be a sluggish way of activity, with no great results over long time spans. On a qualitative scale of beings there is no perfect, but at best a very rudimentary, beginning of the universe.

This is obviously a different creation from that described in the first chapters of Genesis. The fact that the biblical text has a certain logic in the sequence of the six days, for example, that there must be plants before there are animals on the land, does not make this text a description of evolution. The sequence shows rather that the biblical author was aware of the necessities of life. The essential statements of this text, namely, that everything is created by God and that everything created is good, are not necessarily linked to the worldview of the author; they have to be considered in their meaning within a fundamentally changed vision of the universe. It has changed from a world of being to a world of becoming. Hence it did not start in perfection. Obviously, the notion of the Creator acting as the supreme sovereign, with everything coming forth immediately and perfectly at the divine command, does not correspond to the history of the universe. God did not impose the divine self. It seems inappropriate to postulate a very special act of original creation complemented by an act of continued creation maintaining the universe in being. It seems easier to understand God's way of creation if we do not dissect the act of creation into phases. We should rather consider it as one act, which in God's eternity is one and is unfolded in time into its differentiality.

The best way to represent the creation's relation to the Creator—and obviously this is a subjective vision, but it appears compatible with the evolving universe—can be called *creatio appellata*, the called-forth creation. Its basic idea is that this universe is called forth by God out of nothingness toward God. The process of becoming is the answer of creation. The whole process, being the continued attempt to answer God's creative and creating call, is the ongoing creation. There is no first act followed by manipulating the stuff the world is made of. The act that brought forth the beginning of the process and the act that keeps the process going is one and the same call from God on which everything's existence depends, by which everything is maintained in being.

This basic image of God's calling forth the universal process of becoming out of nothingness needs some qualifications that avoid an interpretation linked with the notion of the Creator in classical theology, who was in the first place seen as the almighty God. The universe, though in certain aspects still a demonstration of the Almighty—the immensity of the universe with its billions of galaxies is obviously in need of an almighty Creator—is not in the first place a demonstration of God's almightiness.

As has been shown, God is not imposing on God's creatures. God is infinitely patient, not rushing the world into being in six days. God's calling forth the universe out of nothingness—what we have learned to call *creatio ex nihilo* in theology—is not bringing forth ready-made creatures, but produces the most simple structures and elements, which we still find abundantly in the universe. We should be aware that this is what becomes visible to us, what belongs to the horizon of our perception. How the whole process begins escapes our range of perception; we do not even know if any particles are needed for the whole process of union to begin. The condensed state out of which the Big Bang emerges might well be a transitory state preceding it. Even the seemingly endless time from this point in history, which to us appears as a beginning, to the appearance of the first stars and the first planets, might be only a relatively short while for the Creator patiently waiting for the answer to the divine creative call. If the endless spaces filled with billions of galaxies make us recognize the infinite power of the Creator, these endless times make us perceive the Creator as infinitely patient.

God's way of creating is not a demonstration of power, which would force everything called into being to go directly to God. We might suppose with Moltmann that specifically the Holy Spirit is at work in creation.[11] But the Spirit would certainly not be at work as a designer, laying out blueprints for the future. God seems not to make things happen, but to allow them to happen. As we have seen in chapter 2, the basic process of evolution and of creation is "becoming through union." Elements need to unite to reach a higher level of being. This process of union is maintained by God's persistent creative call. Evidently, God is not pushing elements together and forcing them to unite.

We can even state that the less the elements—particles, protons, atoms, molecules—are evolved, and the lower their level of being, the less they unite. The enormous mass of background radiation, which is for all practical purposes not available for any union, and which represents one billion times the remaining mass of the universe, is a clear hint in this direction. God is visibly not pushing the elements: if that were so, most elements in the universe would escape God's pressure. A better understanding, compatible with the evolutionary reality of creation, would be to see God acting from within the elements. The innermost reality of anything would be conceived as the presence of God, or rather as God's call to come to God. There are two aspects in this way of seeing God at work.

The omnipresence of God would in this way take a new meaning: not an abstract being everywhere, but the concrete immanence of God calling neighboring elements to unite. This immanence of God calling from the inside of the elements leaves intact the integrity of the element. Without this presence of God's call, elements would fall back into nothingness. The lower the elements are situated on the scale of becoming, the less they are open to the future. Only a very few hydrogen atoms will ever enter into combination with other elements or will evolve into higher atoms. It appears that the chances to reach a higher level are extremely limited at these low levels of evolution. But there is no pressure.

If God calls forth the elements to unite, God does not force them together. God's call is not the command of a dominant power. God entices neighboring elements to unite. There is no outside pressure, only an inside tendency toward the neighboring element. Thus the Creator limits the power of the divine creative call toward union to the level of the element. God never imposes self, but lets the neighboring element and the element itself be what they are: infinitely small elements existing by some infinitely small similitude to the Creator, whose presence within them seems to be adequate to this similitude. The divine creative call from within the element thus makes itself similar to the element, without exercising power.

On the level of human relations we have a name for this kind of accepting the other, by offering oneself without imposing oneself: love.

This becomes even more evident when we look at the second aspect of the way God creates by calling from the inside. There is no direct way for the element to go to God. It can answer the call of the Creator only by uniting itself with another element. The human element, the human person, experiences as love the force that unites with another human element without imposing itself: love does not force. In an analogical way, this is applicable to all levels of union, where the other element must always be respected in its integrity and where both become more through union, coming in an infinitesimal way closer to the Creator. Discovering love as the fundamental creative force opens a view that might be considered a very fitting way for God to act. We confess God to be Love, and even if we consider the creative action especially as the action of the Holy Spirit, this would at least fit meaningfully into theological discourse, since the Holy Spirit has often been considered the uniting force of love in trinitarian speculations.

The loving call of God might thus, in theology, be considered the driving force of creation and so of evolution. This in no way contradicts the observations of science. The elements at all levels are exactly what they are. The findings of science are in no way different; the theological statement does not in any way add to a scientific description that in some way was incomplete. But this description is the most exact verifiable description of the concrete reality of creation that we can get. For the eyes of faith, everything found by science is part of the reality allowed to become by God's creative call.[12] This leaves the whole of physics and chemistry and biology untouched, and it does not help to solve problems in any of these sciences. God is not a *deus ex machina* to help scientists who do not have an answer to their problems.

The theological statement is an attempt to describe the relation of this universe to God, to say why there is a universe, why there is evolution, starting in our experience with the Big Bang and reaching its highest level of complexity and consciousness in the human being. The theologian answers the question the scientist as scientist can neither ask nor answer.[13] In this way the theological answer complements the scientific enterprise. Science can, at least to a large extent, describe the universe in its physico-chemico-biological history and even in its human history. Theology, as the way to express the meaning of the revealed truths of faith in their relatedness to the present state reached by the evolving creation, tells us how God acts in this world, God's creation.

If the interpretation of the facts we learned about evolution and about the process of union as the basic structure of the evolving world is correct, then, seen with the eyes of faith, this universe exists because it is held in existence and in its ongoing process of becoming by the creative call of divine love, infinitesimally present in all creatures. The Pauline reference to Christ as the τὸ πλήρωμα τοῦ τὰ πάντα ἐν πᾶσιν πληρουμένου "the fullness of him who fills all in all" (Eph. 1:23),[14] can perhaps find a new interpretation in this way, showing that God is present by God's call in everything, that everything has its existence in this call, without becoming identified with God. This is not a pantheistic understanding of God's immanence, but what could be correctly named panentheistic. The interpretation proposed should be understood in this way. The *Oxford Dictionary of the Christian Church* defines "panentheism" as follows: "The belief that the Being of God includes and penetrates the whole universe, so that every part of it exists in Him but (as against pantheism) that His Being is more than, and is not exhausted by, the universe."[15] If we abstract from the ontological language, we can see panentheism in God's immanent calling forth of all creation.

This presence of God in the creation, God's immanence, is for the Christian theologian inevitably linked with the question of the God whom we believe one in three persons. Within the classical ontologically impregnated language there have always been difficulties in understanding this mystery of faith. We shall have to ask if something is changed once we leave behind us this world of being to live in the world of becoming. There certainly will be difficulties unsolved, as there are in the classical teaching on the Trinity. But be that as it may, if our interpretation of this universe as marked by becoming through union is correct, then we have no choice but to address the mystery of the Trinity as related to this becoming world.

THE TRINITY: CREATOR OF THE BECOMING UNIVERSE

In a nondualistic vision of creation it has always been perceived that the world, creation, has a double aspect in its relation to the Creator: it is both transcended and indwelt. On the one hand, the Creator transcends the creation infinitely. The Creator is the totally other. In this perception of God there is no way to speak about God in terms related to this creation, which are the only positive terms we have at our disposal. This leads to *theologia negativa*, which can state only what God is not. In relation to the evolving world we may state negatively that God is not evolving from less to more. In this perspective, everything we might say positively about God falls short of God's reality, and we may state that there is no way to speak about God, but only a way to speak to God in prayer and worship and silence.

This way of apophatic theology was predominant in the theology of the triune God, more precisely when speaking about what is called the immanent Trinity, that is about the inner divine reality. The unity of the one God in three persons has always been declared to be a revealed mystery, which cannot be known by human reason. Reason may know about God's existence; this is what Thomas Aquinas tried to prove by the five ways,[16] but knowledge of the Trinity surpasses human knowledge in every way.[17] Thus Aquinas, following the Augustinian tradition most radically, separated the tract *De Deo Uno* from the tract *De Deo Trino*.[18] The separation of the trinitarian God in three persons from the notion of the one God has led to a loss of the Trinity in Christian praxis, which Karl Rahner deplored. Formally, Christians hold their trinitarian faith, but we should not be deceived: "Christians, for all their orthodox profession of faith in the Trinity, are almost just 'monotheist' in their actual religious existence. One might almost dare to affirm that if the doctrine of the Trinity were to be erased as false, most religious literature could be preserved almost unchanged throughout the process."[19] Kant denounced how little the traditional presentation of the doctrine of the Trinity is fruitful for the praxis of the Christian: "From the doctrine of the Trinity, taken literally, nothing whatsoever can be gained for practical purposes, even if one believed that one comprehended it—and still less if one is conscious that it surpasses all our concepts."[20]

For centuries theology, though verbally confessing the Trinity, was speaking only of God. Rahner noted,

> There are probably several modern, scientific and extensive Christologies which pay no particular attention to *which* precisely of the divine hypostases has taken on human nature. The average theological text-book today operates in fact with the abstract concept of a divine hypostasis—a concept which is however a very analogous and precarious unity. It does not operate with the concept of exactly the second person in God as such. It asks what it means that God became man, but not what it means in particular that the Logos, precisely as himself in contradistinction to the other divine persons became man.[21]

This reduction of the Trinity to a group of perfectly equal hypostases is such that, ever since Augustine, "contrary to the tradition preceding him, it has been more or less agreed that each of the divine persons could become man. From which it follows that the Incarnation of the second person in particular throws no light on the special character of *this* person within the divine nature."[22] This has led to a practical isolation of the tract on the Trinity in dogmatics: "To put it crudely (and of course with some exaggeration and generalization): once this treatise has been dealt with, it does not recur again in dogmatic theology. Its general function with regard to the whole is only vaguely seen. The mystery appears to have been revealed merely for its own sake."[23]

This rather harsh critique of traditional scholastic theology in 1960 is at least partly overcome by Rahner's work, and in Protestant theology. Taking seriously the point of this criticism, that the specificity of the divine hypostasis in the Incarnation be taken into consideration for a theology of the Trinity, a broad literature has been developed on the Trinity seen in the perspective of salvation.[24] It centered on the notion that the economic Trinity—the Trinity engaged in the world, in salvation—cannot be separated from the immanent Trinity, from the inner trinitarian life. There has been a movement away from the Greek philosophical notion of God as *actus purus*, "who in blissful security . . . always possesses what he is. He does not have to become it first,"[25] and toward the biblical God, who during the whole history of Israel revealed the divine self less as the unchanging Supreme Being than as an acting God angered and exasperated by God's people.

Theology moved away from the Greek notion of the one Supreme Unchanging Eternal Being toward a God who is deeply involved in creation. But on a closer look at this involvement, we find a strange limitation of the argument to a God-human relation. Formally, one repeats: "Neither, therefore, is the Christian profession of an unchangeable and unchanging God in his eternally complete fullness merely the postulate of a particular philosophy. It is also a dogma of faith, as was once again explicitly defined in the First Vatican Council (D.S. 3001)."[26] But Rahner states immediately after this sentence: "But still it is true: the Word *became* flesh."[27] The consequence is that the tension between faith in the Unchanging Supreme Being, the *actus purus*, and in the God of history, who involves the divine self in this world, most explicitly when the Logos becomes man, has now led to a silence about the eternal God, about the Creator.[28] An important discovery of modern theology is: "God can become something."[29]

Here is not the place to go into a full analysis of the consequences of the profound changes in theology of the Trinity for the understanding of salvation and for the understanding of human beings. But it should have become clear that "traditional theology and philosophy of the schools gets into a dilemma"[30] when faced with this tension. We have left behind the world of being, with its ontology culminating in the Supreme Being, in the notion of the unchangeable eternal God. We have become aware that this universe as creation is a process, starting in our experience from a point of a nearly pure multiple with scarcely any information, to become a universe of matter, life, and mind. We have recognized the process as a process of union bringing forth new realities, new levels of being. Now we might ask whether the classical formulation of the dogma defining the triune God as three persons who are ὁμοούσιοι, of one substance, one nature, should be revised within the context of a metaphysics of union.

Obviously, this is not an attempt to question the doctrine of the triune God in its revealed content. But since all language used is always a language of a time determined by the metaphysical horizon of that time, we have no longer the ability to think within the horizon of a static world, even though we still have our habits of thinking linked to classical formulations. This is a real obstacle: we have not yet fully elaborated a metaphysics of union, of the becoming universe, though we are used to a very clear and refined (but no longer very meaningful) language of our philosophical tradition from Plato and Aristotle to Thomas Aquinas and Bonaventure, to Kant[31] and Hegel. Therefore, we have difficulty in liberating ourselves from the habits of thought we have taken for so long as laws of being and of thinking. To give just one example: we are used to accepting the classical statement that the more cannot come from the less. To use the Lucretian statement: *De nihilo nihil.* But in the history of the universe we see this happen very often: from a relative *nihil*—we can neither encounter nor think the absolute *nihil*—we see something new come forth. The whole story of evolution, the whole story of creation is just this: continuous becoming of something new from a relative *nihil*. And this something new is never fully resting in itself. Its own reality is a continued process of being united in itself. Being is thus a temporary aspect of the general process of becoming.

If this is correct, our arguments based on the *analogia entis* need at least some revision: we will need to change to an *analogia fientis*, of which the *analogia entis* is only a temporary aspect. We shall return to this point.

Keeping this in mind as important and real, we can still state with the classical *analogia entis* that there cannot be anything in this universe totally different from God. If this were possible, there would be something totally alien to God. But everything that has come into being exists, becomes, thanks to some similitude with God, however infinitesimal it may be. All that has come to be exists because it participates by some likeness to God. In the perspective of the *creatio appellata*, God calls forth the elements to become more and more similar to God. And to be similar to God should no longer be expressed by the notion of existing, but of becoming, of uniting.[32]

According to the metaphysics of union, the basic process of evolution is the ongoing union of elements on ever higher levels of becoming. Whatever exists, exists as long as its elements are united. In union and by union the process of becoming brings forth new levels of being, new levels of similitude with God. Although according to the principles of negative theology we cannot draw conclusions from the level of creatures to the divine level, it is not incoherent to ask if, in view of God's reality, we can speak about being independently of what we know about being in God's creation. If the Teilhardian definition of being is correct, then the definition of being has some importance for human talk about God's being. This way of speaking about God is at least as justified, if the definition of *esse* is correct, as the classical ascription of being to God. Since we are no longer living in a static world of being, we have to understand how God reflects in the world of becoming. Since we recognize the process of becoming in creation as a process of union driven by the creative call of divine love, we may ask if there is an analogy to this basic process in God.

We look for such an analogy under a double aspect: if union defines being, then not only is union present in God, but God is absolute union, much as we used to say that God is absolute being. In a strict monotheistic vision this would create difficulties, since God would appear to be composed of united elements. If we saw God as absolutely one, God would need some partner to unite with. The monotheistic God in the strict sense would need to create a world to exist in union with. The world would need to be coeternal with God so that God might unite with it. God and creation would be linked to each other. God's transcendence would be only relative, since God would need the universe to unite with in order to exist. As Creator of a universe in which being is defined by union, the strictly monotheistic God would lose God's absolute transcendent nature; with the world in its evolutionary process the monotheistic God does not seem compatible.

One answer is that God becomes a factor in the universal process, being submitted to some higher organizing force, as in Alfred North Whitehead's vision of the process-world. In this vision

> God can be termed the creator of each temporal actual entity. But the phrase is apt to be misleading by its suggestion that the ultimate creativity of the universe is to be ascribed to God's volition. The true metaphysical position is that God is the aboriginal instance of this creativity, and is therefore the aboriginal condition which qualifies its action. It is the function of actuality to characterize the creativity, and God is the eternal primordial character. But of course, there is no meaning to "creativity" apart from its "creatures," and no meaning of "God" apart from the creativity and the "temporal creatures" and no meaning to the temporal creatures apart from "creativity" and "God."[33]

This is a special case of pantheism: God as the function of creativity. In general, this integration of the monotheistic God into the universe, the pantheistic answer, is the only rational solution to the problems raised by an evolving world of becoming through union. The world must be coeternal with God to be God's necessary partner in a universal process of union. This pantheistic way of thinking of God does not correspond to the God in whom Christians believe.

Maintaining the strict monotheistic concept of God isolates God from the world. God would not be a process of union—God would be composed of elements if the Godhead resulted from union—but a Supreme Being. If God were in need of union to exist, God would be in need of the world. We would be back to some kind of Whiteheadian solution. Or God would be totally other, a statement often made in theology. But this monotheistic, isolated God would not be the God of a world in which being is supported by union. God would be God being perfection in the divine self, creating in almightiness a perfect world, well ordered to the slightest detail. This would be the world as it appeared in the Middle Ages. It is a childhood world in which everything is taken care of, in which only human beings are not functioning mechanically, because they have been set free by the will of God, and in which human beings are aliens, put there to be tested. Disobedience against the will of God is punished, often immediately by consequence of the disruption caused by human misbehavior. In such thinking, linked with a strict monotheism, one reaches the conclusion that certain evils such as illnesses are God's punishment for human failure to live according to God's will. Evidently, as a consequence of this understanding of God, there is the burden of the theodicy problem: Who is this God who lets evils hit sinners and innocents without discrimination?

Perhaps humankind had to live for a certain while in this perfect world of its childhood. Evils were understood as punishments, a vision that came under attack in the Hebrew Scriptures, especially in the book of Job, and more explicitly in the Christian Scriptures.[34] The more people reflected on this interpretation of evil, the less acceptable it became. Enough theologians, especially among Christian and Islamic fundamentalists, interpret the appearance of AIDS as God's punishment. But in general praxis this kind of argument is no longer accepted since Voltaire raised the question of a just God after the earthquake of Lisbon in 1755. The monotheistic, almighty God, Creator of the ordered world where everything is directed by divine volition, is confronted with the unsolved and unsolvable problem of evil that could be avoided. Most times this argumentation ignores the fact that the real world, the real creation, does not correspond either to the perfectly ordered world or to the monotheistic God. This evolving creation does not correspond to a God-vision based on Aristotelian or Platonic ontology.

The strictly ordered world of the monotheistic God is not found in the real universe, as has been amply shown. The world is structured on all levels by union. The world in this way tries to resemble, as much as it is able, God who creates it, who calls it forth to the divine self by the divine call of love. Thus God, as the *Urbild* of all that is created, cannot be strictly one being, unchanging in all eternity. We cannot deduce the reality of the Trinity from the process of union that keeps this universe getting closer to God by its evolution. But we may state that this revealed reality of the eternally united trinitarian God is reflected in the universal process of evolution by progressing union.

Christian tradition presented one God in three persons as a *mysterium magnum*, beyond any possibility of human understanding. And this is true in a world conceived through a metaphysics of being. In a certain way the immutable eternal God, the absolute Being, has always been difficult to understand as Trinity related to this world. The God of Abraham, Isaac, and Jacob could hardly be brought to coincide with the notion of absolute immutable Being. Rahner needs to insist on the unchanging God by postulating that "here ontology has to be adapted to the message of faith and not be schoolmaster to this message."[35]

This is a strange postulate, reminiscent of times when theologians tried to tell science how the heavens work. Ontology is not an arbitrary construction of the human mind but the result of the most comprehensive endeavor to understand the universe, to understand creation. As such it is part of God's revelation. Greek philosophy deeply influenced the Christian understanding of the one God and the Chalcedonian formulas to express the triune God as one God in three hypostases having all the same essence, being according to their nature interchangeable. Can these formulas and the ontology they imply be maintained even though the world both were developed in is no more?

We do not live anymore in a cosmos, in a well-ordered world as created by the demiurge of Plato's *Timaeus* or by the God of Israel as described in the first chapters of Genesis. Nor was the human being placed as an alien (Plato) or as a special creation (Genesis) in a static cosmos to be tested there. But obviously, that was the general perception of the world, of creation, and of the human's place in it. For many centuries that was the way God revealed the divine self through God's creation. If we look at the medieval interpretation of creation, we realize that it was order-centered. The Creator "arranged all things by measure and number and weight" (Wisd. of Sol. 11:20).[36]

Accordingly, medieval theologians had precise answers. They knew how to distinguish and to draw the line between true faith and heresy. In a way—this analogy may hurt convinced scholastic scholars, and we trust they will excuse it—these theologians remind us of adolescents who know it all, who have not fathomed the limits of their knowledge and the infinitude of their ignorance. If we consider the growth of humankind as part of the ongoing creation, then this statement should be expected: God did not appear the same at all times, even in the history of Israel. The God of Abraham, Isaac, and Jacob appeared as the God of all only long after the Exodus, but even then as the mighty God of Israel, who is the only God: "All the peoples of the earth may know that the Lord is God; there is no other" (1 Kings 8:60).

For many years the God of Israel appeared to the people as a tribal God, and that was probably the only way the early Israelites and the peoples around them were able to think of God. God behaved toward Israel like a parent: requiring the children to follow strict rules without God's giving any reason, but forgiving when they had broken the rules and repented. We may see here the way God appeared to humankind in its late childhood, which was followed by the medieval adolescence, where God appeared as the universal, almighty, unchanging,[37] eternal Supreme Being, who had everything well ordered and well under control, allowing human freedom by a free decision of God's own.

The ontology linked with this adolescent view of reality seems to need to be replaced. This should not be astonishing if we look at the history of revelation, which continues at least at the level of the continued creation. We live no longer in the cosmos, but in a world of becoming. To this world corresponds the metaphysics of union, even though we have only its rough sketch. Since being is defined in this metaphysics by union, one might state that God needs to unite the divine self. If this were stated about a monotheistic God, God would need to be thought of as a composite or as in need of the universe, as the Whiteheadian God is. Both notions are unsatisfactory. The Whiteheadian concept leads to the integration of God into the universal process as a factor, and the notion of composite unity demands matter out of which God was composed. In this way, both the eternity of God and God's transcendence would be jeopardized. To think God triune—that is, God who cannot be thought of as one without being triune—opens a perspective for the metaphysics of union.

Since according to this metaphysics being is realized by union, and exists only as this union is realized anew in every moment, absolute being is to be defined by absolute union. The highest level of union known to us is interpersonal union, which is realized in humans only in a weak way. In God the three persons are one in eternal total love, renewed at all moments of eternity: naturally, this is human talk, which has no real way to speak about eternity. The old dictum of God as *actus purus* receives a new meaning: it is the eternally renewed and always already fully realized act of union in perfect love uniting the three divine persons of the Trinity, the Father, the Son, and the Holy Spirit. Human imagination cannot grasp the fullness of this union in divine love. Human love, the love we know, may try to give oneself to the other, but it always falls short of this goal. In the Trinity there is no shortcoming of the loving relation. Each person of the Trinity is one with the others in total love. Being united in perfect love beyond all human comprehension, the three divine persons are one God. The mystery of the perfect loving union may allow for the paradoxical statement that each divine person, in perfect union with the others, acts as one God.

This statement has to be qualified by a reminder that union is not fusion: union differentiates. One becomes more oneself in union with the other. The traditional differentiation in Father, Son, and Holy Spirit should be more than just a relational differentiation. This theory was developed within the horizon of an ontological metaphysic, for which everything had its nature in its essence. In this view, any person of the Trinity could take the place of the other. In the metaphysics of union there cannot be an essential identity among the three persons: they become what they are in their union. They are one God, united in such a way that each person participates fully in the others.[38] We may state that the more profoundly the three divine persons are united in love, the more they are differentiated persons far beyond human understanding.

We have to strain our imagination to the utmost limit here, and still we are far from being able to speak about the Trinity in an adequate way. What has been said may hint at the reality covered by the words of revelation, spoken in a time when there was little knowledge of the real history of the universe, of God's ongoing creation. But even in the framework of knowledge of those past times, the revelation of the Trinity was not comprehended, and the interpretations, for example of Augustine, fall short of allowing a clear understanding of the revealed triune God. Any theological attempt to speak about the Trinity in the framework of an evolutionary understanding of creation will be even more difficult, since we have to transpose a barely understood revelation into a new horizon. What has been said about the Trinity in the horizon of an evolving world is most certainly far less clear and less elaborate than the ideas worked out in the obsolete horizon of a static universe. We have at best been able to get a first glimpse at a new way of understanding the revelation of the triune God, the unity of God in three persons as a condition of God's triune existence.

However much the mystery of the inner life of the Trinity remains veiled to the believer, it appears evident that the triune God is the eternal living and realized perfect union of the three divine persons. This union being perfect, there is no need for God to create a world to unite with. The trinitarian God transcends creation and does not need it. The Trinity is absolutely free in the decision to create a world that is invited to participate in God's life.

Theologians have tried to distribute the roles of the three divine persons in relation to creation. Pauline texts, especially the letter to the Colossians, clearly attribute a central role in creation to the second person of the Trinity, the Son: "For in him all things in heaven and on earth were created, things visible and invisible, whether thrones or dominions or rulers or authorities— all things have been created through him and for him. He himself is before all things, and in him all things hold together" (1:16–17). Therefore, the question occurs: How are we to understand the creative role of the Logos within the Trinity? The metaphysics of union changes the perspective so that we can explore in a renewed way what might be said about the three persons in God and their specificity. But we have to leave these questions here, hoping that we can return to them at another time.

But one point seems obvious in the context of this discussion on creation, namely, that of the *vestigia trinitatis*. Eberhard Jüngel quotes some analogies proposed by theologians through the ages: Augustine with his psychological interpretation: memory, intellect, and will; Anselm of Canterbury: source, river, and mouth; Luther: being, form, and potentia; again Luther: grammar, dialectic, and rhetoric; Joachim of Fiore: the three ages of the world, the age of the Father, the age of the Son, and the age of the Spirit.[39] This notion of *vestigia trinitatis* had fallen into disrepute, as well in Catholic apologetics as in Protestant theology, where Barth strongly opposed this notion.[40] "In recent Catholic apologetics, the normal thing is to reject sharply any effort at discovering presentiments of this mystery outside the New Testament"[41]—this statement of Rahner has the consequence, according to him, that for the school theology there cannot be any *vestigia trinitatis*. But the isolation of the tract on the Trinity, which finds its fullest expression in this radical refusal even to consider the notion of the *vestigia*, must be wrong. "The thing is impossible! For the Trinity is a mystery of *salvation*."[42] And salvation is concerned with this creation.

It may be true that the ontological understanding of the universe left little room to find any *vestigia* that would be acceptable to any Protestant or Catholic theologian. The strong isolation of revelation from the self-revelation of God in God's creation hampered further any such search for traces. But if we take seriously the *analogia fientis,* we may say with some confidence that this creation in its structures of becoming is *ad similitudinem Trinitatis*. Anything that evolves to some higher status of being does so by union, reflecting the absolute being in the absolute eternal act of divine union. Thus evolution leads us closer to God, answers the loving call of the Creator by imitating the divine union in infinitesimal approximations, by union with other elements on the level of becoming reached so far.

The most evident *vestigium trinitatis* is not in the first place to be seen in any tripartite reality somehow reflecting the three persons, but in the very process of becoming through union. Union brings forth new realities, which in their becoming being reflect more and more the divine reality. We should not forget in this context that a person can come to be only in relation to other persons; there cannot be one individual person alone.[43] It is by union, which differentiates, that creation, and therefore humans, can come closer to God. Union among humans respecting their personhood[44] is realized in love. Therefore, to say that God is love is more than a moralizing statement: it concerns the central force of union in the Trinity, which is the central force of creation.

There seems to be no other way to get closer to the triune God. As Teilhard once stated, the commandment of love has ceased to be a purely moral instigation to become the ontological principle of evolution, of creation. This creation will reach its goal, the point it is invited to reach, only if love will more and more become the dominating force opening new avenues into the future. Whatever this future dominated by the force of love might be, it seems barely compatible with exaggerated individualism and self-realization as the main interest of humans. What Teilhard has called the noosphere cannot develop a humanly acceptable supporting structure if it is not dominated by love. Creation, called to share in God's life, can lose its chance by an individualistic refusal to love. For, as the great personalistic philosophers of the first half of this century have shown, one gains personhood not in realizing oneself, but in loving the other. Paradoxically, those who love realize themselves without searching for self-realization. The dominant force of evolution is only dimly visible on the earlier, lower levels of evolution, though it clearly is distinguishable as the force of union. On the human level in the eyes of faith, which see the trinitarian God as the *Urbild* to be imitated by creation, it becomes the decisive force. To draw closer to the triune God, to continue the path of creation, there is only one law: "love one another."[45] There is no other way into the future leading to the fullness of creation invited to share the life of the Trinity. This is the answer God expects to the divine faithful creative call of love.

Having discovered with some confidence one *vestigium trinitatis* in the evolving creation, we have to ask if the other great parameters of evolution allow us to discover more than this one, and if they permit us to recognize new aspects of the Creator and the divine intent in this universe.

CREATIO INFORMATA

One of the parameters found, as we have seen, is information: evolution wins stability on higher levels of being by storing information, with typical means of storage corresponding to the level of becoming reached. Since information is not matter, though it may be stored materially,[46] we concluded that an important factor in evolution is rather spiritual than material. There is no doubt that information is causally effective: whatever we know and use of the fruits of technology has information as its *causa formalis*. Without the information created by engineers there would be no car. Without the information stored in the genes there would be no living creatures. Without the knowledge contained in language, and handed down from generation to generation, there would be no human beings.

The importance of this nonmaterial reality of information was known to classical metaphysics, and all information was considered to be stored in the memory of God. Plato's doctrine of ideas, the eternal forms, of which material things are only faded shadows, saw ideas as created by God. The Good not only knows the eternal ideas, but gives them being.[47] We find this same kind of ontological idealism in Whitehead's eternal nature of God, which contains all the possibilities that might be realized in the process of universal evolution.[48] The information is there; it is informing matter by realizing the steps of evolution through union. But though we know, at least to some extent, how the information is realized through evolution, it appears very difficult to show in what way the information in God's omniscience is transferred to the evolving creatures. On the one hand, if God is the absolute plenitude of union and therefore of being, of information, everything is somehow informed by its similitude to God, by its participating in some infinitesimal way in the information present in God. On the other hand, we do not see God impressing information on the evolving universe.

There is an analogy to this difficulty of seeing the way in which God might transfer information to evolving creatures. Human thoughts, inventions, volitions, in short all conscious human actions, have consequences, first in the brain and then in human actions, influencing the body and changing the world around us. But though we experience this, we do not understand how this transfer of information—of a spiritual reality—into material reality is possible: science by analyzing the brain has not been able to make it comprehensible that we can do science.

The spiritual reality of information is most obvious in human language, oral or written. The information communicated is absolutely independent of the specific medium: the text may be written in red, blue, or green ink, but the information is not different in its content. And this information causes changes in the brain, where it is stored in a way barely understood.[49] We know that information, this immaterial entity, is real and is actively efficient in the material world, but we do not know in what way knowledge, by essence immaterial, can be used, can be realized. How is the will transformed into movement? How are our plans to build (a car, a house) transformed into efficient action? We are sure it happens, but the transfer of information into informed activity is not understandable in the accepted scientific way of explanation. It is essentially unexplained, but real.

János Szentágothai,[50] a Hungarian neurophysiologist, has tried to avoid the Scylla of dualism and the Charybdis of reductionism. "There has to be an acceptable third way between the essentially reductionist and the dualist interpretations," he asserted in a 1984 paper, and he proposed the notion of downward causation as a possible answer. Downward causation is vaguely defined when he states that "whatever it is, our mind can causally interfere with the physiological operations of our brain circuits." The same idea of downward causation had been proposed by Donald T. Campbell in 1974 concerning hierarchically organized systems[51] and in 1983 by Nobel laureate Roger W. Sperry[52] as top-down causation. Without their indicating a mechanism or a way in which the transfer from the spiritual to the material is realized, the fact of this transfer is acknowledged by some outstanding scholars in the field of neurology.

Arthur Peacocke has adopted this idea of top-down causation to answer the question of how God could act in this world. Having reminded us that in the evolving world complex systems as a whole influence lower levels, as "the conscious brain states could be top-down causes at the lower level of [neurons],"[53] he sees here an opening for a new understanding of God's interaction with the creation. This notion of top-down causation "points to a way in which we could think divine action making a difference in the world, yet not in any way contrary to those regularities and laws operative within the observed universe which are explicated by the sciences applicable to the level of complexity and organization in question."[54] This use of analogy seems very helpful, for it opens the possibility to "model more convincingly that interaction, dialogue even, between human decisions and actions, on the one hand, and divine intentions and purposes, on the other."[55] This is especially true for the understanding and the possibility "of prayer, worship and the sacraments."[56]

This phenomenon is certainly true, and it would be really convincing if we had a better understanding of how we influence our neurons by our thinking and willing. As it is, we use a mysterious fact to understand better the mystery of how God informs God's creation. We may certainly embrace the notion of top-down causation, and therewith we could lay to rest a number of questions. For a certain number of informations actively integrated into the universe escape our understanding: it is extremely difficult to understand that they are there. The most astonishing informations of this kind, where we do not know their origin, are linked with the earliest times of the universe and the conditions that evolved then. Where do the laws of physics come from? Are they there by chance, or were they defined before the world was created? The idea of multiple universes—of which we will never know anything for lack of ability to receive data from outside our universe—could allow that the universe we live in is just one among an infinite number of universes that by chance had the right laws and the right constants (the right Coulomb constant, the right value for the gravitational force)[57] to allow for the evolution of life and consciousness. Perhaps our universe is the only one in a multiple-universe hypothesis that would search for meaning.

It should be clear that this multiple-universe hypothesis is not in contradiction to the Creator God and creation: all these infinitely numerous universes would still be God's creation, and they could be understood as the expression of God's absolute generosity in creating a world that is not predetermined. On the one hand, there is no absolute logical necessity to have the anthropic principle explained by some information coming from outside, from the Creator. On the other hand, there is no proof for the multiple-universe hypothesis, and top-down causation is by no means excluded as a possible model.

Since we see it at work through our inner experience, there is no reason to exclude the top-down model from our understanding of how God interacts with the world. It would be very helpful to our understanding of God's response to our prayers, a response that sometimes takes the form of miracle (e.g., when sudden healing really occurs).[58] It would be hard to understand God's answers to prayers, which often only praying persons perceive, by another model than top-down causation. The notion fits very well with the concept of grace, especially with the Christian notion of sacraments. The Eucharist can be well seen as bread and wine transformed, receiving a new information. It seems justified to explore the model of top-down causation as the way of God's interaction with the universe.

The universe is not consistently guided by top-down information creating a well-ordered universe. As we have seen, there is some order in the universe, and the higher levels of evolution show a higher level of order, which is the expression of the information stored and realized at that level. But in general this creation is not order-dominated. If God interacts with this universe analogously to the top-down causation model, this is unlikely to be the only way God is related to this universe. It seems that top-down causation is exceptional, especially in the beginning of the universe. It might be imagined to have fixed the values of the constants of the universe, or the source of the constants, if they could ever be reduced to an original state producing them by some necessity. But then, because of the billions of years before the earth was formed, it is hard to believe in a constant top-down causation. At least we do not see a dense flow of information coming from God.

The structure of the *creatio appellata*, with God's creative loving voice calling the elements through elements toward union, does not point in this direction. Should we consider this call toward union as a kind of top-down causation? At least it might be advisable to hesitate before we regard the universe as under the influence of divine top-down causation. It could be a way of reintroducing the God who acts primarily as the Almighty. This would bring back the old problems of theodicy. On the other hand, we see barely any quantitatively dominant evolutionary trend in the universe as a whole. This history of becoming is rather localized. There is no forcing to union. Union creates new information, new structures, which the Creator lets appear, rather than causes them to appear as specific informed structures. The top-down model has an explanatory function when God speaks to humankind through prophets, when God listens to prayers, when God's grace reaches the human person. Thus top-down causation as the model of God's interaction with creation is helpful to make certain events thinkable as God's action in the history of God's creation, without being the only model to be applied.

God supporting God's creation, supporting matter/spirit on its way to higher levels of complexity, centreity, consciousness, spirituality by God's never-failing creative call, seems to be the normal way God interacts with this universe. God calls forth the universe to become more and more similar to God. Becoming more realized information, becoming more creative of information—as happened most visibly on the human level—makes the universe essentially spiritual, and that means to a certain extent similar to God. This should not make us forget that God's loving creative call is in its own way the basic information in this universe. It is not imposing information, but offering the possibility to create information, if only it is grasped—provided the conditions are there. This always present offer, this always present call of God, should correctly be called grace. Since grace is the active love of God for God's creation, since the supportive force of the evolutionary history of the universe is God's love, we may say that the whole of creation is grace.

Grace presumes freedom: freedom on the side of the giver and of the receiver. As we have seen, freedom is another hallmark of God's creation, and its evolution makes it another means to understand the evolutionary process, to understand God's creation and the Creator.

CREATIO LIBERA

We have seen that the story of evolution tells us the story of freedom becoming more and more prevalent in the history of the universe. Is freedom an illusion, finally submitted to the top-down causation we just have recognized as a possible way for God to interact with God's creation? Is top-down causation the rule or the exception? It certainly is a helpful notion for seeing how God's interference in this world as an answer to our prayers may be compatible with what science knows about the laws of nature.

For a traditional theological understanding of creation, this perception of the rise of freedom through evolutionary history creates problems. Theologians were convinced that there is no trace of freedom anywhere in the realm of animals. Descartes did not invent the animal/machine *ab ovo*; he just translated into mechanical language the conviction of all the Scholastics. Everything natural is following the eternal law of God; everything is predetermined, even though secondary causes are fully respected. Descartes translated this total predetermination into a mechanical structure according to the general understanding of the heavens in his time: the heavens having become mechanical, so did everything else. Until modern times the stars, and especially the seven planets, had governed as secondary causes any physical movement on the earth. When the spiritual forces taking care of the movement of the planets were eliminated, it was evident that everything had to become purely mechanical.[59]

In the scholastic world everything was put in place by the will of God, who influenced the will of humans to will what humans wanted to do, whether in good or in evil. Free will in this view became subordinate to God's will, who made the will of humans to will freely. By distinguishing secondary causes from God's causation one leaves room for normal science and theology to go on undisturbed. Aquinas might have been quite happy with the notion of top-down causation. We also cannot forget that the sixteenth century was marked by disagreement about God's providence and free will, which logically exclude each other.

Within the Catholic tradition, Bañez held the Thomistic position, defending in his doctrine "the necessity and nature of *praemotio physica* for *any* action of a creature,"[60] whereas Molina taught that God "in his *scientia media* knows conditionally future free actions from their objective ideal reality."[61] The one insisted on divine providence and predestination, the other on the reality of free will. The fight between these schools was violent: each anathematized the other. Both positions, that of the defenders of human free will and that of the defenders of divine providence, had been maintained within the church's tradition. Exclusiveness of one position as proposed by predestinationism, which declared that God from all eternity had destined one part of humanity to beatitude and the rest to damnation,[62] had been refuted by the church since antiquity, but the dilemma between human freedom and all-encompassing divine providence and predestination remained. To end the Molina-Bañez disagreement, Roman authority's solution was to forbid each side to call the other heretical.

The basic roots of the understanding of an all-encompassing divine providence determining everything that happens in the universe is linked with the conviction that this universe is created to be perfectly ordered, so as finally to restore the disturbed heavenly order.[63] The Middle Ages were fascinated by creating order structures, especially those realizing the number seven, which imitated the heavenly order presented to humankind in the seven planets. The understanding was that everything physical happening on earth is caused by the movement of the seven planets, which are themselves moved by the firmament and thus finally by the First Mover. This chain of causes linked all natural events directly to God's action, whose eternal will predetermined everything happening on earth. Yet the notion of freedom was vigorously defended by all theologians, some making rather paradoxical statements, especially when they tended to insist more on predetermination.

There is probably no rational solution to the dilemma. As Karl Rahner states: "How God can create natural freedom in spite of its radical dependence and how the salutary act can be given as a free act by the grace of God—such questions are left to be freely discussed in the schools."[64] The dilemma is a constant challenge to the human mind. That humans are dependent on God's grace and can nevertheless act freely—another aspect of the predestination-freedom dilemma—was discussed for centuries, and "since the 18th century theological controversy on the subject has stagnated."[65] Perhaps it is wise to follow the advice of Rahner:

> In order really to "understand" the problem grace—freedom, to let it have its proper weight and to accept it, it is necessary to return to the frame of mind of a person at prayer. He receives himself, is, and gives himself back to God, by accepting the acceptance as an element in the gift itself. If one assumes that attitude of prayer (and by so doing in fact accepts the "solution" of the problem), there is no begging of the question, nor flight from it. One is only accepting what one undeniably is, both real and yet derivative, a creature which produced in freedom and is produced as grace as it acts.[66]

The dilemma of predestination and freedom, of grace and freedom, has never been solved rationally, and we should not be surprised that this problem stays with us in an evolving world. The essential difference between the older theological view and a theological understanding within an evolving framework is to be found in the fact that freedom is not an exceptional gift to humans, while all other things and living creatures are strictly submitted to mechanistical determinisms. Freedom evolves step-by-step, until on the human level with reflectivity it reaches the ability to know about itself. Animals have some freedom; they are free to a certain degree. Humans *know* that they are free, that they decide on their own what they want to do and what not. And they know they are responsible for what they do.

If we look at the history of evolution, we see little evidence that God acted by predestinating everything that has happened. The history of evolution can be read as a comprehensible story—it is possible that it happened that way—but at no point in the past would it have been possible to predict the future steps of the evolutionary process. As we have seen, disorder or the lack of recognizable order, as in the quasi-isotropic distribution of background radiation,[67] is more prevalent in the universe than highly ordered structures that are necessary to support life and thought. If there is global predestination of every particle in the universe, it is at least not very evidently signaled in God's creation. The world looks rather as if God were hiding God's predestinating activity.

The best we can say about the preordained orientation of the evolutionary process might be drawn from the fact that, before the background of the universe without order, the evolutionary process producing order, complexity, centreity, life, consciousness, information, and freedom—all aspects of the same process—remains unexplained, if no further factor is introduced, such as the one "Karl Popper has called a propensity in nature. Popper argued[68] that a greater frequency of occurrence of a particular kind of event may be used as a test of whether or not there is inherent in the sequence of events (equivalent to throws of a die) a tendency or propensity to realize the event in question."[69]

A propensity of this kind, or a loaded die, is to be presumed when events happen more often than the statistical probability would allow. Peacocke sees this propensity present at the level of processes governed by the second law of thermodynamics, and he finds that "this *propensity for increased complexity* is also manifest in the history of living organisms."[70] Though the majority of materialistic biologists would shrink from this conclusion, he thinks it correct to say "that there is a propensity towards increased complexity in the evolution of living organisms." This propensity does not mean necessity. It does not allow for predictability in any particular case. Biological systems might tend toward higher complexity, but enough such systems have not changed since the Precambrian. The propensity is far from being a kind of predetermination or predestination, though the trend in global evolution— scientists have a tendency to make abstraction from the nonevolving creatures when talking about evolution—becomes visible as a propensity toward complexity on ever new levels, which imply new ways of realizing complexity.

Teilhard de Chardin, who first introduced the notion of complexity to measure the level of evolution, indicated that there is a close relation between the increasing level of complexity and increasing levels of consciousness. Though Teilhard made quite clear that the one is not the cause of the other, the correlation between them could hardly be denied. This propensity is further correlated with what Peacocke describes as an *"increase of information-processing ability."*[71] In general we might state that there is a propensity in the evolving universe toward greater complexity, consciousness, and information handling. The latter is a basically matter-transcending capacity, pointing to a creation that is moving toward more spirit.

As predestination this propensity is the best approximation we may find in the ongoing process of the universe. Without this propensity, which might be understood as the effect of the sustained call of the Creator to join the divine self through becoming more spiritual, through becoming able to encounter the Creator, there would be no evolution.

But we see that this approximation can hardly be identified with the traditional understanding of predestination. The latter was experienced with the steady movements of the heavens, the planets and the firmament, the cosmic order. With the discovery of inertia and gravitation, predetermination of the heavenly movements became a rather deistic idea, and with the disappearance of the heavenly order, which made room for a chaotic distribution of billions of galaxies, it is difficult today to see the determining, ordering hand of the Creator at work. Despite the astrological statements in newspapers and magazines, most of us no longer believe in Mars or Jupiter determining our actions, nor do we hold the lack of cooperation of the sun in conception responsible for the failure of a pregnancy.

This raises the question whether predestination, certainly a possibility for the almighty God, is actually exercised by God. The view offered by God's creation does not show any strong indication of predestination. The enormous amounts of unused evolutionary energy lost in background radiation and in black holes, where millions of sunlike stars seem to lose the little information they had acquired in the form of chemical elements and simple molecules, do not point to a predetermining Creator who preordains everything in creation. The Creator does not seem interested in predetermining and preordaining creation. With no strong indicator for predestination in the creative process of evolution, we have to ask ourselves if the idea of predestination itself is linked to the obsolete static universe in which humankind lived until the last century. It was a world that relied on an all-ordaining Creator who made the "sun rise on the evil and on the good."[72]

Today it is hard to say these words meaningfully. Taught through scientific exploration of creation the chaotic structures of God's universe with some localized features of order, we find ourselves in a temporarily stabilized solar system, which as such does not rely immediately on God's daily intervention to bring out the sun. We find ourselves exposed to a large scale of possible accidents, such as from earthquakes to more or less disastrous asteroid impacts in the past. The earthquake of Lisbon in 1755 made many intellectuals doubt the existence of God, the Creator, because they saw God as the preordaining, predetermining God who knew everything in advance, and who as the good God should have prevented such a disaster that killed just and unjust people alike. Today such an argument is hardly convincing: we have learned that geologic structures do not follow rules of morality, that plate tectonics are not preordained to strike in certain places at specific dates.

This passivity of God exposes us to a world less reliable than a world perfectly controlled by God, a control exercised by a chain of secondary causes, as the Middle Ages saw it. Our desire for more security might make us indulge in speculations about the necessity of predetermination, preordaining, and predestination. But what if God chooses not to exercise a predetermining power? Creation lacks any strong signs of determinism; the signs in our experience dissolve into statistical distributions corresponding in each case to a certain level of evolution. God's evolving creation rather indicates that there is no predestination exercised by the Creator. Berthold von Regensburg remarked that there is no being in the universe with power over the human free will except "God alone, and He does not want to exercise it."[73] Likewise God does not seem to want to exercise divine power of predestination in creation in general. Only at certain points there might have been some coercive directional influence, especially if this universe with its fine-tuned beginning is the unique universe, but the general movement of the evolving creation is hardly understandable as following the orders of a prede-termining God.

This creation appears to be a freely and painfully evolving universe. God seems to have eliminated any direct pressure to go in a certain direction. The only orientation supported by the vectors of growing complexity, informa-tion, and consciousness seems to move toward the evolution of freedom. The least we might say is that the Creator seems much more concerned with a desire to see freedom freely evolve than with imposing the divine will on creation. The waste in the universe then begins to make sense. The lower the evolutionary level, the less were the chances of going a step in the direc-tion of more complexity. The quasi-endless times before the process of evo-lution reached a somewhat advanced level are as impressive as the small amount of matter that finally reached the level of life and thinking.[74] This is part of the price paid for freedom to evolve. Freedom of the creation was ev-idently more important to the Creator than imposing the divine will by pre-ordaining everything, which would have been more economical.

As we have stated,[75] we might thus speculate that God's intention in cre-ating this world is not to establish a perfect order, to impose the divine will, but to call forth in love a creation that will one day become able to answer in love God's creative call. And God accepts not only the price of a wasteful uni-verse, but the even heavier price of evil. There cannot be any free evolution without necessary evils such as death or without statistically avoidable evil. When things can go wrong, sooner or later some will go wrong. Only in a sta-tic and strictly determined world can evil be avoided. Illness, accidents, and untimely deaths are part of the price. We may be upset by seeing this price accepted by the Creator, but there is no rationally thinkable way to have the evolution of freedom without concomitant evil. Still, it is hard to accept the statement that God accepted the price of the appearance of evil on all levels of evolution so that freedom could reach the level of human freedom.

This difficulty in understanding the presence of evil in God's creation is not new. Classical theology referred to the problem as *mysterium iniquitatis*. Today we can see an unavoidable relation between the structure of the free-dom-oriented creation and the appearance of evil. The price the Creator was ready to pay for the existence of freedom may appear extremely high. The mystery is perhaps much more in the fact that this world was so important to the Creator, as a free world answering the call of Love, that God accepted the unthinkable evil: that the Child of God, the Logos, became man and died the most horrible death on the cross. Whoever tries to solve the problem of evil, at least in a Christian perspective, should meditate on the mystery of the cross, the ultimate price paid so that human freedom might exist.[76] This may indicate how highly God values the reality of freedom.

The great mystery of creation would reside less in the old dilemma of the predestinating God and human free will than in God's love that refrains from imposing an evil-avoiding order, to let the creatures become free to love God. If the interpretation presented is not erroneous, this level of freedom being realized in humankind needs the constant support of the loving creative call of God. As on all levels of evolution, the call goes through the neighbor to the individual person, who can answer this call to love God by loving the human neighbor, by entering into union with him or her.[77] God does not call the human person directly as God, imposing the divine self. God makes the divine self present rather through other human beings by sending prophets. Then, in full coherence with the divine creative intention, the Logos, the Word of God, becomes man, leaving human beings free to love him or to refuse him.[78] The creative call of divine love, calling everything out of nothing by the way of evolution, by creative union, sustains the creation on all levels. However far creation may go astray, the Creator does not withdraw the divine sustaining call of love. Humans are no exception: they exist as everything else because they are held in existence by the loving call of the Creator. Humans can reject themselves; they may seek only themselves. God does not withdraw the divine loving call that is to be answered by love.

The creation that exists only because it is called forth by the loving Creator reaches in the human being the ability to answer or to refuse God's offer of love. On the human level it becomes evident that the creative power at work in this universe is far less the almighty will of the Creator than God's grace that penetrates the whole universe. Everything in this universe is held in existence by God's grace, by God's love.

God's love is infinitely patient, as is documented by the slow answer of the universe: God never did withdraw this creative love. Nor does God withdraw God's grace from anyone. One may refuse to love God, to love one's neighbor, but God's offer of love, of grace, is never withdrawn. Even the sinner, the human who refuses God, may freely grasp at any time the patiently offered love that pervades the whole universe. In a precise sense we may say that the whole of creation is grace. And creation, having become *capax Dei* in humankind, is called upon to answer in love the Creator, in adoration of that eternal Love.

APPENDIX: STUDY QUESTIONS

The following questions are intended to assist readers in their study and understanding of the text. The questions have been successfully used with both college students and an ecumenical adult reading group familiar with neither theology nor the sophistication of modern science.

CHAPTER 1. Theology of Creation as a Permanent Task

1. Before beginning, what is your understanding of theology?
2. Is it your experience that interest in religion is increasing or decreasing? On what do you base your opinion?
3. What is the historical meaning of *sola scriptura* (only scripture)? What is the historical background of the origin of this term?
4. What is the meaning of religious fundamentalism? Give two examples.
5. How do theology and natural theology differ?
6. Compare the presuppositions of theology and of the natural sciences.
7. Explain Eddington's metaphor about ichthyologists to describe the philosophy of materialism.
8. Discuss the possibilities of a general theology for humankind.
9. What is your understanding of Christian *tradition*? Does it agree with the post-Tridentine interpretation of *depositum fidei* (the deposit of faith)? Why was this post-Tridentine interpretation modified at Vatican Council II? Do you see any strengths and weaknesses in these interpretations?
10. Does theology prove the existence of God? What is the reasoning to support your response?
11. Can the existence of God be proven through reflection on the laws of nature? What is the reasoning to support your response?
12. Why should the theologian be aware of how contemporary science understands the universe?
13. Why are criteria of self-evidence and clarity not necessarily signs of the truth? Can you think of an example to support your response?
14. What is meant by the statement that philosophy is the handmaiden of theology? Is this a valid statement today?
15. What preparation in the sciences was normally required in medieval times in order for one to be admitted to studies in theology?
16. Why did it take so long for theologians to give up a Ptolemaic understanding of the universe?
17. What were the two approaches applied by medieval Christian theologians to the science of their time?

18. Why was a new emphasis on the *sola scriptura* principle in the sixteenth century significant for the relation of science to Roman Catholic theology?

19. Why is it claimed that Darwin's *Origin of Species* was a more serious threat to Christian theology than Galileo's *Dialogue Concerning the Two Chief World Systems*?

20. Was there unanimous consent among church leaders in the nineteenth century regarding the origin of humankind?

21. How do you distinguish among hypothesis, theory, and fact? In which of these categories is evolution?

22. One of the greatest theologians of the twentieth century was Karl Barth. Propose how some theologians of the Barthian school might treat evolution.

23. Explain the common theme in the two mottoes *depositum fidei* and *sola scriptura*. Why does an evolutionary environment challenge the traditional understanding of these mottoes?

24. Compare the implications of an evolutionary versus a static Zeitgeist (spirit of the age) for the theologian; for someone in your major field of study. Would an evolutionary Zeitgeist tend to change the interpretation of biblical texts?

25. What advantage does knowledge of science have over other forms of knowing? Why does the more true usually come later in science?

26. Discuss the implications of an evolutionary Zeitgeist on an interpretation of the doctrine of infallibility. Evaluate doctrinal alternatives and their implications.

27. Why is it proposed that theology recognize itself as provisional in its historical formulations? What are the advantages and disadvantages of this proposal?

28. Would you agree that science is an ultimate criterion by which to evaluate the legitimacy of theological doctrine? Are there other criteria?

29. What source is suggested in the text to obtain an authentic statement about the basic content of Christian faith? What two propositions are recommended? What is your conclusion?

CHAPTER 2. The Universe as Process of Becoming: God's Creation

1. Explain the meaning of the term "God of the gaps"?

2. What can the theologian know about the eternity of the world from faith and from reason?

3. Reflecting on their data about nature, scientists sometimes discuss the existence of God. Is this likely to be a central question for theologians? Why or why not?

4. What is the difference in conclusion between models of the universe based on strict determinism and models based on chaos theory?

5. Is there disagreement among scientists about the age of the universe? What is the best estimate?

6. Describe the anthropic cosmological principle. What is the basis for its attractiveness to some scientists? What is the danger for those who invoke it as an argument favoring a creator?

7. How has the classic view of an orderly universe assumed by scholastic theology been changed by modern science?

8. Briefly describe the accepted big bang model of an expanding universe.

9. Why is it proposed in the text that emphasis on quantitative aspects of evolution is not particularly helpful in deriving meaning for human life?

10. Why does our knowledge about the past of the universe differ from our knowledge about its future?

11. Explain in words or diagrams the reasoning in arguments like S. J. Gould's "humans are like a grain of dust in a quasi infinite universe." Why do you agree or disagree?

12. To understand human evolution is it best to start with humans as they are now or as they were at the beginning of time? Why?

13. What is the meaning of body-soul dualism in human beings? Why has this dualism traditionally been accepted by theologians?

14. How would you argue the case for human beings as unified centers made up of multiple parts?

15. What are some of the common features present in humans and other primates? How do humans differ from other primates?

16. Using examples, explain what is meant by the radius of perception to describe evolution.

17. Describe in your own words how unity becomes more elusive and unclear as complexity decreases in nature.

18. What is meant by the statement that in nature the whole can be more than the sum of its parts? Give an example.

19. Is the unity in life explained by the laws of chemistry? Do the elements in a union lose their identity?

20. Explain the meaning of this statement: "The evolutionary process proceeds by union of elements into higher unities in which something new comes into existence."

21. What opportunity would be available to science if there were a "God of the gaps"?

22. What is meant by the statement that "being is realized and maintained union"?

23. Given the biblical tradition of humans created in the image and likeness of God (Gen. 1:26), why might it be reasonable to speculate about God as "the supreme being in union" rather than merely "the supreme being"?

24. Explain the interpretation of 1 John 1:4, "God is love," within the perspective of a metaphysics of union. Discuss the relation of science and theology within this perspective.

CHAPTER 3. Consciousness in the Universe—of the Universe

1. What does it mean to say that in humans evolution has reached a stage of reflection?

2. How would you argue against the statement that the study of the evolution of consciousness is anthropocentric and an epiphenomenon?

3. What is the reductionist basis for the argument that there is no orientation to evolution? How is the argument falsified?

4. How would you describe the meaning of consciousness? Distinguish between human and animal consciousness.
5. What is the sign common to all stages of consciousness in evolution?
6. Why can a holistic and not a reductionistic approach be used in the text to observe behavior regarding consciousness?
7. What is meant by saying that evolution follows a path of statistical improbability?
8. What is the difference between classical orthogenesis in evolution and what is proposed in the text?
9. Is the emergence of consciousness a proof of evolution?
10. Why can science-based arguments to prove the existence of God be poor arguments? What is your opinion?
11. What is the starting point for philosophy and for theology in trying to understand the universe? Why has traditional philosophy withdrawn from its traditional role in this endeavor?
12. Why was the account of creation in the book of Genesis compatible with cosmology until recent times?
13. What was the origin of natural laws according to medieval theologians? Discuss the role of order in this worldview.
14. What is the relation of deterministic eternal physical laws in modern science to medieval thinking?
15. Do scientists today have the same understanding of order in the universe as during the Enlightenment?
16. Explain why the observation of stars in the sky as exemplifying a peaceful and orderly existence is deceptive.
17. Why is it improbable that a simple wave function could describe everything in the universe?
18. How do you respond to the common argument that all living forms are of the same status, including humans?
19. Why can it be said that our material universe is neither a masterpiece of economics nor a masterpiece of order?
20. What is meant by the statement that the whole process of evolution brings forth new qualities and not mere modifications of properties? Give some examples.
21. Why can one make the statement that the human quest for meaning is also the quest of the universe itself?
22. Identify signs of the finite character of the universe.
23. What is the purpose of the biblical story of creation?
24. What does it mean to say that in humans the universe transcends itself?
25. How does one use analogy to predict the qualities of God?
26. What is meant by the biblical notion of human beings as the image of God (*imago Dei*)?
27. Why is eternity difficult to explain? What is *theologia negativa*? How did the church fathers use *theologia negativa* to discuss eternity?
28. What is the difference proposed between the concept of time as understood by classical physics and by evolutionists? Explain why one of the two seems more compatible for understanding the relation of the universe to the Creator.

CHAPTER 4. The Evolution of Information:
A Hallmark of God's Creation

1. What has been the central interest of modern information theory? How has information been measured?
2. Despite the power of computers to outperform humans, particularly in mathematics, give two limitations intrinsic to computers.
3. Within an evolutionary context, why can it be claimed that the occurrence and value of information is not measurable in bits? Give an example of how a bit is unable to distinguish the meaning of information.
4. When is information meaningful?
5. What appears to be the relation of the complexity of a living structure to its informational content?
6. Why is it said that at the atomic level information and structure are not distinguishable?
7. What is the difference between molecules on the prelife level and the DNA molecule?
8. Has research on the structure of the brain elucidated how we recognize meaning?
9. Explain the interpretation of soul, *anima forma corporis,* as the informing reality of an organism.
10. In what sense is information essentially immaterial?
11. What is meant by informed behavior? Is informed behavior instinctive or does it derive from learning, e.g., learning by watching other animals?
12. Why is there need for a scale to analyze the evolution of information?
13. Evaluate the statement that "a body of laws that would precisely regulate all natures" was unknown "until Galileo, Kepler, and Descartes."
14. What is common to the beliefs of both Thomas Aquinas and Albert Einstein about the laws of nature? Is there a difference in their opinions?
15. What is the origin of biological information according to Neo-Darwinist theories? What is your own opinion?
16. Why did the immutability of species, accepted by Linnaeus, not remain acceptable to the scientific community?
17. What is the origin of new information in history?
18. What three qualitative levels may be proposed to describe the evolution of information, since there is no generally acceptable quantitative scale?
19. What is meant by saying that the level of communication of information by matter is related to the level of its structure?
20. How does genetic information stored in living matter differ from information stored in nonliving matter?
21. How do animals remember? Give an example of an animal using memory.
22. How do the quality and range of memory relate to evolution?
23. Describe two systems of information storage in living creatures that are not found in preliving matter.
24. What is the new dimension of storage of information found in humans?

25. Why was the invention of writing a significant step in evolution?

26. Why is information an immaterial factor in such systems as writing, photography, and electronic storage?

27. With respect to communicating information, what is the difference between pre-living and living matter?

28. It is said that communication on the human level has become multidimensional and that the medium used is irrelevant to the content. Give some examples of this phenomenon.

29. What does it mean to say that as evolution continues, information becomes a matter-independent entity?

30. Explain the thesis that the evolution of information traces a path from materiality to spirituality.

31. Is it true to say that through information humankind has reached a new level of likeness to the Creator?

32. Why is it proposed that analysis of the evolution of information makes mystical experience easier to understand, though not scientifically verifiable? How can this proposal be related to the biblical theme of humans as images of God?

CHAPTER 5. Evolution of Freedom in God's Creation

1. What did medieval theologians consider to be the origin of human freedom?

2. What is the source of the tendency for scientists to believe in a deterministic universe?

3. Why has the scientific community shown relatively little interest in research on human freedom?

4. What is the origin of animal behavior according to the Scholastics, and according to Descartes?

5. What was the definition of life according to the Scholastics? Why do you agree or disagree with this definition?

6. Give some examples to show that instinct alone cannot explain animal behavior. Does animal research find an abrupt gap between human freedom and the behavior of animals?

7. Why are clarifications of the degrees of freedom in animal and human behavior significant?

8. In what sense do protons and neutrons exercise freedom?

9. How could both Heisenberg uncertainty and chaos theory permit "God of the gaps" as answers to questions about nature?

10. What is meant by the statement that the chance of an event's occurring in the universe may be approximately known within the vector of possibilities open to the element involved?

11. Explain, using a bell curve, what is meant by saying that the interesting events in evolution always happen within the range that is highly improbable at the limits of the statistical distribution.

12. Why does the application of probability and statistics inevitably eliminate a strictly deterministic explanation of evolution?

13. Show on a typical probability-distribution curve how a new species can emerge in evolution. What is the role of DNA in this emergence?
14. Why are structures needed in an evolutionary universe?
15. Give an example of a specialized structure in evolutionary history that limits its vector of freedom.
16. Explain how bodily human evolution seems to have terminated, and yet new human abilities have developed. How could this type of analysis of evolution be applied to the economic job market?
17. Explain how genetics limits the freedom of animal species more than that of the human species.
18. Name the factors that limit human development.
19. What is meant by the proposition that individual freedom must be balanced by structures within a context of the emergence of change? What institution has offered this structure for modern secularized societies?
20. Verify or falsify with an example the proposition that rigid structures halt evolution.
21. What images would you recommend to describe models for a dynamic church and for a static church?
22. Why can evolutionary development be painful? How can this development affect a person's Christian faith?
23. Explain what is meant by the statement that "natural evil is quite common in the story of evolution."
24. "If God cannot eliminate evil, then he is powerless; if he does not want to do it, he is envious; that he wants to do it and can do it is contradicted by common experience." How does one respond: (a) understanding the universe to be static and deterministic; (b) understanding evolution to occur by strict orthogenesis; (c) applying a statistical model proposed in the text; (d) in your own view?
25. What scientific data reveal that death has been an essential condition of evolution?
26. Do animals suffer both physical and psychic pain? Do you agree with those who try to prevent all scientific research because of potential cruelty to animals?
27. What is meant by the statement that moral evil seems to be a new dimension in evolution?
28. Do the positive and negative aspects of human beings, becoming *capax Dei*, seem more easy to understand in a deterministic or a nondeterministic world?
29. What is your interpretation of the statements about the goodness of creation in Genesis 1:4, 10, 12, 18, 21, 25, 31, in view of so much waste and suffering found in an evolutionary universe?

CHAPTER 6. God, Creator of the Evolving Universe

1. What is the difference, if any, between how a person looks at the process of evolution as scientist and as theologian?
2. "The [Holy] Spirit is the principle of creativity on all levels of matter and life. He creates new possibilities and in these anticipates the new designs and 'blueprints'

for material and living organisms. In this sense the Spirit is the principle of evolution." Why do you agree or disagree with this statement?

3. What was God doing before the creation of the world?

4. Philosophers, theologians, and scientists throughout history have discussed the eternity of the universe. How would you discuss eternity from each perspective?

5. How does the change in theological vision from a static to a dynamic evolving universe affect the interpretation of the first chapters of Genesis? Include in your explanation (a) interpretations that creation is "good," and (b) the role of Adam, Abraham, and Moses.

6. Why is a model of *creatio appellata* (creation called forth) proposed instead of an original and continued creation?

7. How can viewing the universe as evolutionary translate traditional theological emphases of God as almighty to an emphasis on the Creator's patience?

8. In a metaphysics of union, (a) what is meant by the proposition that the lower the level of an element's being, the less its tendency to unite? (b) Within this model of understanding creation through the union of elements, how is God conceived to be present? (c) How is this understanding of God's presence similar to the human experience of love?

9. (a) What is the meaning of analogy in science and in theology? (b) Relate the metaphysics of union of elements by analogy to the scriptural confession of God as Love? (c) Why does, or why doesn't, this theological understanding end up as a "God of the gaps"?

10. (a) What is panentheism? (b) How can panentheism clarify the text of Ephesians 1:25 that refers to Christ as "the completeness of Him who fills the universe, all in all"?

11. What is the difference in Christian tradition between what can be known about the existence of God and how God exists?

12. (a) What is at the root of tension in Christian tradition between the God of Greek philosophy and the God of the bible? (b) At what point in history do you think this tension could become most explicit?

13. (a) Within an evolutionary context, what is the distinction between the analogy of being (*analogia entis*) and the analogy of becoming (*analogia fientis*)? How can this distinction be applied to understand the universe as creation called forth (*creatio appellata*)?

14. (a) God is described in classical Western thought as *ipsum esse subsistens* (absolute being itself), and all other beings inasmuch as they exist possess relative similarities to God. How can the same principle be applied to a metaphysics of union in an evolutionary universe? (b) Why is Alfred North Whitehead's panentheism not acceptable to many Christian philosophers and theologians?

15. (a) Are the appearance and spread of AIDS around the planet God's punishment? (b) Discuss theological issues raised by this question, e.g., as in the book of Job. (c) Are there ontological (philosophical) roots in Western thought that support this understanding of punishment by God?

16. What are the Chalcedonian formulas that are traditionally accepted by Christians?

17. How does the understanding of God change with time, e.g., Moses; Abraham, Isaac, and Jacob; medieval worldview; process philosophy; Schmitz-Moormann?

18. Based on a metaphysics of union, what does it mean to say of the Trinity that the more perfect the union, the more differentiated the persons?

19. (a) Do you think that humanity will ever fully understand the Trinity? Why or why not? (b) How can a metaphysics of union clarify our knowledge about the tri-une God?

20. Can union among creatures in evolution draw them closer to God? Why or why not?

21. (a) How can the statement "God is love" (1 John 4:8) be more than a statement about morality? (b) Why can a philosophy based on individualism be a rejection of the real world, not only morally, but also metaphysicallly?

22. Give an example of spiritual information that is stored in matter.

23. How is a plan for action stored in the brain in order to be transformed into action?

24. (a) What does top-down causation mean? (b) How would you explain to someone the analogical application of this notion to prayer and the Christian sacraments? (c) Discuss the application of top-down causation to creation called forth (*creatio appellata*).

25. (a) What is the meaning of a multiple-universe hypothesis? (b) What physical criteria would you suggest to predict whether human life could develop in another universe? (c) Do multiple-universe hypotheses question the existence of God?

26. Discuss the meaning of God's grace in a theology of creation?

27. (a) Describe Thomas Aquinas's solution to the dilemma of human free will in a deterministic universe. (b) What was the theological issue left unsolved after the Molina-Bañez controversy in the sixteenth century? (c) What is your solution to this question?

28. (a) Explain the difference between predeterminism and propensity toward com-plexification in biological evolution. (b) How can each of these tendencies be related to a movement toward spirit?

29. (a) Discuss the price paid for freedom to evolve within creation. (b) Do you see this approach making more sense than the traditional view within a static model of creation. Why or why not? (c) What might be the role of Jesus of Nazareth in an evolving model?

30. How can the metaphysics of union support a Christian understanding of Jesus' words in Matt. 25:30–45? If so, in what sense?

31. (a) What is the meaning of the statement that "the whole of creation is grace"? (b) Is the proposition reasonable, given the evolutionary creation found by modern science? (c) Does the proposition modify your understanding of the Creator God? If so, in what sense?

NOTES

Introduction

1. This does not imply that any special theory of evolution is accepted: one must distinguish between the fact and the theories to explain the fact, which may be of limited value.
2. Steven Weinberg, *The First Three Minutes* (London: Andre Deutsch, 1977).
3. Paul Davies, *The Mind of God: The Scientific Basis for a Rational World* (New York: Simon & Schuster, 1992).
4. Cf. Arthur Peacocke, John C. Polkinghorne, Ian Barbour.
5. In this book *sciences* and *science* refer to the natural sciences, and only rarely to the "human sciences."
6. Cf. Nancey Murphy, *Theology in the Age of Scientific Reasoning* (Ithaca, N.Y.: Cornell University Press, 1990).

1. Theology of Creation as a Permanent Task

1. Lev. 11:6; Deut. 14:7.
2. Thomas Aquinas, *Summa Theologica* 1a.1, 2c.
3. *Address of Pope John Paul II to International Theological Commission on December 2, 1994, Crux of the News,* 16 January 1995, 5.
4. Cf. William Paley, *Natural Theology: Or, Evidences of the Existence and Attributes of the Deity, Collected from the Appearances of Nature* (Philadelphia: n.p., 1814).
5. A typical statement along this line of thinking is "One cannot make that argument airtight *until concepts like knowledge and creativity have been successfully translated into the language of physics*" (David Deutsch and Michael Lockwood, "The Quantum Physics of Time Travel," *Scientific American*, March 1994, 74, italics added). In the last century, in a more popular version, Jules Verne in his *Voyage au centre de la terre* had its protagonist, a German professor, declare: *The miracles of nature, great as they may be, can always be explained by physical laws.*
6. Sir Arthur Eddington, *The Philosophy of Physical Science* (Cambridge: Cambridge University Press 1939), 16.
7. Karl Rahner, ed., *Sacramentum Mundi: An Encyclopedia of Theology* (New York: Herder & Herder, 1970), 6:234.
8. Ibid., 6:235.
9. A number of modern religions and movements try to do just that: e.g., the Baha'i and many of the New Age movements, as well as recent enterprises like the World Council of Religions and other efforts to formulate a universally acceptable world ethics. They usually are an expression of the inability of traditional religions, as expressed by their theologies, to speak to persons in the modern world.

10. This presentation will refer primarily to the Roman Catholic tradition.

11. Karl-Heinz Weger, "Tradition," *Sacramentum Mundi*, 6:270.

12. Vincentius Lirinensis *Commonitorium* n. 22, M.L. 50:649: "Quid est depositum? Id est quod tibi creditum est, non a te inventum, quod accepisti, non quod excogitasti; rem non ingenii sed doctrinae, non usurpationis privatae sed publicae traditionis; rem ad te perductam non a te prolatam; in qua non auctor debes esse sed custos, non institutor sed sectator, non ducens sed sequens, 'Depositum' inquit 'custodi' (1 Tim. 6, 20); catholicae fidei talentum inviolatum illibatumque conserva . . . magnopere curandum est *ut teneamus quod ubique, quod semper, quod ab omnibus creditum est.* . . . Intellegatur . . . illustrius quod ante obscurius credebatur. . . . Eadem tamen quae didicisti doce, ut cum dicas nove non dicas nova."

13. Weger, "Tradition," *Sacramentum Mundi*, 6:270.

14. Ibid., 6:271.

15. Ibid., 6:271–72.

16. Vatican II, *Unitatis Redintegratio*, art. 11.

17. Anselm of Canterbury, *Cur Deus homo* (Darmstadt: Wissenschaftliche Buchgesellschaft, 1993), 12.

18. Cf. Friedrich Christian Lesser, *Théologie des Insectes ou Démonstration des Perfections de Dieu dans tout ce qui concerne les Insectes*, traduit de l'Allemand, M. P. Lyonnet (Paris: Hugues-Daniel Chaubert-Laurent Durand, 1745); Paley, *Natural Theology*.

19. Michael Buckley, S.J., *At the Origins of Modern Atheism* (New Haven, Conn.: Yale University Press, 1987).

20. This argument was still used by Gerhard Mercator in the treatise "De fabrica mundi," introducing his atlas. During the Middle Ages, it was considered a physical proof for spherical shape of the earth. "Mercator aus der Sicht mittelalterlicher Theologie," in *Mercator—ein Wegbereiter neuzeitlichen Denkens*, edited by Irmgard Hantsche, Duisburger Mercator-Studien, Bd. 1 (Bochum: Universitätsverlag Dr. N. Brockmeyer, 1994), 1–11.

21. This is an everyday experience: e.g., it is evident that one cannot penetrate a stone wall with one's head.

22. This event was quoted also by Protestant scholars of that time as proof for geocentrism, e.g., in one of his "Table Talks" held in 1539, Martin Luther is quoted as saying: "People gave ear to an upstart astrologer who strove to show that the earth revolves, not the heavens or the firmament, the sun and the moon. . . . This fool wishes to reverse the entire science of astronomy; but sacred Scripture tells us [Josh. 10:13] that Joshua commanded the sun to stand still, and not the earth." Translated and quoted by Andrew D. White, *A History of the Warfare of Science and Theology in Christendom* (New York: Appleton, 1896), 1:126.

23. It is probably one of the weaknesses of human sciences like psychology that they strive for the ideal of measurement and calculable proof. This limits their field of research by leaving out of consideration the most human qualities like values, which cannot be evaluated by statistical measurements.

24. Cf. Pierre Glorieux, *Répertoire des Maîtres en Théologie au XIIIᵐᵉ siècle* (Paris: n.p., 1933–35).

25. Johannes de Sacrobosco, *Tractatus de sphaera mundi* (Paris, c. 1235). This was a reference book often revised through the centuries. Cf. Bernard of Trillia, *Quaestiones in Sphaeram Joannis de Sacro Bosco* (c. 1250). Galileo, who studied at the Collegium Romanum, used for teaching his course of astronomy in Padua the edition revised by the Jesuit Christopher Clavius, who was also involved in the recalculation of the calendar. Philip Melanchthon reedited the "Sacrobusco" for use in the Lutheran School of Theology in Wittenberg. The teaching on the heavenly bodies and discussion of related subjects were quite common in the thirteenth century, e.g., Dirk of Freiburg, *De universitate entium; de animatione caeli; de elementis in quantum sunt partes mundi; de intelligentiis et motoribus coelorum.*

26. It has been said that NASA engineers have made calculations based on a Ptolemaic model rather than a Newtonian model in order to determine the position of the planets because of the former's greater preciseness. This oral information has not been confirmed in writing by the agency.

27. Cf. the most comprehensive text on the Galileo case: Annibale Fantoli, *Galileo: For Copernicanism and for the Church,* trans. George V. Coyne, S.J., Studi Galileiani, vol. 3 (Vatican City: Vatican Observatory Publications, 1994). Galileo was right in defending the Copernican view, but his proof based on the tides was wrong. The first convincing proof for the heliocentric system was the observation of the Bradley Aberrations in the eighteenth century.

28. Albertus Magnus, *Mineralia* l.2 tr. 2 c.1: "Scientiae enim naturalis non est simpliciter narrata accipere, sed in rebus naturalibus inquirere causas."

29. Albertus Magnus, *Meteoral* 3 tr. 1 c.21: "Quae probatio (per sensum) in naturis rerum certissima est, et plus dignitatis habet quam ratio sine experimento."

30. Albertus Magnus, *De vegetalibus et plantis* [ed. Meyer-Jessen, 340, n. 1]: "Experimentum enim solum certificat in talibus, eo quod de tam particularibus naturis syllogismus haberi non potest."

31. E.g., Richard C. Dales, *The Scientific Achievement of the Middle Ages* (Philadelphia: University of Pennsylvania Press, 1989).

32. *Summa contra Gentiles* II, 3: "Sic ergo patet falsam esse quorumdam sententiam, qui dicebant nihil interesse ad fidei veritatem qui de creaturis quisque sentiret, dummodo circa Deum recte sentiatur, ut Augustinus narrat De origine animae (c.4 et 5). Nam error circa creaturas redundat in falsam de Deo scientiam, et hominum mentes a Deo abducit."

33. M. M. Davy, *Les sermons universitaires parisiens de 1250–1251, Études de Philosophie médiévale* 15 (Paris, 1931), 231–37: "Non moventur motu proprio sed sequntur motum firmamenti, sic et veri claustrales non debent moveri propria voluntate sed motu firmamenti scilicet Dei. . . . Sed multi motu contrario moventur, sequentes proprias voluntates, et propter hoc dicit Daniel (VIII, I, 10) Cornu arietis deiecit de stellis et conculcavit eos. . . . Stella . . . in uno loco fixa est, sic religiosi et clerici fixi debent esse ut loca sua non mutent. . . . Sed quidam sunt qui contrarium faciunt." Cf. ibid. for sermon of William of Auvergne on the order of the cosmos, which is presented as the model to be followed (149–53).

34. Cf. Berthold von Regensburg, *Vollständige Ausgabe seiner Predigten,* mit Anmerkungen von Franz Pfeiffer, mit einem Vorwort von Kurth Ruth (Berlin, n.d.), 1: 48–64; 2:233–37.

35. *Summa Theologica* 1a.68, 1; cf. Augustine *De Genes. ad litt.* lib 1, cap. 18 [Corpus Scriptorum Ecclesiae Latinorum, 28,27]: "In hujusmodi quaestionibus duo sunt observanda. Primum quidem, ut veritas Scripturae inconcusse teneatur. Secundum, cum Scriptura divina multipliciter exponi possit, quod nulli expositioni aliquis ita praecise inhaereat, ut si certa ratione constiterit hoc esse falsum, quod aliquis sensum Scripturae esse credebat, id nihilominus asserere praesumat: ne Scriptura ex hoc ab infidelibus derideatur, et ne eis via credendi praecludatur."

36. Bonaventura *Breviloquium* pars secunda, de creatura mundi c. 5: "Scriptura, ordinate *narrat* quantum ad doctrinae sufficientam, licet non ita explicite describat distinctionem orbium nec caelestem nec elementarium, parvum aut nihil dicat de motibus et virtutibus corporum superiorum et de mixtionibus elementorum et elementatorum. . . . Ratio autem ad intelligentiam praedictorum haec est: quia, cum primum principium reddat se nobis cognoscibile et per *Scripturam* et per *creaturam*, per librum *creaturae* se manifestat ut principium *effectivum*, per librum *Scripturae* ut principium *reparativum*."

37. Without a geological theory fossil shells could easily be accommodated with the Great Flood.

38. We probably overestimate the effects of this principle on the theological praxis of the early Reformation, which did not break radically with the traditional teaching of theology. In Wittenberg, students learned physics using the manual written by Philip Melanchthon, to which he refers quite often in his theological opus. In Geneva, theologians used the *Physica Christiana* by Lambertus Danaeus (Lambert Daneau); this book had eighteen reprints, more than any of his theological writings.

39. "If there were a real proof that the Sun is in the center of the universe, that the Earth is in the third heaven, and that the Sun does not go round the Earth but the Earth round the Sun, then we would have to proceed with great circumspection in explaining passages of Scripture which appear to teach the contrary and rather admit that we did not understand them than declare an opinion to be false which is proved to be true. But, as for myself, I shall not believe that there are such proofs until they are shown to me." Letter to Foscarini, published in Galileo's *Opere*, 12:159–60; cf. Giorgio de Santillana, *The Crime of Galileo* (Chicago: University of Chicago Press, 1955), 98–100.

40. E.g., Friedrich Christian Lesser, *Théologie des Insectes*, 6: "Si vous parlez d'une Pierre, d'une Fourmi, d'un Moucheron, d'une Abeille, votre discours est une espece de démonstration de la puissance de celui qui les a formées; car la sagesse de l'Ouvrier se manifeste pour l'ordinaire dans ce qui est le plus petit. Celui qui a étendu les Cieux, & qui a creusé le lit de la Mer n'est point different de celui qui a percé l'aiguillon d'une Abeille, afin de donner passage à son venin," Basil in *Hexaemeron*. [When you speak about a stone, an ant, a fly, a bee, your discourse is a kind of demonstration of the power of the one who formed them; for the wisdom of the Worker manifests itself ordinarily in the smallest things. The one who has stretched the heavens and dug the bed of the ocean is not at all different from the one who has pierced the sting of the bee to let through its poison. (Translated by Karl Schmitz-Moormann, hereafter designated "S-M.")] The original German was published in the seventeenth century. (I could not locate a copy.) There are a large number of similar publications with titles like Lithotheology or Hydrotheology. They are based on observation and laid the ground for a number of branches of mod-

ern science. The numerous references to the church fathers are no longer quoted in modern theological manuals.

41. These ideas had been discussed for more than a hundred years. Pierre Louis Moreau de Maupertuis (1698–1759) had developed the idea that chance mutations would be selected because of environmental pressures and this would explain the structural changes observed in the living world.

42. Charles Darwin, *The Origin of Species by Means of Natural Selection* (London, 1859; New York: Avenel Books, 1979).

43. *Osservatore Romano* 19.9.1946: "Si talis opinio amplectanda esse videatur, *quid fiet de numquam mutandis catholicis dogmatibus, quid de fidei unitate et stabilitate?*" (italics added).

44. Cf. the *Message of His Holiness John Paul II,* in *Physics, Philosophy and Theology: A Common Quest for Understanding,* edited by Robert John Russell, William R. Stoeger, S.J., and George V. Coyne, S.J. (Notre Dame, Ind.: University of Notre Dame Press, 1988). Unfortunately, there seems to be little haste to take up this challenge.

45. J. H. Newman, Doc. A.18.21, Birmingham Oratory. Quoted from N. Max Wildiers, *Wereldbeeld en teologie: Van de middeleeuwen tot vandaag* (Antwerpen: Standaard Wetenschappelijke Uitgeverij, 1973), 275 n. 75.

46. J. H. Newman, *Sundries,* 83. Quoted from N. Max Wildiers, *Wereldbeeld en teologie,* 275 n. 75.

47. Gen. 1:31.

48. Cf. Karl Schmitz-Moormann, ed., *Schöpfung und Evolution: Neue Ansätze Zum Dialog Zwischen Naturwissenschaften und Theologie,* Schriften der Katholischen Akademie in Bayern, vol. 145 (Düsseldorf: Patmos, 1992), 56 n. 54.

49. Cf. Karl Rahner, S.J., *Theological Investigations,* vol. 1 (Baltimore: Helicon Press, 1961), 11. Denziger was the first editor of the *Enchiridion Symbolorum,* the latest edition of which was done by Karl Rahner, who proposed (oral communication) compiling an anti-Denziger using the same sources, not the same quotations, used in Denziger.

50. Eccles. 3:14.

51. Gen. 1:27.

52. Tertullian *Adv. Marcionites* 4, 5: Corpus Scriptorum Ecclesiae Latinorum 47, 430. "In summa, si constat id verius quod prius, id prius quod [ab initio], id ab initio quod ab apostolis, pariter utique constabit id esse ab apostolis traditum, quod apud ecclesias apostolorum fuerit sacrosanctum." (Emphasis added in text extract.)

53. This does not exclude the possibility that something new may come into existence under the label of *reform.*

54. Michael J. Buckley, S.J., *At the Origins of Modern Atheism* (New Haven, Conn.: Yale University Press, 1987), 27.

55. Rom. 8:22.

56. During the 1950s, when four Jesuits of the theological faculty of Lyon were forbidden to teach, the state of affairs was described with a short formula: *Beatus vir qui non habet ideas novas: vir tutus appellatur* (Blessed is the man who has no new ideas: he is called safe).

57. There are many ways to excommunicate: e.g., to take away one's faculty position, and therefore one's living, can be as effective as a formal anathema.

58. Cf. Rudolf Bultmann, *Jesus Christ and Mythology* (New York: Charles Scribner's Sons, 1958), 35–44.

59. We shall return to this point later, especially in chapter 5 and passim.

60. Cf. Steven Weinberg, *Dreams of a Final Theory: The Search for the Fundamental Laws of Nature* (New York: Pantheon Books, 1992). But also cf. Paul Davies, *The Mind of God* (New York: Simon & Schuster, 1992), 165–69.

61. Wolfhart Pannenberg, *Toward a Theology of Nature: Essays on Science and Faith* (Louisville: Westminster/John Knox Press, 1993), 74, 113 n. 3; cf. Karl Barth, *Church Dogmatics,* 4 vols. (Edinburgh: T. & T. Clark, 1936–62), 3:1 (1945).

62. Karl Rahner, "Science as a 'Confession,'" in *Theological Investigations,* vol. 3 (New York: Seabury Press, 1974), 385–400.

63. Cf. Thomas Forsyth Torrance, *The Ground and Grammar of Theology* (Charlottesville: University of Virginia Press, 1980).

64. Bernard Lonergan, *Method in Theology* (New York: Herder & Herder, 1972).

65. Nancey Murphy, *Theology in the Age of Scientific Reasoning* (Ithaca, N.Y.: Cornell University Press, 1990).

66. Arthur Peacocke, *Theology for a Scientific Age: Being and Becoming—Natural, Divine, and Human,* enlarged ed. (Minneapolis: Fortress Press, 1993), 18.

67. Pannenberg, *Toward a Theology of Nature,* 79.

68. Cf. Peacocke, *Theology for a Scientific Age,* 280–81.

69. This claim, specific for the Enlightenment, is itself not scientific, but belongs in the domain of the religion of reason, for which the French Revolution built temples. We are reminded that the claim that religion needs justification is not a very reasonable postulate. As Arthur Eddington stated, it is "somewhat of an anomaly that among the many extraphysical aspects of experience, religion alone should be singled out as specially in need of reconciliation with the knowledge contained in science" (Sir Arthur Eddington, *Science and the Unseen World* [New York: Macmillan, 1929], 29).

70. Some persons seem to accept only their own authority, but who would listen to oneself and hear something new?

71. *Summa Theologica* 2a2ae.174, 6c. principio: "Fides nostra in duobus principaliter consistit: primo quidem, in vera Dei cognitione . . . secundo in mysterio incarnationis Christi."

2. The Universe as Process of Becoming: God's Creation

1. Cf. Joseph I. Silk, "Road to Nowhere," *Scientific American,* January 1995, 93: "Even observational cosmologists have entered the God stakes. George Smoot, the leader of the National Aeronautics and Space Administration team that discovered fluctuations in the cosmic microwave background, described his achievement as seeing 'the face of God.' Paul Davies, seldom far from the forefront of cosmology, has already written two books in which he identifies God as a quantum cosmologist. Never bashful, Stephen W. Hawking declared God unnecessary."

2. Inaugural lecture to the Lucasian Chair at the University of Cambridge, titled "Is the End in Sight for Theoretical Physics?"

3. Cf. Robert John Russell, Nancey Murphy, and C. J. Isham, eds., *Quantum Cosmology and the Laws of Nature: Scientific Perspectives on Divine Action* (Vatican City and Berke-

ley, Calif.: Vatican Observatory Publications; the Center for Theology and the Natural Sciences, 1993).

4. Cf. especially for the argument from design, William Paley, *Natural Theology: Or, Evidences of the Existence and Attributes of the Deity, Collected from the Appearances of Nature* (Philadelphia: n.p., 1814).

5. Cf. his *Biology of Ultimate Concern* (New York: New American Library, 1967).

6. It is interesting to find this argument reappear as a recorded natural response to a scientific lecturer, without acknowledgment of its origin in history. Cf. Paul Davies, *The Mind of God: The Scientific Basis for a Rational World* (New York: Simon & Schuster, 1992), 223.

7. *Summa Theologica* 1a.2, 3.

8. A term used by Pierre Rousselot in *Les Yeux de la Foi* (Paris, 1914), translated into German, *Die Augen des Glaubens* (Freiburg: Herder, 1963).

9. Cf. Hans Küng, *Existiert Gott?* (München: Piper, 1978); English: *Does God Exist?* (Garden City, N.Y.: Doubleday, 1980).

10. Cf. Theodor Schneider, ed., *Handbuch der Dogmatik* (Düsseldorf: Patmos Verlag, 1992); Christian Link, *Schöpfung* (Gütersloh: G. Mohn, 1991); Jürgen Moltmann, *Gott in der Schöpfung: ökologische Schöpfungslehre* (München, 1985), English translation by C. Kaiser, *God in Creation: A New Theology of Creation and the Spirit of God* (San Francisco: Harper & Row, 1985).

11. Two important questions still not really answered concern the origin of galaxies and the age of the universe. There are observations of distant galaxies indicating an age of more than 15×10^9 years. This age would be incompatible with the standard model, which could be saved by reintroducing the cosmological constant λ. This reintroduction has been proposed by the Bonn group around Priester, who estimate an age of $\approx (35 \pm 5) \times 10^9$ and a λ of 10^{-52}.

12. Cf. Steven Weinberg, *The First Three Minutes* (London: Andre Deutsch, 1977).

13. The Cosmic Background Explorer; cf. *Scientific American*, January 1990; spring 1993.

14. This timescale has many difficulties. On the one hand, the universe seems to be expanding faster than expected, which makes the universe younger, in the eight-billion-year-plus range. On the other hand, the observation of very old, red-colored elliptic galaxies at great distances hints that the universe is older. Cf. *Science*, 13 May 1994, 906–7. The Bonn group around Priester even estimates an age of thirty-five billion years.

15. Cf. John Barrow and Frank J. Tipler, *The Anthropic Cosmological Principle* (Oxford: Clarendon Press, 1986); George Gale, "The Anthropic Principle," *Scientific American*, December 1981, 154–64.

16. Cf. "The Newtonian Settlement," in *Physics, Philosophy and Theology: A Common Quest for Understanding*, edited by Robert John Russell, William R. Stoeger, S.J., and George V Coyne, S.J. (Vatican City: Vatican Observatory, 1988), 81–102.

17. It was often quoted by the medieval Scholastics, e.g., by Bonaventure.

18. Ilya Prigogine, *From Being to Becoming* (San Francisco: Freeman, 1980), 214.

19. "Space-time," the term used more often, corresponds to the geometrization of time and does not integrate the "arrow of time." Time is irreversible in our experience, although physics teaches that we may reduce aging and experienced time by moving at great

speeds. Internal movements of an organism can be reduced by high speeds up to limits set by the speed of light.

20. A few other atoms such as lithium formed in the beginning, which do not add much to the overall mass, although they are of theoretical interest for physicists.

21. These points of order are the necessary condition for science to be possible: science can exist only where order and structure exist.

22. This is visible in ecological movements that want to maintain nature as it is, or better: was.

23. Cf. chapter 5 and passim.

24. Frank J. Tipler, *The Physics of Immortality: Modern Cosmology, God, and the Resurrection of the Dead* (New York: Doubleday, 1994); cf. the review of this book by Silk, "Road to Nowhere," 93–94.

25. Cf. Stephen Jay Gould, "The Evolution of Life on the Earth," *Scientific American*, October 1994, 84–91; see the graph on p. 86.

26. This way of speaking is not certain: it would be correct in an inflationary universe; otherwise radiation would create space.

27. A measure of the improbability of an event: the more there are, the less probable. Normally, statisticians stop at a probability of four standard deviations in their descriptive statistics.

28. As long as it was a dogma in chemistry that amino acids need life to be produced, one might have considered this a proof for life in the universe. But the spontaneous evolution of amino acids in the Miller-Urey laboratory experiments has shown that we can expect amino acids out there. Cf. George Wald, "The Origin of Life," *Scientific American*, August 1954, 44–53.

29. But any approach based on reason is anthropocentric, be it physics expressed in mathematical terms, or biology based on human systematization.

30. Dollo's law, named after the French scientist, states that there is no regressive evolution, e.g., from mammals to fish.

31. Cf. the research of Thure von Üxküll on the limited worlds of animals.

32. Since the speed of light is the fastest way to communicate any information, our knowledge of the past is limited by the speed of light: we cannot perceive simultaneously an actual event happening today several light-years away; we perceive the distant galaxies as they were billions of years ago. Cf. Stephen Hawking, *A Brief History of Time* (New York: Bantam, 1988), 24–29.

33. E.g., Plato's *Phaidros* or the myth of Re in the last book of his *Republic*; see also *Die Schöpfung in den Religionen* (Sankt Augustin: Steyler, 1990); Jean-Pierre Longchamp, *La Création du monde* (Paris: Desclée de Brouwer, 1990).

34. This widespread position makes people talk "brain-language": the brain thinks, coordinates, and has ideas, as if it were not the organ of a whole person, but a separately existing entity.

35. This is not the place to discuss in detail the possibility of human survival into the realm of eternity. The possibility of transformation does at least not exclude an eternal future for humans.

36. Cf. the statements of Pius XII in his encyclical *Humani generis* of 1950.

37. For a rather short moment this taboo was broken in Alexandria by Herophilus and Erasistratus, but after some years dissections were abandoned. Although Galen knew that in his time the taboo prevailed, he dissected animals such as macaques and certain ungulates. The practice of dissection reappeared in the Middle Ages first in Italy, a region dominated by church influence. In 1316, Mondino dei Luzzi wrote the first dissection manual, *Anatomia*. Dissections of human corpses were ordered by Pius V, formally breaking the still-present taboo; thus the Middle Ages opened the door for great anatomists like Vesalius. Cf. David C. Lindberg, *The Beginnings of Western Science: The European Scientific Tradition in Philosophical, Religious and Institutional Context, 600 B.C. to A.D. 1450* (Chicago: University of Chicago Press, 1992), 119–22, 342–45.

38. Chimpanzees hunt on their own, and the hunter has the right of ownership of the prey. Others beg by stretching out their hands, but they do not try to rob the successful hunter. Even the alpha animal, though getting a better part, respects the right of the hunter. Cf. Arndt Kortlandt, "Handgebrauch bei freilebenden Schimpansen," in *Handgebrauch und Verständigung bei Affen und Frühmenschen*, edited by Bernhard Rensch, Symposium der Werner-Reimers-Stiftung für Anthropogenetische Forschung (Bern und Stuttgart: Verlag Hans Huber, 1968), 59–102; Geza Teleki, "The Omnivorous Chimpanzee," *Scientific American*, January 1973, 32–47.

39. E.g., excluding the selfish individual from sharing a food source.

40. Cf. the work of Rensch with the chimpanzee Julia, who learned to open twenty-five differently closed boxes containing visible tools to open another box and finally to open a box with a banana, or with a magnet to slide a coin through a complicated maze by studying the maze first and then getting the coin out in the shortest possible way. Bernhard Rensch and J. Röhl, "Spontanes Öffnen verschiedener Kistenverschlüsse durch einen Schimpansen," in *Zeitschrift für Tierpsychologie* (Berlin: Verlag Paul Parey, 1967), 476–89; Bernhard Rensch and J. Röhl, "Wählen zwischen zwei überschaubaren Labyrinthwegen durch einen Schimpansen," in *Zeitschrift für Tierpsychologie* (Berlin: Verlag Paul Parey, 1967), 216–31.

41. Cf. Ann James Premack and David Premack, "Teaching Language to an Ape," *Scientific American*, October 1972, 92–99; Michael P. Ghiglieri, "The Social Ecology of Chimpanzees," *Scientific American*, June 1985, 102–13.

42. Some animals may have ranges of perception not shared by our biophysical potential. We do not perceive polarized or ultraviolet light, as bees do, or ultrasounds as bats do, or magnetism as homing pigeons seem to do. But we are able to use instruments to make up for these "deficiencies."

43. When hunting with guns started, deer were much more easy prey than now when guns are spotted by deer and avoided. Today hunters must hide and surprise the deer from ambush.

44. Cf. Gerald M. Edelman, "Cell-Adhesion Molecules: A Molecular Basis for Animal Form," *Scientific American*, April 1984, 118–29; James H. Schwartz, "The Transport of Substances in Nerve Cells," *Scientific American*, April 1980, 152–59; Corey S. Goodman and Michael J. Bastiani, "How Embryonic Nerve Cells Recognize One Another," *Scientific American*, December 1984, 58–77; Mark S. Bretscher, "How Animal Cells Move," *Scientific American*, December 1987, 72–93.

45. Gerd Binnig and Heinrich Rohrer, "The Scanning Tunneling Microscope," *Scientific American*, August 1985, 50–69.

46. Gary J. Feldman and Jack Steinberger, "The Number of Families of Matter," *Scientific American*, February 1991, 70–77.

47. The origin and the meaning of this word are not evident. There is a German word corresponding to it, meaning a kind of cottage cheese. In German the word is also used to designate nonsense: one may say in this sense that all this is "quark." The term was, it seems, first introduced as a fun word.

48. The up-quarks carry a charge of +2/3 and the down-quarks carry a charge of -1/3. Thus the proton has a charge of 1, and the neutron has a charge of 0.

49. 1 electron volt (energy unit) = 1×10^{-28} grams (mass unit).

50. Cf. Claudio Rebbi, "The Lattice Theory of Quark Confinement," *Scientific American*, February 1983, 54–65.

51. This mark of all reality has been known by philosophers of all ages, but the question of the origin and becoming of unity has rarely been addressed.

52. Cf. Rebbi, "The Lattice Theory of Quark Confinement," 54–65.

53. Relatively small amounts of other light elements such as lithium also form.

54. The number of neutrons is closer to the number of protons among the lighter elements. In heavier elements the number of neutrons usually exceeds the number of protons. Thus the nuclei of the four isotopes of uranium contain 92 protons and 140 to 143 neutrons.

55. Cf. J. Mayo Greenberg, "The Structure and Evolution of Interstellar Grains," *Scientific American*, June 1984, 124–35; Roy S. Lewis and Edward Anders, "Interstellar Matter in Meteorites," *Scientific American*, August 1983, 66–77.

56. Cf. Harold C. Urey, "The Origin of Life," *Scientific American*, October 1952, 53–61; George Wald, "The Origin of Life," *Scientific American*, August 1954, 44–53; Richard E. Dickerson, "Chemical Evolution and the Origins of Life," *Scientific American*, September 1978, 70–109; John Horgan, "In the Beginning . . . ," *Scientific American*, February 1991, 116; A. G. Cairns-Smith, "The First Organisms," *Scientific American*, June 1985, 90–101.

57. Cf. Nigel Unwin and Richard Henderson, "The Structure of Proteins in Biological Membranes," *Scientific American*, February 1984, 78–95; Harvey F. Lodish and James E. Rothman, "The Assembly of Cell Membranes," *Scientific American*, January 1979, 48–63; Mark S. Bretscher, "The Molecules of the Cell Membrane," *Scientific American*, October 1985, 100–109.

58. Cf. Edelman, "Cell-Adhesion Molecules: A Molecular Basis for Animal Form," 118–29.

59. Teilhard de Chardin, *Les directions de l'Avenir*, Oeuvre t. 11 (Paris: Seuil, 1973), 208.

60. This notion of matter describes a state of nonbeing, whereas concrete matter, as Thomas Aquinas stated, is already formed (informed) matter.

61. This term, introduced by G. Soehngen at Bonn, and generally accepted today among German theologians, refers to the thought of St. Thomas himself, as opposed to scholastic interpreters.

62. This is not an evaluation of the theological content of that story, but refers to the way in which God is depicted as the all-powerful one whose word creates the world.

63. See chapter 6.

64. Eccles. 1:9.

65. The modern overestimation of the individual is in this view evidently regressive. For the notion of the person cf. Martin Buber, *I and Thou*; Romano Guardini, *Welt und Person*; and Emmanuel Mounier, *Personalism*.

3. Consciousness in the Universe—of the Universe

1. The recently observed circular speed of matter close to the halo of the 87 A Nova probably indicates the presence of a black hole with a mass of more than a million times the mass of the sun.

2. There is naturally a theory about a future: the black hole will create a stronger curvature and form a bubble out of which finally a miniuniverse might arise, first linked by a wormhole, and finally becoming independent. Cf. Paul Davies, *The Mind of God: The Scientific Basis for a Rational World* (New York: Simon & Schuster, 1992), 71. There are a few open questions. Because this would be another universe, we could never have any proof of its existence. And since mass would disappear out of our universe, there would be a violation of the first law of thermodynamics. But this latter point might be a wrong presumption. Some physicists speculate that this law might apply only locally.

3. Cf. the last sentences of Steven Weinberg, *The First Three Minutes* (London: Andre Deutsch, 1977).

4. Cf. Barry E. Turner, "Interstellar Molecules," *Scientific American*, March 1973, 50–69; Eric J. Chaisson, "Gaseous Nebulas," *Scientific American*, December 1978, 164; M. A. Gordon and W. B. Burton, "Carbon Monoxide in the Galaxy," *Scientific American*, May 1979, 54–67; Alan H. Barrett, "Radio Signals from Hydroxyl Radicals," *Scientific American*, December 1968, 36–59.

5. Some privately funded research continues.

6. C. J. Isham, "Quantum Theories of the Creation of the Universe," in *Quantum Cosmology and the Laws of Nature, Scientific Perspectives on Divine Action,* edited by Robert John Russell, Nancey Murphy, and C. J. Isham (Vatican City: Vatican Observatory Publications, 1993), 49–89.

7. On this point some neurologists might disagree, claiming that the brain is the mind. That is true and not true. The point is, in which way we interpret matter. Teilhard speaks about *matière/esprit*, and if one accepts this concept, there is a meaningful way of taking the brain for the form of matter, in which its spirituality becomes most evident. The Teilhardian way of thinking in this field may be aligned with the holistic interpretation, which tries to overcome the exclusive dualistic-monistic alternative as represented by Descartes for the dualistic view and T. H. Huxley and materialistic scientists for the monistic view. Cf. Giuseppe del Re, ed., *Brain Research and the Mind-Body Problem: Epistemological and Metaphysical Issues—Proceedings of a Round Table Discussion Held at the Pontifical Academy of Science on 25 October 1988* (Ex Aedibus Academicis in Civitate Vaticana: Pontificia Academia Scientiarum, 1992); John R. Searle, Paul M. Churchland, and Patricia Smith Churchland, "Artificial Intelligence: A Debate," *Scientific American*, January 1990, 25; John R. Searle, "Is the Brain's Mind a Computer?" *Scientific American*, January 1990, 26–31.

8. The sometimes heard claim that in principle it should be possible to write a wave function for every living being is rather pretentious. The function describing a simple bacterium has never been written, and it is more than doubtful that it ever will be written. And even if such a formula could be written, it would hardly tell us why there is a life and what is life.

9. Cf. e.g., Alan H. Guth and Paul J. Steinhardt, "The Inflationary Universe," *Scientific American*, May 1984, 116–30.

10. Thus the recent decision by the U.S. Congress to support funding of research of the human genome, which represents a quantitatively negligible reality in the universe. Congress canceled funding for a supercollider, which would have searched for other rare realities.

11. Postulated particles that are extremely rare, such as monopoles and the top quark, are searched for with very costly experiments. Cf. Richard A. Carrigan Jr. and W. Peter Trower, "Superheavy Magnetic Monopoles," *Scientific American*, April 1982, 106–19. One of the greater experiments in search for those particles is performed in the Gran Sasso installation in Italy.

12. Coherence is one of four fundamental criteria commonly used to test the validity of a scientific theory. The other three are agreement with data, scope of the theory, and fertility for an ongoing research program. Cf. Ian Barbour, *Religion in an Age of Science* (New York: Harper & Row, 1990), 1:34–36.

13. Giuseppe del Re, *Brain Research and the Mind-Body Problem*.

14. There is one similar influence to be registered in the history of life, when archaea developed the ability to use photons as an energy source to break the chemical bond between oxygen and carbon, and set the oxygen free. This process "poisoned" the environment of the majority of living beings at that time, the anaerobic bacteria. But though this event changed the whole atmosphere, it was nevertheless not a diversified action as is that of humankind.

15. Today people have become more aware of this far-reaching capacity so that the protection of the environment becomes a serious preoccupation of many.

16. E.g., Rensch in Münster trained a chimpanzee to slide a coin through a complicated maze. The coin would get her a bar of chocolate from a vending machine. The chimpanzee observed the glass-covered maze for a few minutes and then slid the coin with a magnetic handle error-free through the maze to get her chocolate.

17. Cf. Karl von Frisch, *The Dance Language and Orientation of Bees* (Cambridge: Harvard University Press, 1967); Wolfgang H. Kirchner and William F. Towne, "The Sensory Basis of the Honeybee's Dance Language," *Scientific American*, June 1994, 74–80.

18. See the experiments by Thure von Üxküll.

19. Having built its nest, the wasp paralyzes a caterpillar by stinging and brings it to the nest. Leaving it at a distance from the nest, the wasp verifies the nest. Meanwhile if one displaces the caterpillar to a short distance, the wasp will find it, bring it back to the place where it was first put, and verify the nest again. If displacement of the prey is repeated, the wasp will repeat the whole procedure hundreds of times. The wasp visibly has some perception of its environment, but it cannot integrate a minor change in the sequence of its behavior.

20. See James H. Thomas, "The Mind of a Worm," *Science* 264 (1994): 1688–89.
21. Eric R. Kandel, "Small Systems of Neurons," *Scientific American*, September 1979, 66–78.
22. Cf. A. O. D. Willows, "Giant Brain Cells in Mollusks," *Scientific American*, February 1971, 68–75; Donald Kennedy, "Small Systems of Nerve Cells," *Scientific American*, May 1967, 44–65; Charles M. Lent and Michael H. Dickinson, "The Neurobiology of Feeding in Leeches," *Scientific American*, June 1988, 98–103.
23. Cf. Manfred Eigen, William Gardiner, Peter Schuster, and Ruthild Winkler-Oswatitsch, "The Origin of Genetic Information," *Scientific American*, April 1981, 88–119; Julius Rebek Jr., "Synthetic Self-Replicating Molecules," *Scientific American*, July 1994, 48–55.
24. We may remember in this context that humans are the only species whose consciousness embraces the dimension of time and with this ability creates the awareness of the history of the universe.
25. P. J. E. Peebles, *Principles of Physical Cosmology* (Princeton, N.J.: Princeton University Press, 1993), 5.
26. Cf. the Miller-Urey experiment in the early 1950s. See Richard E. Dickerson, "Chemical Evolution and the Origins of Life," *Scientific American*, September 1978, 70–109; George Wald, "The Origin of Life," *Scientific American*, August 1954, 44–53; Harold C. Urey, "The Origin of Life," *Scientific American*, October 1952, 53–61. In the first half of 1993 Miller recognized that the great hope of elucidating the origins of life had not come true: we do not know much more than we did in 1953.
27. Edouard Le Roy and Teilhard de Chardin stated that in the first quarter of this century. From there the notion of complexity and complexification made its way into the biological sciences as well as into general scientific discourse, mostly without any reference to the source. There are exceptions: the French paleontologist Jean Piveteau in the 1960s publicly insisted on Teilhard's priority in introducing the notion of complexity into the life sciences.
28. In this worldview any event is strictly determined, with the exception of human free will, which is free because God wills it so.
29. Cf. Steven Weinberg, *Dreams of Final Theory: The Search for the Fundamental Laws of Nature* (New York: Pantheon Books, 1992).
30. Cf. the sermons of Berthold von Regensburg on the seven planets: Berthold von Regensburg, *Vollständige Ausgabe seine Predigten*, ed. Franz Pfeiffer (Berlin, n.d.), 1:48–64; 2:233–37.
31. Before the age of color television and the space program reaching the moon, on a summer night in a small village in France, I showed some elderly peasants Saturn through a small amateur telescope, and I was impressed by how thankful they were to have been allowed to see such beauty.
32. Cf. Peebles, *Principles of Physical Cosmology*, 35.
33. Cf. George Gamow, "Modern Cosmology," *Scientific American*, March 1954, 54–65; Victor E. Viola and Grant J. Mathews, "The Cosmic Synthesis of Lithium, Beryllium and Boron," *Scientific American*, May 1987, 38–45.
34. Hans A. Bethe and Gerald Brown, "How a Supernova Explodes," *Scientific American*, May 1985, 60–87.

35. But there are justified doubts about this claim: since the initial conditions are unknowable according to quantum physics, such a wave function cannot be written concretely. So far, even to write a wave function of the electron in a hydrogen atom seems close to the limit of scientific possibilities. The wave function of the universe, Ψ_U, is an expression of the belief in determinism by the scientist who postulates it rather than a concrete possibility that it could be written. It seems incompatible with the indeterminate evolving reality of the universe.

36. In an interview Gerald Edelman of the Neurosciences Institute in La Jolla, California, declared that "while biology needs physics to describe the physical world, physics is not sufficient to describe the biological process." If this is so, then it is not understandable that he claims that biology should be able to explain the spiritual, the mind, and consciousness; these need the biological processes just as they need the physical ones. See *Frankfurter Allgemeine Zeitung*, Magazin Heft 811, 15 September 1995, 54-55.

37. Some materialistic scientists do not acknowledge this fact. By repeating, without reason, that all living forms are of the same status, they suppress the evidence of their own existence. Either they consider themselves strangers in this universe—a pre-evolutionary notion wherein humans were created and set apart as strangers in the garden from which they were expelled later—or they consider themselves rooted in the evolutionary process: in this case they are the ones who study the universe. No other animal or living structure containing DNA does it. As long as they do not recognize and explain this difference, they cannot be taken seriously.

38. The question whether other planets contain living beings is yet unanswered. The billions of galaxies give a rather high probability to a positive answer, but the special conditions necessary for life to arise, such as correct distance to a planet's sun, right composition, correct spin to avoid great temperature gradients, and a correct magnetic field to prevent damaging cosmic radiation, make a negative answer probable.

39. See chapter 5.

40. We are reminded in this context that in a concrete and realistic way life started some 3.5 billion years ago. The thread of life starting ages ago was never cut, though life went through changes. If it had been cut, we would not be here.

41. Cf. Stan Woosley and Tom Weaver, "The Great Supernova of 1987," *Scientific American*, August 1989, 32-41; Ray Jayawardhana, "A Dark Matter Recipe Is Tested—and Found Wanting," *Science* 264 (1994): 1845.

42. Cf. Rudolf Otto, *The Idea of the Holy* (London: Penguin, 1959).

43. Cuvier, who as director of the Museum of Natural History in Paris and at the same time supervisor of the Protestant church of France, repressed Lamarck, and explained the existence of fossils by earlier, less perfect creations, which God abandoned and replaced by others.

44. Bonaventure *Breviloquium* pars secunda, de creatura mundi c. 5: "Scriptura, ordinate *narrat* quantum ad doctrinae sufficientam, licet non ita explicite describat distinctionem orbium nec caelestium nec elementarium, parvum aut nihil dicat de motibus et virtutibus corporum superiorum et de mixtionibus elementorum et elementatorum."

45. See chapter 6.

46. Both usually are good, but not when they are used magically.

47. One consequence of this classical notion of the analogy of being is the definition of evil as a lack of being. Even the devil, a power of evil, exists as a fallen angel in some similitude with God's being.
48. Cf. Plato, *The Republic*, bk. 6.
49. Cf. Lawrence W. Fagg, *The Becoming of Time: Integrating Physical and Religious Time* (Atlanta: Scholars Press, 1995).
50. Quoted from ibid., 249.
51. Cf. Ilya Prigogine, "Time and the Unity of Knowledge," in *Teilhard and the Unity of Knowledge*, edited by Thomas M. King, S.J., and James F. Salmon, S.J. (New York: Paulist Press, 1983), 21–45.
52. Schrödinger does this in his wave function.
53. This statement is not to be read as exclusive.
54. The cyclical aspect of time has importance: it allows for some stability by giving the impression of renewal of the already existing, as we experience by the change of day and night and by the cycle of seasons.
55. Cf. as well Friedrich Nietzsche's well-known statement: "All happiness of earthly man wants deep, deep eternity."
56. Classical metaphysics might speak here of accidentals as compared to the essence of consciousness.

4. The Evolution of Information: A Hallmark of God's Creation

1. Cf. John E. Hopcroft, "Turing Machines," *Scientific American*, May 1984, 86–107.
2. John R. Searle, "Is the Brain's Mind a Computer?" *Scientific American*, January 1990, 26–31.
3. Cf. John Rennie, "Grading the Gene Tests," *Scientific American*, June 1994, 88–97.
4. Michael Kaback, quoted in ibid.
5. Rennie, "Grading the Gene Tests."
6. Most probably this is based on the old structuring of all orders according to the seven planets in the Middle Ages and in antiquity, to which we owe the seven days of the week and the seven ages of human life.
7. Cf. Manfred Eigen, William Gardiner, Peter Schuster, and Ruthild Winkler-Oswatitsch, "The Origin of Genetic Information," *Scientific American*, April 1981, 88–119.
8. Molecules that polarize light, that rotate a beam of light to the left or to the right.
9. Cf. Richard G. Brewer and Erwin L. Hahn, "Atomic Memory," *Scientific American*, December 1984, 50–57.
10. Cf. Steven Weinberg, "The Decay of the Proton," *Scientific American*, June 1981, 64–75; J. M. LoSecco, Frederick Reines, and Daniel Sinclair, "The Search for Proton Decay," *Scientific American*, June 1985, 54–77.
11. To obtain certain crystals, the regulation of temperature and pressure is necessary.
12. Cf. Carlo M. Croce and Hilary Koprowski, "The Genetics of Human Cancers," *Scientific American*, February 1978, 117–25; Frank H. Ruddle and Raju S. Kucherlapati, "Hybrid Cells and Human Genes," *Scientific American*, July 1974, 36–49.
13. Or archaebacteria; cf. Ursula W. Goodenough and R. P. Levine, "The Genetic Activity of Mitochondria and Chloroplasts," *Scientific American*, November 1970, 22–29; J. William

Schopf, "The Evolution of the Earliest Cells," *Scientific American*, September 1978, 110–39.

14. Cf. Gunther S. Stent, "Cellular Communication," *Scientific American*, September 1972, 42–51; Werner R. Loewenstein, "Intercellular Communication," *Scientific American*, May 1970, 78–91; Solomon H. Snyder, "The Molecular Basis of Communication Between Cells," *Scientific American*, October 1985, 132–41; Lubert Stryer, "The Molecules of Visual Excitation," *Scientific American*, July 1987, 42–51.

15. Cf. Julius Axelrod, "Neurotransmitters," *Scientific American*, June 1974, 58–71; Solomon H. Snyder and David S. Bredt, "Biological Roles of Nitric Oxide," *Scientific American*, May 1992, 68–77; David I. Gottlieb, "Gabaergic Neurons," *Scientific American*, February 1988, 82–89.

16. In this context we may remember that death, once linked primarily with the stopping of the heart, i.e., a quasi-mechanical event, is today more often identified with the end of brain functions, with the stopping of brain waves.

17. Cf. Dietrich Schneider, "The Sex-Attractant Receptor of Moths," *Scientific American*, July 1974, 28–35; Edward O. Wilson, "Animal Communication," *Scientific American*, September 1972, 52–71.

18. Cf. Lincoln Pierson Brower, "Ecological Chemistry," *Scientific American*, February 1969, 22–29.

19. Cf. Nicholas B. Davies and Michael Brooke, "Coevolution of the Cuckoo and Its Hosts," *Scientific American*, January 1991, 92–99; James E. Lloyd, "Mimicry in the Sexual Signals of Fireflies," *Scientific American*, July 1981, 138–47; Jürgen Nicolai, "Mimicry in Parasitic Birds," *Scientific American*, October 1974, 92–99; Lawrence E. Gilbert, "The Coevolution of a Butterfly and a Vine," *Scientific American*, August 1982, 110–21; Spencer C. H. Barrett, "Mimicry in Plants," *Scientific American*, September 1987, 76–85; Theodore W. Pietsch and David B. Grobecker, "Frogfishes," *Scientific American*, June 1990, 96–103.

20. Cf. Arndt Kortlandt, "Handgebrauch bei freilebenden Schimpansen," in *Handgebrauch und Verständigung bei Affen und Frühmenschen,* edited by Bernhard Rensch (Bern and Stuttgart: Verlag Hans Huber, 1968), 59–102.

21. Cf. A. O. D. Willows, "Giant Brain Cells in Mollusks," *Scientific American*, February 1971, 68–75.

22. Cf. Robert M. Sapolsky, "Stress in the Wild," *Scientific American*, January 1990, 116–23. Centreity (*Centreité*) is a word introduced by Teilhard to express increasing centeredness as complexity occurs.

23. E.g., wild corn will shed its grains, but farmers have to sow the grains, which they can harvest only because they are not shed. Farmer's corn depends on human effort to continue to exist.

24. Steven Weinberg, *Dreams of a Final Theory: The Search for the Fundamental Laws of Nature* (New York: Pantheon Books, 1992), 10–11.

25. *Summa Theologica* 1a2ae.91, 1c: "Et ideo ipsa ratio gubernationis rerum in Deo sicut in principe universitatis existens legis habet rationem. Et quia divina ratio nihil concipit ex tempore, sed habet aeternum conceptum, ut dicitur *Prov.* 8:23, inde est quod hujusmodi legem oportet dicere aeternam."

26. Ibid., 1a2ae.91, 2c: "Unde cum omnia quae divinae providentiae subduntur a lege aeterna regulentur et mensurentur, ut ex dicis patet, manifestum est quod omnia participant aliqualiter legem aeternam, inquantum scilicet ex impressione ejus habent inclinationes in proprios actus et fines."

27. Stephen W. Hawking, *A Brief History of Time* (London and New York: Bantam, 1988), last sentence.

28. Albert Einstein, *Science, Philosophy and Religion,* a Symposium (New York: Harper, 1941), 211.

29. Albert Einstein, *Mein Weltbild,* ed. C. Seelig (Zürich: Europa Verlag, 1953), 171.

30. Albert Einstein, *Ideas and Opinions* (New York: Laurel Editions, 1973), 285.

31. Eugene Wigner, "The Unreasonable Effectiveness of Mathematics in the Natural Sciences," *Communications in Pure and Applied Mathematics* 13 (1960): 1–12, here 1.

32. Weinberg, *Dreams of a Final Theory,* 157.

33. Einstein, *Mein Weltbild,* 17.

34. Even though it is recognized that acquired immunity is transmitted by chromosomes (cf. J. W. Pollard, "Is Weismann's Barrier Absolute?" in *Beyond Neo-Darwinism: An Introduction to the New Evolutionary Paradigm,* edited by M. W. Ho and P. T. Saunders [London: Academic Press, 1984], 291–314). Darwinian dogmatists continue to repeat rather stubbornly that every evolutionary step is explainable by "undirected mutation and directing selection." Mutation or change (both words mean the same) without any direction would happen by pure chance. But so far no Neo-Darwinist has ever shown how evolution could happen if all the changes happened by pure chance. It would need at least some probability that the changes in the DNA sequence were possible within the concrete framework of this earth.

    If yes, it should give a probable possibility to the following case, where sufficient data are known to calculate the probabilities:

    Data:

    Chimpanzees and hominids diverged 8 million years ago (cf. Yves Coppens, "Eastside Story: The Origin of Humankind," *Scientific American,* May 1994, 88–95).

    The human DNA differs from the chimp DNA by about 1 percent.

    To be generous, let's assume 0.1 percent.

    The length of the human DNA comprises 3×10^9 nucleotides.

    The difference of 0.1 percent makes then for 3×10^6 mutations (changes) on the nucleotide level.

    Since these cannot happen at the same moment, but have to happen successively, and have to happen by pure chance, the probability of the successful change is:

    $P = 1/3{,}000{,}000{,}000$ for the first correct hit.

    For the second hit as well {The number does not diminish, as with selections from a number of possibilities, e.g., calculating the chances of winning in a 6 of 49 lotto game.}

    $P = 1/30{,}000{,}000{,}000$

    For the combination of both

    $P = 1/3{,}000{,}000{,}000 \times 1/3{,}000{,}000{,}000$ etc.

    The total probability of 3×10^6 combined correct hits is then

    $3{,}000{,}000{,}000^{3{,}000{,}000}$

To be sure, we cannot any longer name this number: a 10 with billions of zeros. To have a probability of one, all these mutations must be tried. These mutations must be realized on a population of a few thousand members. With about twenty years of generational reproduction, we have at our disposal 400,000 generations to realize enough mutations that P reaches a value of 1/1000 to respect at least vaguely the claim of pure chance. There would be a need of at least several billion undirected mutations in each generation to create the slightest probability for humankind to evolve from the common ancestor with the chimpanzee. Obviously, this cannot be done, either with respect to the objective timescale or with respect to the necessity of great genetic stability. It seems we have to look for other factors than those acting by pure chance.

There is quite a large discussion under way (cf. Michael Schmitt, "Evolutionstheorie zwischen Krise und Patentrezept," in *Lexikon der Biologie*, edited by Michael Schmitt, Bd. 10 [*Biologie im Überblick*] [Freiburg: Herder Verlag, 1992], 505–10) and even in the renowned journal *Science* the discussion has been opened (cf. Elizabeth Culotta, "Evolutionary Biology: A Boost for 'Adaptive Mutation,'" *Science* 265, no. 15 [July 1994]: 318–19; cf. as well in the same number of *Science* the articles by S. M. Rosenbert et al. [405–7] and P. L. Foster and Jeffrey M. Trimarchi [407–9]).

In 1991, several European scientists were interviewed to give their opinion on Darwinian theories. All made quite clear that Darwinism is no longer defendable as theory. Giuseppe Sermonti (professor of genetics at the University of Perugia, director of the journal *Biologie forum*) stated, when asked about the position of Ernst Mayr: He "is a 'pontifex,' a high priest of the theory, he must *show* that he believes in it! I do not think that once he has returned to his bedroom, alone with himself, he really believes that small chance mutations and natural selection could suffice to produce a dinosaur starting with an amoeba—it is impossible that he believes that!" (*Figaro*, 26 October 1991, 82).

It should be clear. All this is no argument against the fact of evolution; it targets only a specific theory.

35. Cf. J. R. Lucas, "Wilberforce and Huxley: A Legendary Encounter," *Hibbert Journal* 22, no. 2 (1979): 313–30. Huxley became a hero of science more than thirty years after the discussion in Mrs. Isabella Sidgwick's "A Grandmother's Tales," *Macmillan's Magazine* 78, no. 468 (October 1898): 433–34.
36. This is the explanation Stephen J. Gould gave when pressed for an explanation in a TV show. He should have added that we have no real explanation. The statement quoted is a confession of ignorance.
37. Isotopes of a chemical element have slightly different weights and the same chemical properties. The Mendeleyev periodic table of elements is correct insofar as the number of elements is concerned.
38. Cf. James E. Darnell Jr., "RNA," *Scientific American*, October 1985, 68–87.
39. Cf. Lincoln Pierson Brower, "Ecological Chemistry," *Scientific American*, February 1969, 22–29.
40. Cf. James H. Thomas, "The Mind of a Worm," *Science* 264 (1994): 1698–99.
41. Manfred Eigen indicated this to me in oral communication. Cf. as well Ronald E. Kalil, "Synapse Formation in the Developing Brain," *Scientific American*, December 1989, 76–87.

42. Birds grow new neurons each year during the mating period when they compete in singing. Cf. Fernando Nottebohm, "From Bird Song to Neurogenesis," *Scientific American*, February 1989, 74–79.

43. Cf. E. H. Gombrich, "The Visual Image," *Scientific American*, September 1972, 82–97.

44. Cf. Gerald M. Edelman, "Cell-Adhesion Molecules: A Molecular Basis for Animal Form," *Scientific American*, April 1984, 118–29; Mark S. Bretscher, "How Animal Cells Move," *Scientific American*, December 1987, 72–93; Richard O. Hynes, "Fibronectins," *Scientific American*, June 1986, 42–51.

45. Cf. Werner R. Loewenstein, "Intercellular Communication," *Scientific American*, May 1970, 78–91; Gunther S. Stent, "Cellular Communication," *Scientific American*, September 1972, 42–51; Lewis Wolpert, "Pattern Formation in Biological Development," *Scientific American*, October 1978, 154–65; Corey S. Goodman and Michael J. Bastiani, "How Embryonic Nerve Cells Recognize One Another," *Scientific American*, December 1984, 58–77; Mark S. Bretscher, "The Molecules of the Cell Membrane," *Scientific American*, October 1985, 100–109; Solomon H. Snyder, "The Molecular Basis of Communication Between Cells," *Scientific American*, October 1985, 132–41; Michael J. Berridge, "The Molecular Basis of Communication Within the Cell," *Scientific American*, October 1985, 142–52; Erwin Neher and Bert Sakmann, "The Patch Clamp Technique," *Scientific American*, March 1992, 44–51.

46. Cf. Edward O. Wilson, "Animal Communication," *Scientific American*, September 1972, 52–71.

47. Cf. Myron Tribus and Edward C. McIrvine, "Energy and Information," *Scientific American*, September 1971, 179–90.

48. For Thomas Aquinas *materia prima* is a mental construct, pure potentiality without any being, any reality of its own. It is, like Whitehead's eternal nature of God, only real as potentiality of creation in the mind of God the Creator.

49. Philip Hefner, *The Human Factor: Evolution, Culture and Religion* (Minneapolis: Fortress Press, 1993).

50. Cf. Karl Schmitz-Moormann, "Die Ideenlehre Platons im Lichte des Sonnengleichnisses des sechsten Buches des Staates" (Ph.D. diss., München, 1957; Münster, 1959).

51. Pierre Rousselot, *The Eyes of Faith: Answer to Two Attacks* (New York: Fordham University Press, 1990).

5. Evolution of Freedom in God's Creation

1. Cf. Karl Schmitz-Moormann, "On the Evolution of Human Freedom," *Zygon* 22, no.4 (December 1987): 443–58.

2. Cf. Berthold von Regensburg, *Vollständige Ausgabe seiner Predigten*, mit Anmerkungen von Franz Pfeiffer, mit einem Vorwort von Kurth Ruth (Berlin, n.d.), 1:48–64; 2:233–37. "Ez stênt siben sternen an dem himel, dar an sult ir lesen unde tugende lernen. . . . Und alsô hât unser herre die sternen ouch geschaffen, die habent gar grôze kraft über alliu dinc diu ûf erden sint under dem himel. Als er den steinen und den wurzen unde den worten kraft hât gegeben, alsô hât er ouch den sternen kraft gegeben, daz sie über alliu dinc kraft hânt, ân über éin dinc. Sie haben kraft über böume und über wînwahs, über loup und gras, über krût und wurze, über korn und allez daz, daz sâme treit, über die Vo-

gel in den lüften und über diu tier in dem Walde und über die vische in dem wâge und über die würme in der erden: über allez samt daz under dem himel ist, dar über hât unser herre den sternen kraft gegeben, wan über éin dinc: dâ hât nieman keine kraft über noch keine macht, weder sterne noch wurze noch wort noch steine noch engel noch tiuvel noch nieman wan got alleine; der wil sîn ouch nicht tuon, der wil nicht gewaltes drüber hân. Daz ist des menschen frîiu willekür: dâ hât nieman gewalt über danne dû selber" (1:50).

3. *Summa Theologica* 1a2ae.78, 1c. Thomas refers to Aristotle Eth. III,1 (1110b 28), stating that "every evil man is ignorant."

4. See the writings of Victor Frankl, who in Nazi concentration camps resisted by searching for meaning in his life by doing something meaningful.

5. The German constitution guarantees this freedom of teaching and research as one of the unchangeable rights; in praxis the supreme court has limited this freedom to teaching and research on the university level.

6. Mechanistically minded philosophers and scientists will continue to argue that there has been some infinitesimally small cue making the donkey act this way or the other. Unfortunately, they cannot measure it. See also work with ants in Prigogine's laboratory at Brussels. Cf. Ilya Prigogine, "Time and the Unity of Knowledge," in *Teilhard and the Unity of Knowledge*, edited by Thomas M. King, S.J., and James F. Salmon, S.J. (New York: Paulist Press, 1983), 33.

7. *Summa Theologica* 1a.19, 10c: "Alia animalia, quae naturali instinctu moventur ad aliquid non dicuntur libero arbitrio moveri."

8. Ibid., 1a.75, b ad 1: "Quod ergo dicitur quod homo et alia animalia habent simile generationis principium, verum est quantum ad corpus."

9. Ibid., 1a.75, b: "Nam anima brutorum producitur ex virtute aliqua corporea, anima vero humana a Deo."

10. Ibid., 1a.18, 3c: "Et hujusmodi sunt plantae, quae secundum formam inditam eis a natura movent seipsas secundum augmentum et decrementum."

11. Ibid.: "Nam ea quae non habent nisi sensum tactus, movent solum ad seipsa motu dilatationis et constrictionis, ut ostrea, parum excedentia motum plantae."

12. Ibid.: "Est eis inditus a natura, cujus instinctu ad aliquid agendum moventur per formam sensu apprehensam."

13. Freud, once having published the case, lost all interest in the man.

14. Cf. N. Tinbergen, "The Curious Behavior of the Stickleback," *Scientific American*, December 1952, 22–38: "This insignificant fish has a ceremonious sex life. To attract females the male builds a house, changes color and does a kind of dance, a ritual singularly useful to the study of instinct."

15. Cf. Konrad Z. Lorenz, "The Evolution of Behavior," *Scientific American*, December 1958, 67–82.

16. Cf. Jack P. Hailman, "How an Instinct Is Learned," *Scientific American*, December 1969, 98–108.

17. It need not be spoken language; sign language, too, is a good start, which can be supplemented later by spoken language in children who cannot hear.

18. Whoever has translated a book knows that this is in reality an impossible task: *tradutori: traditori*.

19. They were sometimes brought into the human community, but when it appeared useless to try to make them accept life in a human community, they were left alone to live in the forests.

20. This "woodman" accompanied by a chimpanzee can still be found in some choir stalls of monasteries and in churches in Brittany.

21. Cf. also Michael P. Ghiglieri, "The Social Ecology of Chimpanzees," *Scientific American*, June 1985, 102–13; Ann James Premack and David Premack, "Teaching Language to an Ape," *Scientific American*, October 1972, 92–99; Geza Teleki, "The Omnivorous Chimpanzee," *Scientific American*, January 1973, 32–47; Charles B. Ferster, "Arithmetic Behavior in Chimpanzees," *Scientific American*, May 1964, 98–107.

22. This term should be understood in the general meaning of an open angle, not in the strict mathematical sense, where a vector is an oriented line. The notion of some orientation is naturally linked with the notion of an angle, open in a certain direction, that excludes possibilities outside its sidelines.

23. The recent announcement by a Bonn group that it had produced preferably one enantiomer by applying a magnetic field has been withdrawn: one member of the group had manipulated the data. Cf. Daniel Clery and David Bradley, "Underhanded 'Breakthrough' Revealed," *Science* 265, no. 1 (July 1994): 21.

24. E.g., plutonium and the other transuranium elements.

25. Cf. Theodosius Dobzhansky, *The Biology of Ultimate Concern* (New York: New American Library, 1967).

26. For those interested in a technical discussion of this interpretation and the importance of Bell's inequalities, cf. A. A. Grib, "Quantum Cosmology, the Role of the Observer, Quantum Logic," in *Quantum Cosmology and the Laws of Nature*, edited by Robert John Russell, Nancey Murphy, and C. J. Isham (Vatican City: Vatican Observatory Publications, 1993), 163–83.

27. Cf. Stephen H. Kellert, *In the Wake of Chaos* (Chicago: University of Chicago Press, 1993).

28. It might be helpful to remember at least the basic notions of a statistical distribution, which is known as the bell curve. It is the description of any distribution of events that are not strictly determined, but that center on a mean value. It is similar to the binomial distribution, which in its simplest form is the probable outcome of flipping coins. This distribution corresponds to the development of the binomial $(a + b)^n$, where n corresponds to the number of flippings. In short series of two flippings there will be, if repeated often enough, a distribution of multiples of 1 (2 heads) : 2 (1 head, 1 tail) : 1 (2 tails), if series of three are thrown, there will be multiples of 1 (3 heads) : 3 (2 heads, 1 tail) : 3 (1 head, 2 tails) : 1 (3 tails), and so on. With two flippings the probability of 2 heads is 1:4, with three the probability of 3 heads is 1:8, etc., with 10 flippings the probability of 10 heads is 1:1024 with a distribution of 1:10:45:120:210:252:210:120:45:10:1. This distribution can be transcribed into Pascal's triangle:

1

1 2 1

1 3 3 1

1 4 6 4 1

1 5 10 10 5 1

1 6 15 20 15 6 1

1 7 21 35 35 21 7 1

1 8 28 56 70 56 28 8 1

1 9 36 84 126 126 84 36 9 1

1 10 45 120 210 252 210 120 45 10 1

etc.

The binomial distribution is useful with discrete values (either head or tail, no value between); the Gaussian distribution applies to continuous values and results in a bell curve:

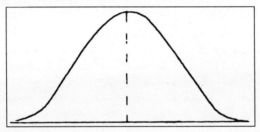

What we see in everyday life are events close to the mean of the distribution; only exceptionally do phenomena in the extremes appear. The greater the number of possibilities, the rarer the events in the extremes. E.g., throwing ten times two dice instead of two coins will statistically result in ten double sixes in a row only once in 3,656,158,440,062,976 attempts.

29. We do not know what was first: the DNA or the living structure. Cells can survive for a certain time without DNA, and DNA alone is not alive. The anthropomorphic talk about selfish genes does not make much sense. Nobody so far has shown us genes with special desires, but some living creatures in our world show desires without any recognizable reference to their genes. The genes are not a special entity, but an integrated part of the whole living creature, including its potential for procreation.

30. The French biologist Lucien Cuénot introduced this term.

31. The idea of placing a small group of people on an island and leaving them there for the future without any contact with the rest of humanity, as proposed in the exhibition on evolution by the Field Museum in Chicago titled "From Dinosaurs to DNA" (1995), is impossible in such a closed world as the earth. There could be further evolution into a new species of humans if a group of humans left the earth to land on some other planet in another solar system: they would most probably go on a trip with no return, and as a small group might develop new properties. But this is science fiction, as is the island proposal.

32. N.B. As a general rule the bestsellers of the day will not enter the collections of great literature. Goethe was rarely played on the stage in Weimar; the front-runner was Kotzebue. Who is Kotzebue? The same phenomenon is found in science literature. The bestseller of the nineteenth century was Ludwig Büchner's *Kraft und Stoff*, first published in 1855, reedited twenty-one times in Germany, translated into more than seventeen languages. Who knows it today?

33. It appears that most religions outside the Judeo-Christian tradition are not prone toward the evolution of democracies. The only tendency toward some kind of democratic feature might be found in China, where access to the ruling class of mandarins was based on success in examinations and not on a family's rank. A substantial number of the new mandarins passing the critical examinations came from the lower classes of society. The societal structures created by Islam seem to have difficulties with the idea of democracy, as had Christian churches in the last century. Hinduism is in its very nature not democratic.

34. Eccles. 1:9.

35. E.g., the nailsmith lost his job the day machines made nails much faster. Many typists will lose their job the day computers can write from dictation.

36. Lactantius *De ira Dei* 13.

37. *Werke*, 18:712.

38. The often-proposed pulsating universe, which is based on speculations about more and more questionable dark matter, neutrino masses, and other possible sources of extra gravity, is more a kind of philosophical postulate in an axiomatically eternal world than a theory based on observed data; the data point rather to an open or a flat universe.

39. Stephen Langdon, *Babylonian Penitential Psalms* (Paris, 1927): "Mankind as many as there be [commit] sin . . . the food that belongs to God I have eaten."

6. God, Creator of the Evolving Universe

1. *Catechism of the Catholic Church* (Mahwah, N.J.: Paulist Press, 1997), 374–79.

2. Karl Rahner, ed., *Sacramentum Mundi*, 6 vols. (New York and London: Herder & Herder; Burns & Oates, 1970), 6:174a.

3. Theodor Schneider, ed., *Handbuch der Dogmatik* (Düsseldorf: Patmos Verlag, 1992), 226–28.

4. Karl Rahner, *Theological Investigations* (New York: Seabury Press, 1993), 18:5. Roman theologians have learned at least on this point: the new catechism does not deny unbaptized children access to heaven.

5. Schneider, *Handbuch der Dogmatik*, 206–36.

6. N.B. What are material organisms? How do they differ from living ones? The German text, twice using the article, is talking about two different kinds of organisms.

7. Jürgen Moltmann, *God in Creation: An Ecological Doctrine of Creation* (London: SCM Press, 1986), 100.

8. It is painful to see Moltmann use the term "open systems," a term taken from thermodynamics describing systems that need energy input to subsist, to postulate the universe as an open system, which is asking for a constant energy input from outside the universe. This would be in plain contradiction with the first law of thermodynamics.

9. *Summa Theologica* 1a.46, 2c: "Dicendum quod mundum non semper fuisse sola fide tenetur, et demonstrative probari non potest. . . . Et hujus ratio est, quia novitas mundi non potest demonstrationem recipere ex parte ipsius mundi."

10. Arthur Peacocke, *Theology for a Scientific Age: Being and Becoming—Natural and Divine,* enlarged ed. (Minneapolis: Fortress Press, 1993), 100.

11. This has become a trend in modern theology; we shall return to this point in the section "The Trinity: Creator of the Becoming Universe."

12. Cf. Thomas Aquinas, arguing for the need of faith and following in his arguments Moses Maimonides, in *Sancti Thomae de Aquino Expositio super Librum Boethii de Trinitate* (Leiden: Brill, 1955), 61: "Propter multa praeambula, quae exiguntur ad habendam cognitionem de Deo secundum viam rationis. Requiritur enim ad hoc fere omnium scientiarum cognitio, cum omnium finis sit cognitio divinorum; quae quidem praeambula paucissime consequuntur" (q. III, a. 1, r. 3) [Because of the many preconditions that must be fulfilled to have knowledge of God by way of reasoning. For this a knowledge of nearly all sciences is required, since the goal of all is the knowledge of divine matters; these preconditions are rarely fulfilled].

13. As long as he or she speaks as a scientist. The person might try to be a theologian, with more or less success, depending largely on his or her theological education.

14. Cf. 1. Cor. 12:6: ὁ δὲ αὐτὸς θεὸς ὁ ἐνεργῶν τὰ πάντα ἐν πᾶσιν (the same God who produces all in everyone); 1 Cor. 15:28: ὁ θεὸς τὰ πάντα ἐν πᾶσιν (God may be all in all).

15. F. L. Cross and E. A. Livingstone, eds., 2d rev. ed. (Oxford: Oxford University Press, 1983), 1027, here quoted from Peacocke, *Theology for a Scientific Age,* 371; the notion of panentheism need not be understood in the restricted sense it has acquired in process theology; for a critical appraisal of it see Peacocke, *Theology for a Scientific Age,* 371–72.

16. *Summa Theologica* 1a.2, 3.

17. Ibid., 2a2ae.171, 3c: "Quae excedunt universaliter cognitionem omnium hominum, non quia secundum se non sint cognoscibilia, sed propter defectum cognitionis humanae: sicut mysterium Trinitatis" [Those truths which universally surpass the knowledge of all men, not because they are intrinsically unknowable, but because of a defect in human knowledge. An example of this is the mystery of the Trinity]. Cf. *Summa contra Gentiles* IV, c. 2–16: "De his quae de ipso Deo supra rationem credenda proponuntur, seu de Trinitate" [Those things concerning God's self which are above reason and are proposed to our belief, such as (belief in) the Trinity. (Translation by Karl Schmitz-Moormann.)].

18. Ibid., 1a.2–26: "Primo namque considerabimus ea quae pertinent ad essentiam divinam" [First, . . . his nature]; 1a.27–43: "Secundo, ea quae pertinent ad distinctionem personarum" [Secondly, the distinction of persons (in God)].

19. Rahner, "Remarks on 'De Trinitate,'" *Theological Investigations* (Baltimore: Helicon Press, 1966), 4:79.

20. Immanuel Kant, *Der Streit der Fakultäten* (Leipzig: Philosophische Bibliothek, n.d.), 34 (quoted from John J. O'Donnell, *The Mystery of the Triune God* [London: Sheed & Ward, 1988], 19).

21. Rahner, "Remarks on 'De Trinitate,'" 4:79.

22. Ibid., 80.

23. Ibid., 82.

24. Cf. Rahner, *Theological Investigations* (multiple articles related to the subject); Eberhard Jüngel, *God as the Mystery of the World* (Edinburgh: T. & T. Clark, 1983); O'Donnell, *The Mystery of the Triune God*, 184; many more publications also rethink the theology of the Trinity in reference to Christology. A good overview of the present stage of thinking can be found in the text of John O'Donnell.

25. Rahner, *Foundations of Christian Faith* (New York: Seabury, 1978), 219.

26. Ibid.

27. Ibid.

28. Typically, John J. O'Donnell, in his excellent representation of present teaching on *The Mystery of the Triune God*, offers only four pages on the subject of creation, mostly on the theme of salvation. How the triune God is related to the concrete creation is barely touched upon, using the notion of *diastasis* proposed by Urs von Balthasar. The whole discussion is mostly concerned with the possibility of human freedom, but the question how things do become and how God is related to this becoming is not even asked.

29. Rahner, *Foundations of Christian Faith*, 220.

30. Ibid., 219.

31. It might be helpful to be reminded that Kant was unable to think of any evolutionary becoming: "The smallness of the degrees of difference between the species is (because the number of species is so great) a necessary consequence of their number. But a blood relationship among them such that either one genus would be coming forth out of another or all out of one single original genus or even out of one single procreating womb would entail ideas which are so monstrous that reason recoils from it" (Immanuel Kant, *Gesammelte Werke*, Akademie-Ausgabe, 8:54).

32. Because there is no fully developed language of a metaphysics of union, we cannot avoid reverting often into a language of the metaphysics of being. As one may realize, there is not even an appropriate word available to talk about becoming: to *be* has one clear meaning; *become* is a composite word with divergent meanings. This difficulty exists in most languages: French: *devenir;* Latin: *fieri;* German: *werden;* Greek: γίγνομαι. This indicates how much we are slaves of our metaphysical past.

33. Alfred North Whitehead, *Process and Reality: An Essay in Cosmology* (New York: Macmillan, 1929), 343.

34. Cf. John 9:2–4.

35. Rahner, *Foundations of Christian Faith*, 221.

36. Thomas Aquinas in his two summae quotes the words *omnia mensura et numero et pondere disposuisti* more often than any other words from the Hebrew Scriptures, with the exception of Genesis 1:1, 1:26, 1:27, and 1:31, which immediately concern the creation.

37. The unchanging God was, among other aspects, the necessary condition for the validity of the eternal law, the law of nature.

38. One might be tempted to say that each participates fully in the essence of the others, but this would be to succumb to the language of ontology, which we try to avoid.

39. Eberhard Jüngel, *God as the Mystery of the World* (Grand Rapids: Eerdmans, 1983), 348 n.

40. Cf. ibid., 348.

41. Rahner, "Remarks on 'De Trinitate,'" 4:86.

42. Ibid., 87.

43. The German psychiatrist von Auersperg, in a talk given at a conference at Vezelay in the 1960s, stated that "one chimpanzee is no chimpanzee," implying that the same is true for humans.

44. Forcing persons together according to the French Revolution's slogan—"Liberté, Égalité, Fraternité ou la Mort"—is not furthering union, but individualization, making persons faceless numbers.

45. John 13:34.

46. Materialistic scientists often insist on the fact that all information needs energy to be created or to be stored. The important point of the quality of this energy is completely neglected. The slice of bread eaten by Einstein is used to create quite other information than the bread eaten by a journalist.

47. Cf. Karl Schmitz-Moormann, "Die Ideenlehre Platons im Lichte des Sonnengleichnisses des sechsten Buches des Staates" (Ph.D. diss. München, 1957; Münster, 1959).

48. Cf. Whitehead, *Process and Reality.*

49. Theories vary from molecular storage (engrams) to electrical links among neurons. But the means of storage differ from the informational content: we cannot know what a person knows by studying her brain. She can tell us, and a neurologist may inform us about brain damage that prevents storage in the brain, as in Alzheimer's disease. It is like writing in a book: if pages are blotted with ink, eaten by worms, or burned, we can no longer read the information because the matter it was stored in is defaced. But we might find the same information in an undamaged book, as another person with an undamaged brain might have the same knowledge. This analogy should not be pushed. It does not say that mind and brain are different entities; this is an impression caused by neurological study of the brain's physiology. It is preferable to speak of the thinking human being, whose higher spiritual capacities have registrable effects in its physiology. An analogical statement can be made about life and the coordination of material elements in the living entity. A human being is a spiritual entity, with a functioning brain.

50. Cf. János Szentágothai, "Downward Causation?" *Ann. Rev. Neurosci.* 1 (1984): 1–11; János Szentágothai, "The Brain-Mind Relationship," in *The Brain-Mind Problem: Philosophical and Neurophysiological Approaches,* edited by B. Guyas (Leuven: Leuven University Press, 1987), 63–115; and János Szentágothai, "About a Paradigm of Neural Organization," in *Brain Research and the Mind-Body Problem: Epistemological and Metaphysical Issues— Proceedings of a Round Table Discussion Held at the Pontifical Academy of Science on 25 October 1988,* edited by Guisepe del Re, Pontificiae Academiae Scientiarum Scripta Varia 79 (Ex Aedibus Academicis in Civitate Vaticana: Pontificia Academia Scientiarum, 1992), 61–64.

51. Donald T. Campbell, "'Downward Causation' in Hierarchically Organised Systems," in *Studies in the Philosophy of Biology: Reduction and Related Problems,* edited by F. J. Ayala and T. Dobzhansky (Oxford: Blackwell, 1983), 178–86.

52. Roger W. Sperry, *Science and Moral Priority* (Oxford: Blackwell, 1983).

53. Peacocke, *Theology for a Scientific Age,* 158.

54. Ibid.

55. Ibid.

56. Ibid.

57. Cf. John Barrow and Frank J. Tipler, *The Anthropic Cosmological Principle* (Oxford: Clarendon Press, 1986).

58. Though usually we avoid talking about miracles today—they are in this world of science often a cause of disbelief—they are still happening, as in Lourdes, where a number of medically controlled (by nonbelieving medical doctors), well-documented sudden healings have occurred.

59. One might recall in this context that French scientists at first rejected the heavenly mechanics of Newton because with the force of gravity he reintroduced new ghostly factors into the heavens.

60. Rahner, *Sacramentum Mundi*, 2:424.

61. Ibid., 2:425.

62. As proposed by the presbyter Lucidus: cf. *Epistola Fausti ad Lucidum presbyterum* and *Exemplar libelli Lucidi presbyteri*, Migne, PL 125, 79–82. Cf. the pseudo-Augustinian *Liber Praedestinatus, Liber secundus, sub nomine Augustini confictus*, Migne, PL 53, 621–28; see the vigorous refutation by Prosper of Aquitaine, *Pro Augustino Responsiones ad Capitula Objectionum Gallorum Calumniantium*, Migne, PL 51, 155–74.

63. Disturbed by the fall of the angels.

64. Rahner, *Sacramentum Mundi*, 2:361.

65. Ibid., 2:426.

66. Ibid., 2:427.

67. Another analogy to this lack of order is thick fog: no visual orientation is possible.

68. At the World Philosophy Congress, Brighton, August 1988, reported in *The Guardian*, 29 August 1988, here quoted from Peacocke, *Theology for a Scientific Age*, 65, 356 n. 37.

69. Peacocke, *Theology for a Scientific Age*, 65.

70. Ibid., 66.

71. Ibid., 68.

72. Matt. 5:45.

73. Cf. supra chapter 5, n. 2.

74. Even if there are other inhabited planets in the universe, the amounts of matter involved will always be quantitatively insignificant.

75. Chapter 5, at end.

76. This leads into the subject of Christology, which seems to need some fundamental revision to show Christ as the *Redemptor* or, to use a more adequate term, the *Salvator* of this universe.

77. Cf. Matt. 25:30–45.

78. This aspect of a future Christology needs further development.

BIBLIOGRAPHY

Aertsen, Johannes Adrianus. *Nature and Creature: Thomas Aquinas's Way of Thought*. Leiden: E. J. Brill, 1988.

Albert, David Z. *Quantum Mechanics and Experience*. Cambridge: Harvard University Press, 1992.

Albrecht-Buehler, Guenter. "The Tracks of Moving Cells." *Scientific American*, April 1978, 68–89.

Alkon, Daniel L. "Learning in a Marine Snail." *Scientific American,* July 1983, 70–85.

Allégre, Claude J., and Stephen H. Schneider. "The Evolution of the Earth." *Scientific American,* October 1994, 66–75.

Andersen, Svend, and Arthur R. Peacocke, eds. *Evolution and Creation: A European Perspective*. Aarhus: Aarhus University Press, 1987.

Anselm of Canterbury. *Cur Deus homo*. Darmstadt: Wissenschaftliche Buchgesellschaft, 1993.

Armbruster, Peter, and Gottfried Münzenberg. "Creating Superheavy Elements." *Scientific American,* May 1989, 66–75.

Atkins, P. W. *Creation Revisited*. Oxford and New York: W. H. Freeman, 1992.

Atkinson, Richard C., and Richard M. Shiffrin. "The Control of Short-Term Memory." *Scientific American,* August 1971, 82–91.

Aubert, Roger. "Die modernistische Krise." In *Handbuch der Kirchengeschichte,* edited by Hubert Jedin, 6:489–92. Freiburg: Herder, 1985.

Aviezer, Nathan. *In the Beginning . . . : Biblical Creation and Science*. Hoboken, N.J.: Ktav Publishing House, 1990.

Axelrod, Julius. "Neurotransmitters." *Scientific American,* June 1974, 58–71.

Bagoot, Jim. *The Meaning of Quantum Theory: A Guide for Students of Chemistry and Physics*. Oxford: Oxford Science Publications, 1992.

Bailey, Lloyd R. *Genesis, Creation, and Creationism*. New York: Paulist Press, 1993.

Barbour, Ian. *Ethics in an Age of Technology: The Gifford Lectures 1989–1991*. Vol. 2. San Francisco: HarperSanFrancisco, 1993.

——— . *Religion in an Age of Science: The Gifford Lectures 1989–1991*. Vol. 1. New York: Harper & Row, 1990.

Barger, Vernon D., and David B. Cline. "High-Energy Scattering." *Scientific American,* December 1967, 76–91.

Barish, Barry C. "Experiments with Neutrino Beams." *Scientific American,* August 1973, 30–47.

Barrett, Alan H. "Radio Signals from Hydroxyl Radicals." *Scientific American,* December 1968, 36–59.

Barrett, Spencer C. H. "Mimicry in Plants." *Scientific American,* September 1987, 76–85.

Barrow, John. *The Theories of Everything: The Quest for Ultimate Explanation*. Oxford: Oxford University Press, 1991.

——— . *The World Within the World*. Oxford: Clarendon, 1988.

Barrow, John, and Frank J. Tipler. *The Anthropic Cosmological Principle*. Oxford: Clarendon, 1986.

Barrow, John D., and Joseph Silk. "The Structure of the Early Universe." *Scientific American,* April 1980, 118–29.

Barth, Karl. *Church Dogmatics*. 4 vols. Edinburgh: T. & T. Clark, 1936–62.

Bayer, Oswald. *Schöpfung als Anrede: zu einer Hermeneutik der Schöpfung*. 2d enlarged ed. Tübingen: J. C. B. Mohr (Paul Siebeck), 1990.

Becker, Thomas. *Geist und Materie in den ersten Schriften Pierre Teilhard de Chardins*. Freiburger theologische Studien 134. Freiburg, Basel, and Wien: Herder, 1987.

Bennett, Charles H., and Rolf Landauer. "The Fundamental Physical Limits of Computation." *Scientific American,* July 1985, 48–71.

Bentley, David, and Ronald R. Hoy. "The Neurobiology of Cricket Song." *Scientific American,* August 1974, 34–52.

Bergold, Ralph. *Der Glaube vor dem Anspruch der Wissenschaft*. Frankfurt am Main: Peter Lang, 1991.

Berridge, Michael J. "The Molecular Basis of Communication Within the Cell." *Scientific American,* October 1985, 142–52.

Bertalanffy, Ludwig von. *General Systems Theory: Foundations, Development, Applications*. Harmondsworth: Penguin University Books, 1984.

Berthold von Regensburg. *Vollständige Ausgabe seiner Predigten*. Ed. Franz Pfeiffer. Foreword by Kurth Ruth. Berlin, n.d.

Bethe, Hans A., and Gerald Brown. "How a Supernova Explodes." *Scientific American,* May 1985, 60–87.

Binnig, Gerd, and Heinrich Rohrer. "The Scanning Tunneling Microscope." *Scientific American,* August 1985, 50–69.

Binns, Emily. *The World as Creation: Creation in Christ in an Evolutionary World View*. Wilmington, Del.: M. Glazier, 1990.

Birch, Charles. *On Purpose*. Kensington, Australia: New South Wales University Press, 1990.

Blondel, Maurice, and Pierre Teilhard de Chardin. *Correspondance commentée*. Commentator Henri de Lubac. Paris: Beauchesne, 1965.

Bohm, David. *Wholeness and the Implicate Order*. London: Routledge & Kegan Paul, 1980.

Bosshard, Stefan Niklaus. *Erschafft die Welt sich selbst?: die Selbstorganisation von Natur und Mensch aus naturwissenschaftlicher, philosophischer, und theologischer Sicht*. Freiburg: Herder, 1985.

Bouyer, Louis. *Cosmos: The World and the Glory of God*. Petersham: St. Bede's Publications, 1988.

Bretscher, Mark S. "How Animal Cells Move." *Scientific American,* December 1987, 72–93.

——— . "The Molecules of the Cell Membrane." *Scientific American,* October 1985, 100–109.

Brewer, Richard G., and Erwin L. Hahn. "Atomic Memory." *Scientific American,* December 1984, 50–57.

Brooke, J. H. *Science and Religion: Some Historical Perspectives.* Cambridge: Cambridge University Press, 1991.

Brower, Lincoln Pierson. "Ecological Chemistry." *Scientific American,* February 1969, 22–29.

Brown, James Cooke. "Loglan." *Scientific American,* June 1960, 53–63.

Brümmer, Vincent, ed. *Interpreting the Universe as Creation: A Dialogue of Science and Religion.* Kampen: Kok Pharos, 1991.

Buber, Martin. *I and Thou.* New York: Scribner's, 1958.

Büchner, Ludwig. *Kraft und Stoff, empirisch-naturphilosophische Studien in allgemeinverständlicher Darstellung.* New York: E. Steiger, 1871.

Buckley, Michael, S.J. *At the Origins of Modern Atheism.* New Haven, Conn.: Yale University Press, 1987.

Buffon, Georges Louis Leclerc Comte de. *Histoire Naturelle.* 44 vols. Paris, 1749–89.

Bühler, Pierre, and Clairette Karakash, eds. *Science et foi font système: Une approche herméneutique.* Geneva: Labor et Fides, 1992.

Bultmann, Rudolf. *Jesus Christ and Mythology.* New York: Charles Scribner's Sons, 1958.

Busignies, Henri. "Communication Channels." *Scientific American,* September 1972, 98–113.

Cairns-Smith, A. G. "The First Organisms." *Scientific American,* June 1985, 90–101.

Calvin, William H. "The Emergence of Intelligence." *Scientific American,* June 1994, 100–107.

Campbell, John H., and William J. Schopf, eds. *Creative Evolution?!* Boston: Jones and Bartlett, 1994.

Cantin, Marc, and Jacques Genest. "The Heart as an Endocrine Gland." *Scientific American,* February 1986, 76–81.

Carrigan, Richard A., Jr., and W. Peter Trower. "Superheavy Magnetic Monopoles." *Scientific American,* April 1982, 106–19.

Catechism of the Catholic Church. Mahwah, N.J.: Paulist Press, 1997.

Chaisson, Eric J. "Gaseous Nebulas." *Scientific American,* December 1978, 164–80.

Churchland, Paul M., and Patricia Smith Churchland. "Could a Machine Think?" *Scientific American,* January 1990, 32–39.

Clifford, Richard J. *Creation Accounts in the Ancient Near East and in the Bible.* Monograph Series 26. Washington: The Catholic Biblical Association of America, 1994.

Cline, David B. "Beyond Truth and Beauty: A Fourth Family of Particles." *Scientific American,* August 1988, 60–67.

Cole-Turner, Ronald. *The New Genesis: Theology and the Genetic Revolution.* Louisville: Westminster/John Knox, 1993.

Comte, Auguste. *Discours sur l'esprit positif.* Paris, 1844.

——— . *Rede über den Geist des Positivismus.* Trans. and ed. I. Fetscher. Hamburg, 1956.

——— . *Système de politique positive ou traité de sociologie instituant la religion de l'humanité.* Paris, 1851–54.

Coppens, Yves. *Cosmos as Creation: Theology and Science in Consonance.* Nashville: Abingdon, 1989.

——— . "Eastside Story: The Origin of Humankind." *Scientific American,* July 1994, 88–95.

Coveney, Peter, and Roger Highfield. *The Arrow of Time.* London: W. H. Allen, 1990.

Coyne, George V., S.J., Karl Schmitz-Moormann, and Christoph Wassermann, eds. *Origins,*

Time, and Complexity. Part 1. Studies in Science and Theology—Yearbook of the European Society for the Study of Science and Theology 1, 1993. Geneva: Labor et Fides, 1994.

————, eds. *Origins, Time, and Complexity*, Part 2. Studies in Science and Theology—Yearbook of the European Society for the Study of Science and Theology 2, 1994. Geneva: Labor et Fides, 1994.

Craig, W. L., and Q. Smith. *Theism, Atheism, and Big Bang Cosmology*. Oxford: Clarendon, 1993.

Craig, William Lane. *The Cosmological Argument from Plato to Leibniz*. London: Macmillan, 1980.

————. *Creation and Evolution*. Leicester: Inter-Varsity, 1985.

Crewe, Albert V. "A High-Resolution Scanning Electron Microscope." *Scientific American,* April 1971, 26–35.

Croce, Carlo M., and Hilary Koprowski. "The Genetics of Human Cancers." *Scientific American,* February 1978, 117–25.

Cuénot, Claude. *Pierre Teilhard de Chardin: Les Grandes Étapes de Son Évolution*. Paris: Plon, 1958.

Cupitt, Don. *Creation Out of Nothing*. London and Philadelphia: SCM Press; Trinity, 1990.

Dal Gal. "Il papa S. Pio X." 183. In *Handbuch der Kirchengeschichte*, edited by Hubert Jedin, 6:491. Freiburg: Herder, 1985.

Dales, Richard C. *The Scientific Achievement of the Middle Ages*. Philadelphia: University of Pennsylvania Press, 1989.

Daly, Gabriel. *Creation and Redemption*. Wilmington, Del.: M. Glazier, 1989.

Darnell, James E., Jr. "RNA." *Scientific American,* October 1985, 68–87.

Darwin, Charles. *The Origin of Species by Means of Natural Selection*. London, 1859; New York: Avenel Books, 1979.

Davies, Nicholas B., and Michael Brooke. "Coevolution of the Cuckoo and Its Hosts." *Scientific American,* January 1991, 92–99.

Davies, Paul. *The Mind of God: The Scientific Basis for a Rational World*. New York: Simon & Schuster, 1992.

de Lagarde, Jean, ed. *La Fécondation Mutuelle Entre Science et Théologie; Actes Du Séminaire BENA*. Entveitg, France: Association Béna, 1994.

Dempsey, Elbert. *God's Other Books*. Independence: Herald, 1987.

Derham, William. *Physico-theology: Or, A Demonstration of the Being and Attributes of God, from His Works of Creation, Being the Substance of Sixteen Sermons Preached in St. Mary-le-Bow-Church, London, at the Honourable Mr. Boyle's Lectures in the Year 1711 and 1712; with Large Notes and Many Curious Observations by W. Derham*. 4th corr. ed. London: Printed for W. Innys, 1716.

Deutsch, David, and Michael Lockwood. "The Quantum Physics of Time Travel." *Scientific American,* March 1994, 74.

Dickerson, Richard E. "Chemical Evolution and the Origins of Life." *Scientific American,* September 1978, 70–109.

————. *Dieu, le monde et l'homme: hasard ou projet?* Paris: O.E.I.L., 1988.

————. "The DNA Helix and How It Is Read." *Scientific American,* December 1983, 94–111.

Dobzhansky, Theodosius. *The Biology of Ultimate Concern*. New York: New American Library, 1967.

Dodson, Edward O. *Creation or Evolution: Correspondence on the Current Controversy*. Ottawa: University of Ottawa Press, 1990.

Draper, William. *History of the Conflict Between Religion and Science*. New York, 1874.

Drees, Willem R. *Beyond the Big Bang: Quantum Cosmologies and God*. Chicago: Open Court, 1990.

Dyson, Freeman. *Disturbing the Universe*. New York: Harper & Row, 1979.

Eaton, G. Gray. "The Social Order of Japanese Macaques." *Scientific American*, October 1976, 96–107.

Eaves, L. J., H. J. Eysenck, and N. G. Martin. *Genes, Culture, and Personality: An Empirical Approach*. London: Academic, 1989.

Eberlein, Karl. *Gott der Schöpfer, Israels Gott: eine exegetisch-hermeneutische Studie zur theologischen Funktion alttestamentlicher Schöpfungsaussagen*. Frankfurt am Main: Peter Lang, 1986.

Eddington, Sir Arthur. *The Nature of the Physical World*. Cambridge: Cambridge University Press, 1928.

——— . *New Pathways in Science*. New York: Macmillan, 1935.

——— . *The Philosophy of Physical Science*. Cambridge: Cambridge University Press, 1939.

——— . *Science and the Unseen World*. New York: Macmillan, 1929.

Edelman, Gerald M. "Cell-Adhesion Molecules: A Molecular Basis for Animal Form." *Scientific American*, April 1984, 118–29.

Eigen, Manfred, et al. "The Origin of Genetic Information." *Scientific American*, April 1981, 88–119.

Eigen, Manfred, and Ruthild Winkler. *Das Spiel: Naturgesetze steuern den Zufall*. München: Piper, 1990.

Einstein, Albert. *Ideas and Opinions*. New York: Laurel Editions, 1973.

——— . *Mein Weltbild*. Neue, Vom Verfasser Durchgesehene und Wesentlich Erweiterte Auflage. Ed. C. Seelig. Zürich: Europa Verlag, 1953.

——— . *Science, Philosophy, and Religion: A Symposium* New York: Harper, 1941.

Emerson, Thomas I. "Communication and Freedom of Expression." *Scientific American*, September 1972, 163–72.

Ephrussi, Boris, and Mary C. Weiss. *Evolution and Creation*. Notre Dame, Ind.: University of Notre Dame Press, 1985.

——— . "Hybrid Somatic Cells." *Scientific American*, April 1969, 26–35.

Fagg, Lawrence W. *The Becoming of Time: Integrating Physical and Religious Time*. Atlanta: Scholars, 1995.

Fantoli, Annibale. *Galileo: For Copernicanism and for the Church*. Trans. George V. Coyne, S.J. Studi Galileiani, vol. 3. Vatican City (Notre Dame): Vatican Observatory Publications (Distr. University of Notre Dame), 1994.

Faricy, Robert. "The Heart of Christ in the Spirituality of Teilhard de Chardin." *Gregorianum* 69 (1988): 261–77.

Feldman, Gary J., and Jack Steinberger. "The Number of Families of Matter." *Scientific American*, February 1991, 70–77.

Feldman, Jerome A. "Programming Languages." *Scientific American,* December 1979, 94–117.

Ferris, Timothy. *Coming of Age in the Milky Way.* New York: Morrow, 1988.

Ferster, Charles B. "Arithmetic Behavior in Chimpanzees." *Scientific American,* May 1964, 98–107.

Fiddes, John C. "The Nucleotide Sequence of a Viral DNA." *Scientific American,* December 1977, 54–67.

Flamming, Peter James. *God and Creation.* Nashville: Broadman, 1985.

Fox, Matthew. *Sheer Joy: Conversations with Thomas Aquinas on Creation Spirituality.* San Francisco: HarperSanFrancisco, 1992.

Frisch, Karl von. *The Dance Language and Orientation of Bees.* Cambridge: Harvard University Press, 1967.

Gale, George. "The Anthropic Principle." *Scientific American,* December 1981, 154–71.

Gamow, George. "Galaxies in Flight." *Scientific American,* July 1948, 20–25.

——— . "Modern Cosmology." *Scientific American,* March 1954, 54–65.

Ganoczy, Alexandre. *Schöpfungslehre.* 2d enlarged ed. Düsseldorf: Patmos, 1987.

——— . *Suche nach Gott auf den Wegen der Natur; Theologie, Mystik, Naturwissenschaft— ein kritischer Versuch.* Düsseldorf: Patmos, 1992.

Gelerntner, David. "The Metamorphosis of Information Management." *Scientific American,* August 1989, 66–73.

Gerbner, George. "Communication and Social Environment." *Scientific American,* September 1972, 152–61.

Ghiglieri, Michael P. "The Social Ecology of Chimpanzees." *Scientific American,* June 1985, 102–13.

Gilbert, Lawrence E. "The Coevolution of a Butterfly and a Vine." *Scientific American,* August 1982, 110–21.

Gilbert, Walter, and Lydia Villa-Komaroff. "Useful Proteins from Recombinant Bacteria." *Scientific American,* April 1980, 74–97.

Gilkey, Langdon. *Nature, Reality and the Sacred: The Nexus of Science and Religion.* Minneapolis: Fortress, 1993.

Gisel, Pierre. *La Création, Essai sur la Liberté et la Nécessité, L'histoire et la Loi, L'homme, le Mal et Dieu.* 2d ed. Geneva: Labor et Fides, 1987.

Gleick, James. *Chaos Making a New Science.* New York: Viking, 1987.

Glorieux, Pierre. *God and Creation: An Ecumenical Symposium.* Notre Dame, Ind.: University of Notre Dame Press, 1990.

——— . *Répertoire des Maîtres en Théologie au XIIIme siècle.* Paris, 1933–35.

Goldmark, Peter C. "Communication and the Community." *Scientific American,* September 1972, 142–51.

Gombrich, E. H. "The Visual Image." *Scientific American,* September 1972, 82–97.

Goodall, Jane. *The Chimpanzees of Gombe: Patterns of Behavior.* Cambridge: Belknap Press of Harvard University Press, 1986.

——— . *Through a Window: My Thirty Years with the Chimpanzees of Gombe.* Boston: Houghton Mifflin, 1990.

Goodenough, Ursula W., and R. P. Levine. "The Genetic Activity of Mitochondria and Chloroplasts." *Scientific American,* November 1970, 22–29.

Goodman, Corey S., and Michael J. Bastiani. "How Embryonic Nerve Cells Recognize One Another." *Scientific American,* December 1984, 58–77.

Gordon, M. A., and W. B. Burton. "Carbon Monoxide in the Galaxy." *Scientific American,* May 1979, 54–67.

Gottlieb, David I. "Gabaergic Neurons." *Scientific American,* February 1988, 82–89.

Gould, James L., and Peter Marler. "Learning by Instinct." *Scientific American,* January 1987, 74–85.

Gould, Stephen Jay. "The Evolution of Life on the Earth." *Scientific American,* October 1994, 84–91.

Greenberg, J. Mayo. "The Structure and Evolution of Interstellar Grains." *Scientific American,* June 1984, 124–35.

Guardini, Romano. *Welt und Person.* Nürnberg: Werkbund Verlag, 1937.

Guillaumont, François, ed. *Pierre Teilhard de Chardin et Jean Boussac: Lettres de guerre inédites.* Commentator Henri de Lubac. Paris: O.E.I.L., 1986.

Guth, Alan H., and Paul J. Steinhardt. "The Inflationary Universe." *Scientific American,* May 1984, 116–30.

Haas, Ernst. *Schöpfung und Sündenfall: Das Zeugnis der Biblischen Urgeschichte.* Freiburg im Breisgau: Informationszentrum Berufe der Kirche, 1984.

Habing, Harm J., and Gerry Neugebauer. "The Infrared Sky." *Scientific American,* November 1984, 48–57.

Hailman, Jack P. "How an Instinct Is Learned." *Scientific American,* December 1969, 98–108.

Halliwell, Jonathan J. "Quantum Cosmology and the Creation of the Universe." *Scientific American,* December 1991, 76–85.

Harari, Haim. "The Structure of Quarks and Leptons." *Scientific American,* April 1983, 56–77.

Harrison, Edward R. *Cosmology.* Cambridge: Cambridge University Press, 1981.

Hawking, Stephen W. *A Brief History of Time.* London and New York: Bantam, 1988.

Hayward, Alan. *Creation and Evolution: The Facts and the Fallacies.* London: Triangle, 1985.

Hefner, Philip. *The Human Factor: Evolution, Culture and Religion.* Minneapolis: Fortress Press, 1993.

Hemleben, Johannes. *Teilhard de Chardin in Selbstzeugnissen und Dokumenten.* Reinbek: Rowohlt, 1966.

Hemminger. *Jenseits der Weltbilder: Naturwissenschaft, Evolution, Schöpfung.* Stuttgart: Quell, 1991.

Hengstenberg, Hans Eduard. *Das Band Zwischen Gott und Schöpfung: Entwurf einer Analogia Trinitatis.* 3d rev. ed. Frankfurt am Main: Peter Lang, 1991.

Hirsch, E. C. *Das Ende aller Gottesbeweise.* Hamburg, 1975.

Holbach, Dietrich von. *System der Natur oder die Gesetze der physischen und moralischen Welt.* N.p., 1841.

Hopcroft, John E. "Turing Machines." *Scientific American,* May 1984, 86–107.

Horgan, John. "In the Beginning . . ." *Scientific American,* February 1991, 116.

——— . "Universal Truths." *Scientific American,* October 1990, 108–16.

Huber, William Dennis. *The General Theology of Creation.* Buffalo: ISCS, 1992.

Humphreys, Colin. *Creation and Evolution.* Oxford: Oxford University Press, 1985.

Huth, Werner. *Flucht in die Gewissheit, Fundamentalismus und Moderne.* München: Claudius Verlag, 1995.

Hydén, Holger. "Satellite Cells in the Nervous System." *Scientific American,* December 1961, 62–83.

Hynes, Richard O. "Fibronectins." *Scientific American,* June 1986, 42–51.

Im Anfang schuf Gott Himmel und Erde: im Auftrage des Direktoriums der Salzburger Hochschulwochen als Jahrbuch. Graz: Styria, 1991.

Inose, Hiroshi. "Communication Networks." *Scientific American,* September 1972, 116–29.

Interpreting the Universe as Creation: A Dialogue of Science and Religion. Kampen: Kok Pharos, 1991.

Isham, C. J. "Quantum Theories of the Creation of the Universe." In *Quantum Cosmology and the Laws of Nature, Scientific Perspectives on Divine Action,* edited by Robert John Russell, Nancey Murphy, and C. J. Isham, 49–89. A Series on Divine Action in Scientific Perspective. Vatican City and Berkeley, Calif.: Vatican Observatory Publications; the Center for Theology and the Natural Sciences, 1993.

Ishikawa, Kenzo. "Glueball." *Scientific American,* November 1982, 142–57.

Israel, Martin. *Creation: The Consummation of the World.* London: Collins, 1989.

Jaki, Stanley L. *Genesis 1: Through the Ages.* London: Thomas Moore, 1992.

——— . *Universe and Creed.* Milwaukee: Marquette University Press, 1992.

Jakobson, Roman. "Verbal Communication." *Scientific American,* September 1972, 72–80.

Jayawardhana, Ray. "A Dark Matter Recipe Is Tested—and Found Wanting." *Science* 264 (1994): 1845.

Jerison, Harry J. "Paleoneurology and the Evolution of Mind." *Scientific American,* January 1976, 90–101.

Jüngel, Eberhard. *God as the Mystery of the World.* Grand Rapids, Mich.: Eerdmans, 1983.

Kaiser, Christopher B. *Creation and the History of Science.* London and Grand Rapids: Marshall Pickering; Eerdmans, 1991.

Kalil, Ronald E. "Synapse Formation in the Developing Brain." *Scientific American,* December 1989, 76–87.

Kalinowska, Janina. "Mysterium Septiformis Ecclesiae." *Analecta Cracoviensia* 23 (1991): 307–24 plus 8 hp. Krakowie: Polskie Towarzystwo Teologizne.

Kalisch, Oskar. "Atheismus als Frucht der Wissenschaft—Literarische Spuren eines geistigen Prozesses." *Glaube und Denken, Jahrbuch der Karl-Heim-Gesellschaft* 6. Jahrgang (1993): 67–94.

Kandel, Eric R. "Nerve Cells and Behavior." *Scientific American,* July 1970, 57–71.

——— . "Small Systems of Neurons." *Scientific American,* September 1979, 66–78.

Kant, Immanuel. *Der Streit der Fakultäten.* Leipzig: Philosophische Bibliothek. n.d.

Katechismus der Katholischen Kirche. München-Wien, Leipzig, Freiburg, Linz: Oldenbourg, Benno, Paulusverlag, Veritas, 1993.

Kefatos, Menas, and Robert Nadeau. *The Conscious Universe: Part and Whole in Modern Physical Theory.* New York and Heidelberg: Springer-Verlag, 1990.

Kellert, Stephen H. *In the Wake of Chaos.* Chicago: University of Chicago Press, 1993.

Kemeny, John G. "Man Viewed as a Machine." *Scientific American,* April 1955, 58–67.

Kendall, Henry W., and Wolfgang Panofsky. "The Structure of the Proton and the Neutron." *Scientific American,* June 1971, 60–77.

Kennedy, Donald. "Small Systems of Nerve Cells." *Scientific American,* May 1967, 44–65.

Khoury, Adel Theodore. *So machte Gott die Welt: Schöpfungsmythen der Völker.* Freiburg im Breisgau: Herder, 1985.

King, Thomas M., S.J., and James F. Salmon, S.J., eds. *Teilhard and the Unity of Knowledge.* New York: Paulist Press, 1983.

Kirchner, Wolfgang H., and William F. Towne. "The Sensory Basis of the Honeybee's Dance Language." *Scientific American,* June 1994, 74–80.

Klein, Wolfgang. *Teilhard de Chardin und das Zweite Vatikanische Konzil.* München: Schöningh, 1975.

Knoll, Andrew H. "End of the Proterozoic Eon." *Scientific American,* October 1991, 64–73.

Koch, Traugott. *Das göttliche Gesetz der Natur: zur Geschichte des neuzeitlichen Naturverständnisses und zu einer gegenwärtigen theologischen Lehre von der Schöpfung.* Zürich: Theologischer Verlag, 1991.

Kortlandt, Arndt. "Handgebrauch bei freilebenden Schimpansen." In *Handgebrauch und Verständigung bei Affen und Frühmenschen,* edited by Bernhard Rensch, 59–102. Symposium der Werner-Reimers-Stiftung Für Anthropogenetische Forschung. Bern und Stuttgart: Verlag Hans Huber, 1968.

Kramer, William. *Evolution and Creation: A Catholic Understanding.* Huntington: Our Sunday Visitor, 1986.

Kretzmer, Ernest R. "Communication Terminals." *Scientific American,* September 1972, 130–41.

Krisch, Alan D. "The Spin of the Proton." *Scientific American,* May 1979, 68–99.

Kuhn, Thomas S. *The Structure of Scientific Revolutions.* Chicago: University of Chicago Press, 1962.

Küng, Hans. *Does God Exist?* Garden City, N.Y.: Doubleday, 1980.

Lane, Charles. "Rabbit Hemoglobin from Frog Eggs." *Scientific American,* August 1976, 60–71.

Lanzenberger, Gerhard. *Schöpfung ist Evolution: die Schöpfungsgeschichte der Bibel im Horizont der modernen Naturwissenschaften.* Karlsruhe: INFO, 1988.

Leder, Philip. "The Genetics of Antibody Diversity." *Scientific American,* May 1982, 102–15.

Lederman, Leon. "The Two-Neutrino Experiment." *Scientific American,* March 1963, 60–79.

Lent, Charles M., and Michael H. Dickinson. "The Neurobiology of Feeding in Leeches." *Scientific American,* June 1988, 98–103.

Leroy, P., H. Morin, and S. Soulié, eds. *Pélerin de l'avenir: Le Père Teilhard de Chardin à travers son correspondance.* Paris: Le Centurion, 1986.

Leroy, Pierre, ed. *Dans le sillage des sinanthropes: Lettres inédites de Pierre Teilhard de Chardin et J. Gunnar Anderson.* Paris: O.E.I.L., 1986.

———. *Lettres familières de Pierre Teilhard de Chardin mon ami.* Paris: Le Centurion, 1976.

Leslie, John, ed. *Physical Cosmology and Philosophy.* London: Macmillan, 1990.

———. *Universes.* London and New York: Routledge, 1989.

Lesser, Friedrich Christian. *Théologie des Insectes ou Démonstration des Perfections de Dieu dans tout ce qui concerne les Insectes.* Traduit de l'Allemand. Avec des remarques de M. P. Lyonnet. Paris: Hugues-Daniel Chaubert-Laurent Durand, 1745.

Lewis, John S. "The Chemistry of the Solar System." *Scientific American,* March 1974, 50–65.

Lewis, Roy S., and Edward Anders. "Interstellar Matter in Meteorites." *Scientific American,* August 1983, 66–77.

Lindberg, David C. *The Beginnings of Western Science: The European Scientific Tradition in Philosophical, Religious and Institutional Context, 600 B.C. to A.D. 1450.* Chicago and London: University of Chicago Press, 1992.

Link, Christian. *Schöpfung, Schöpfungstheologie angesichts der Herausforderungen des 20. Jahrhunderts.* Vol. 7,2 of C. H. Ratschow, ed., *Handbuch Systematischer Theologie.* Gütersloh: Gütersloher Verlagshaus Gerd Mohn, 1991.

Lloyd, James E. "Mimicry in the Sexual Signals of Fireflies." *Scientific American,* July 1981, 138–47.

Loder, James E., and W. Jim Neidhardt. *The Knight's Move: The Relational Logic of the Spirit in Theology and Science.* Colorado Springs: Helmers & Howards, 1992.

Lodish, Harvey F., and James E. Rothman. "The Assembly of Cell Membranes." *Scientific American,* January 1979, 48–63.

Loewenstein, Werner R. "Intercellular Communication." *Scientific American,* May 1970, 78–91.

Lonergan, Bernard J. F. *Insight, a Study of Human Understanding.* San Francisco [London]: Harper & Row [Longman, Green & Company], 1978.

Longchamp, Jean-Pierre. *La Création du monde.* Paris: Desclée de Brouwer, 1990.

Lorenz, Konrad Z. "The Evolution of Behavior." *Scientific American,* December 1958, 67–82.

LoSecco, J. M., Frederick Reines, and Daniel Sinclair. "The Search for Proton Decay." *Scientific American,* June 1985, 54–77.

Lovell, Bernard. *Man's Relation to the Universe.* New York: Freeman, 1975.

Lucas, J. R. "Wilberforce and Huxley: A Legendary Encounter." *Hibbert Journal* 22, no. 2 (1979): 313–30.

Luginbuhl, Marianne. *Menschenschöpfungsmythen: ein Vergleich zwischen Griechenland und dem Alten Orient.* Bern and New York: Peter Lang, 1992.

Lukas, Mary, and Ellen Lukas. *Teilhard: A Biography.* London: Collins, 1977.

Lyons, James A. *The Cosmic Christ in Origen and Teilhard de Chardin: A Comparative Study.* Oxford: Oxford University Press, 1982.

McCarthy, John. "Information." *Scientific American,* September 1966, 64–73.

MacKay, Donald M. *The Clockwork Image.* London: Inter-Varsity, 1974.

McMenamin, Mark A. S. "The Emergence of Animals." *Scientific American,* April 1987, 94–103.

McPherson, Thomas. *The Argument from Design.* London: Macmillan, 1972.

Maldamé, J. M. "Christianisme et Science." *Revue Thomiste* 93, no. 3 (1993): 439–62.

Margulis, Lynn. "Symbiosis and Evolution." *Scientific American,* August 1971, 48–61.

Marti, Kurt. *Schöpfungsglaube: die Ökologie Gottes.* 2d ed. Stuttgart: Radius-Verlag, 1985.

Marxer, Fridolin. *Gottes Spuren im Universum: Schöpfungsmystik und moderne Physik.* München: Verlag J. Pfeiffer, 1990.

Matthews, Clifford N., and Roy Abraham Varghese, eds. *Cosmic Beginnings and Human Ends: Where Science and Religion Meet.* Chicago: Open Court, 1995.

Menzel, Randolf, and Jochen Erber. "Learning and Memory in Bees." *Scientific American,* July 1978, 102–11.

Mercator, Gerhard. *Mercator—ein Wegbereiter neuzeitlichen Denkens*, edited by Irmgard Hantsche. Duisburger Mercator-Studien, Bd. 1. Bochum: Universitätsverlag Dr. N. Brockmeyer, 1994.

Mickens, Ronald E. *Mathematics and Science*. Singapore: World Scientific, 1990.

Miller, Stanley L. "The Prebiotic Synthesis of Organic Compounds as a Step Toward the Origin of Life. "In *Major Events in the History of Life,* edited by J. William Schopf, 1–28. Boston: Jones & Bartlett, 1992.

Minsky, Marvin. "Will Robots Inherit the Earth?" *Scientific American,* October 1994, 108–13.

Moe, Michael K., and Simon Peter Rosen. "Double-Beta Decay." *Scientific American,* November 1989, 48–55.

Moltmann, Jürgen. *God in Creation: An Ecological Doctrine of Creation.* London: SCM Press, 1986.

——— . *Trinität und Reich Gottes.* München: Chr. Kaiser, 1980.

——— . *The Trinity and the Kingdom.* San Francisco: Harper, 1981.

Monod, Jacques. *Chance and Necessity.* Trans. A. Wainhouse. London: Collins, 1972.

Montenat, Christian. *How to Read the World: Creation in Evolution.* New York: Crossroad, 1985.

Mooney, Christopher. *Teilhard de Chardin and the Mystery of Christ.* New York: Harper & Row, 1964.

Moore, Edward F. "Artificial Living Plants." *Scientific American,* October 1956, 118–27.

Morell, Virginia. "Decoding Chimp Genes and Life." *Science* 265 (1994): 1172–73.

Morgan, Thomas. *Physico-theology, Or, A Philosophico-moral Disquisition Concerning Human Nature, Free Agency, Moral Government, and Divine Providence.* London: Printed for T. Cox at the Lamb Under the Royal-Exchange, 1741.

Morrin, P. A., et al. "Kin Selection, Social Structures, Gene Flow and the Evolution of Chimpanzees." *Science* 265 (1994): 1193–1201.

Morris, Henry M. *Scientific Creationism.* San Diego: Creation Life Publishers, 1985.

Morris, Richard. *The Edges of Science.* New York: Prentice-Hall, 1990.

——— . *Time's Arrow.* New York: Simon & Schuster, 1984.

Morris, Simon Conway, and H. B. Whittington. "The Animals of the Burgess Shale." *Scientific American,* July 1979, 122–35.

Morrison, Philip. "The Neutrino." *Scientific American,* January 1956, 58–69.

Mott, Sir Neville, ed. *Can Scientists Believe? Some Examples of the Attitude of Scientists to Religion.* London: James & James, 1991.

Mounier, Emmanuel. *Personalism.* Paris: Seuil, 1948.

Neher, Erwin, and Bert Sakmann. "The Patch Clamp Technique." *Scientific American,* March 1992, 44–51.

Neville, Robert C. *God the Creator: On the Transcendence and Presence of God.* Albany: State University of New York Press, 1992.

Newman, Eric A., and Peter H. Hartline. "The Infrared 'Vision' of Snakes." *Scientific American,* March 1982, 116–27.

Nicholls, John G., and David Van Essen. "The Nervous System of the Leech." *Scientific American,* January 1974, 38–53.

Nicolai, Jürgen. "Mimicry in Parasitic Birds." *Scientific American,* October 1974, 92–99.

Nicolas, J.-H. *Synthèse dogmatique: complément de l'univers à la trinité.* Fribourg: Éditions Universitaires, 1993.

Nottebohm, Fernando. "From Bird Song to Neurogenesis." *Scientific American,* February 1989, 74–79.

O'Donnell, John J. *The Mystery of the Triune God.* A Heythrop Monograph. London: Sheed & Ward, 1988.

O'Shaughnessy, Thomas J. *Creation and the Teaching of the Qur'an.* Rome: Biblical Institute, 1985.

Orgel, Leslie E. "The Origin of Life on the Earth." *Scientific American,* October 1994, 76–83.

Otto, Rudolf. *The Idea of the Holy.* London: Penguin, 1959.

Ouince, René d', S.J. *Un Prophète en Procès: Teilhard de Chardin, 1. dans L'église de Son Temps, 2. et L'avenir de la Pensée Chrétienne.* Intelligence de la Foi. Paris: Aubier-Montaigne, 1970.

Pagels, Heinz. *The Dreams of Reason.* New York: Simon & Schuster, 1988.

Pais, Abraham. *Subtle Is the Lord: The Science and Life of Albert Einstein.* Oxford: Clarendon, 1982.

Paley, William. *Natural Theology: Or, Evidences of the Existence and Attributes of the Deity, Collected from the Appearances of Nature.* Philadelphia, 1814.

Pannenberg, Wolfhart. *Toward a Theology of Nature: Essays on Science and Faith.* Louisville: Westminster/John Knox Press, 1993.

Paul, Iain. *Science and Theology in Einstein's Perspective.* Theology and Science at the Frontiers of Knowledge 3. Edinburgh: Scottish Academic, 1986.

Peacocke, Arthur. *Creation and the World of Science.* Oxford: Clarendon, 1979.

———. *God and the New Biology.* London: Dent, 1986.

———. *Intimations of Reality: Critical Realism in Science and Religion.* Notre Dame, Ind.: University of Notre Dame Press, 1984.

———. "Reductionism: A Review of the Epistemological Issues and Their Relevance to Biology and the Problem of Consciousness." *ZYGON: Journal of Religion and Science* 11 (1976): 306–34.

———. *Science and the Christian Experiment.* London: Oxford University Press, 1971.

———. *Theology for a Scientific Age: Being and Becoming—Natural, Divine, and Human.* Enlarged ed. Minneapolis: Fortress Press, 1993.

———, ed. *The Sciences and Theology in the Twentieth Century.* Stocksfield: Oriel, 1981.

Peebles, P. James E., et al. "The Evolution of the Universe." *Scientific American,* October 1994, 52–57.

Peebles, P. J. E. *Principles of Physical Cosmology.* Princeton Series in Physics. Princeton, N.J.: Princeton University Press, 1993.

Penrose, Roger. *The Emperor's New Mind: Concerning Computers, Minds and the Laws of Physics.* Oxford: Oxford University Press, 1989.

Peterson, W. Wesley. "Error-Correcting Codes." *Scientific American,* February 1962, 96–111.

Pierce, John R. "Communication." *Scientific American,* September 1972, 30–41.

Pietsch, Theodore W., and David B. Grobecker. "Frogfishes." *Scientific American,* June 1990, 96–103.

Pike, Nelson. *God and Timelessness.* London: Routledge & Kegan Paul, 1970.

Pinkerton, Richard C. "Information Theory and Melody." *Scientific American,* February 1956, 77–87.

Polkinghorne, John C. *The Faith of a Physicist—Reflections of a Bottom-Up Thinker.* Princeton: Princeton University Press, 1994.

———. *Science and Creation: The Search for Understanding.* London: SPCK, 1988.

Pollard, J. W. "Is Weismann's Barrier Absolute?" In *Beyond Neo-Darwinism: An Introduction to the New Evolutionary Paradigm,* edited by M. W. Ho and P. T. Saunders. London: Academic Press, 1984.

Poundstone, William. *The Recursive Universe.* Oxford: Oxford University Press, 1985.

Premack, Ann James, and David Premack. "Teaching Language to an Ape." *Scientific American,* October 1972, 92–99.

Prigogine, Ilya. *From Being to Becoming.* San Francisco: Freeman, 1980.

Prigogine, Ilya, and Isabelle Stengers. *Order Out of Chaos.* London: Heinemanns, 1984.

Rahner, Karl. "Chalkedon—Ende oder Anfang?" In *Das Konzil von Chalkedon, Geschichte und Gegenwart—Band III: Chalkedon heute,* edited by Aloys Grillmeier, S.J., and Heinrich Bacht, S.J., 3–49. Freiburg, Basel, and Wien: Herder, 1976.

———. *Foundations of Christian Faith.* New York: Seabury, 1978.

———. *Theological Investigations.* 22 vols. New York and London: Crossroad, Seabury, and others, 1960–89.

———, ed. *Sacramentum Mundi: An Encyclopedia of Theology.* 6 vols. New York and London: Herder and Herder; Burns & Oates, 1970.

Rahner, Karl, and Herbert Vorgrimler. *Kleines Konzilskompendium.* Freiburg: Herder, 1974.

Ratzinger, Joseph. *In the Beginning: A Catholic Understanding of the Story of Creation and the Fall.* Huntington: Our Sunday Visitor, 1990.

Re, Giuseppe del, ed. *Brain Research and the Mind-Body Problem: Epistemological and Metaphysical Issues—Proceedings of a Round Table Discussion Held at the Pontifical Academy of Science on 25 October 1988.* Pontificiae Academiae Scientiarum Scripta Varia 79. Ex Aedibus Academicis in Civitate Vaticana: Pontificia Academia Scientiarum, 1992.

Rebbi, Claudio. "The Lattice Theory of Quark Confinement." *Scientific American,* February 1983, 54–65.

Rebek, Julius, Jr. "Synthetic Self-Replicating Molecules." *Scientific American,* July 1994, 48–55.

Regan, David, Kenneth Beverley, and Max Cynader. "The Visual Perception of Motion in Depth." *Scientific American,* July 1979, 136–51.

Rennie, John. "Grading the Gene Tests." *Scientific American,* June 1994, 88–97.

Rensch, Bernhard, ed. *Handgebrauch und Verständigung bei Affen und Frühmenschen.* Symposium der Werner-Reimers-Stiftung Für Anthropogenetische Forschung. Bern und Stuttgart: Verlag Hans Huber, 1968.

Rensch, Bernhard, and J. Röhl. "Spontanes Öffnen verschiedener Kistenverschlüsse durch einen Schimpansen." Reprinted from *Zeitschrift Für Tierpsychologie.* Berlin: Verlag Paul Parey, 1967.

———. "Wählen zwischen zwei überschaubaren Labyrinthwegen durch einen Schimpansen." Reprinted from *Zeitschrift Für Tierpsychologie.* Berlin: Verlag Paul Parey, 1967.

Rousselot, Pierre. *The Eyes of Faith: Answer to Two Attacks.* Translation of *Les Yeux de la Foi.*

Trans. Joseph Donceel. Introduction by John M. McDermott. Trans. Avery Dulles. New York: Fordham University Press, 1990.

———. *Les Yeux de la Foi*. Paris, 1914.

Rowe, William. *The Cosmological Argument*. Princeton: Princeton University Press, 1975.

Rubenstein, Edward. "Diseases Caused by Impaired Communication Among Cells." *Scientific American*, March 1980, 102–23.

Rucker, Rudy. *Infinity and the Mind*. Boston: Birkhauser, 1982.

Ruddle, Frank H., and Raju S. Kucherlapati. "Hybrid Cells and Human Genes." *Scientific American*, July 1974, 36–49.

Ruiz de la Pena, Juan Luis. *Teologia de la creacion*. 2d ed. Santander: Sal Terrae, 1986.

Rukang, Wu, and Lin Shenglong. "Peking Man." *Scientific American*, June 1983, 86–95.

Russell, Robert John, Nancey Murphy, and C. J. Isham, eds. *Quantum Cosmology and the Laws of Nature: Scientific Perspectives on Divine Action*. Vatican City and Berkeley, Calif.: Vatican Observatory Publications; the Center for Theology and the Natural Sciences, 1993.

Russell, Robert John, William R. Stoeger, S.J., and George V. Coyne, S.J., eds. *Physics, Philosophy and Theology: A Common Quest for Understanding*. Vatican City: Vatican Observatory; University of Notre Dame Press, 1988.

Sacrobosco, Johannes de. *Tractatus de Sphaera Mundi*. Paris, c. 1235.

Sagan, Carl. "The Search for Extraterrestrial Life." *Scientific American*, October 1994, 92–99.

Sallantin, Xavier. *Théorie du sens; de l'accord imparfait à l'amour parfait*. Entveigt, France: Association Béna, 1994.

Samuelson, Norbert Max. *The First Seven Days: A Philosophical Commentary on the Creation of Genesis*. Atlanta: Scholars, 1992.

Santillana, Giorgio de. *The Crime of Galileo*. Chicago: University of Chicago Press, 1955.

Sapolsky, Robert M. "Stress in the Wild." *Scientific American*, 1990, 116–23.

Scheffczyk, Leo. *Die heile Schöpfung und das Seufzen der Kreatur*. Weilheim-Bierbronnen: G.-Siewerth-Akademie, 1992.

Schiwy, Günther. *Teilhard de Chardin: Sein Leben und seine Zeit, 1881–1923*. Vol. 1. München: Kösel, 1981.

———. *Teilhard de Chardin: Sein Leben und seine Zeit, 1923–1955*. Vol. 2. München: Kösel, 1981.

Schmaus, Michael. *Der Glaube der Kirche*. St. Ottilien: Eos, 1979.

Schmitz-Moormann, Karl. "Can Theology Be Done Ignoring Science?" *Bulletin Jesuits in Science, Distributed by the International Center for Jesuit Education at the Curia S.J. in Rome* 7 (1991): 12–16.

———. "The Concept of Complexity Seen in the Light of the Evolution of Complexes." In *Origins, Time, and Complexity*, Part 2, edited by George V. Coyne, S.J., Karl Schmitz-Moorman, and Christoph Wassermann, 236–41. Studies in Science and Theology, 1994. Geneva: Labor et Fides, 1994.

———. *Die Erbsünde, Überholte Vorstellung—Bleibender Glaube*. Olten: Walter, 1969.

———. "Evolution in the Catholic Theological Tradition." In *Evolution and Creation: A European Perspective*, edited by Svend Andersen and Arthur R. Peacocke, 121–31. Aarhus: Aarhus University Press, 1987.

———. "The Evolution of Information." In *The Science and Theology of Information*, edited by Christoph Wassermann, Kirby Richard, and B. Rordorff, 172–84. Geneva: Labor et Fides, 1992.

———. "Die Ideenlehre Platons im Lichte des Sonnengleichnisses des sechsten Buches des Staates." Ph.D. diss. München, 1957; Münster, 1959.

———. "On the Evolution of Human Freedom." ZYGON, *Journal of Religion and Science* 22, no. 4 (1987): 443–58.

———. "Science and Theology in a Changing Vision of the World: Reading John Paul's Message." In *John Paul II on Science and Religion: Reflections on the New View from Rome*, edited by Robert John Russell, William R. Stoeger, S.J., and George V. Coyne, S.J. Vatican City: Vatican Observatory Publications, 1990.

———. "Teilhard de Chardin's View on Evolution." In *Evolution and Creation: A European Perspective*, edited by Svend Andersen and Arthur R. Peacocke, 162–68. Aarhus: Aarhus University Press, 1987.

———. "Teilhard théologien." *Études Teilhardiennes* 3 (1970): 63–69.

———. "Theology in an Evolutionary Mode." ZYGON, *Journal of Religion and Science* 27, no. 2 (1992): 133–51.

———. "Theology's Relation to Science." In *Evolution and Creation: A European Perspective*, edited by Svend Andersen and Arthur R. Peacocke, 27–34. Aarhus: Aarhus University Press, 1987.

———, ed. *Schöpfung und Evolution: Neue Ansätze Zum Dialog Zwischen Naturwissenschaften und Theologie*. Akademie-Tagungen. Pope John Paul II et al. Schriften der Katholischen Akademie in Bayern. Düsseldorf: Patmos, 1992.

———, ed. *Teilhard de Chardin in der Diskussion*. Wege der Forschung. Darmstadt: Wissenschaftliche Buchgesellschaft, 1986.

Schneider, Dietrich. "The Sex-Attractant Receptor of Moths." *Scientific American,* July 1974, 28–35.

Schneider, Theodor, ed. *Handbuch der Dogmatik*. Düsseldorf: Patmos Verlag, 1992.

Schopf, J. William. "The Evolution of the Earliest Cells." *Scientific American,* September 1978, 110–39.

———, ed. *Earth's Earliest Biosphere: Its Origin and Evolution*. Princeton: Princeton University Press, 1983.

———, ed. *Major Events in the History of Life*. Boston: Jones & Bartlett, 1992.

Die Schöpfung in den Religionen. Sankt Augustin: Steyler, 1990.

Schramm, David N., and Gary Steigman. "Particle Accelerators Test Cosmological Theory." *Scientific American,* June 1988, 66–73.

Schwartz, James H. "The Transport of Substances in Nerve Cells." *Scientific American,* April 1980, 152–59.

Schwarz, Hans. *Die Biblische Urgeschichte: Gottes Traum von Mensch und Welt*. Freiburg im Breisgau: Herder, 1989.

Scoville, Nick, and Judith S. Young. "Molecular Clouds; Star Formation and Galactic Structure." *Scientific American,* April 1984, 42–53.

Searle, John R. "Is the Brain's Mind a Computer?" *Scientific American,* January 1990, 26–31.

Searle, John R., Paul M. Churchland, and Patricia Smith Churchland. "Artificial Intelligence: A Debate." *Scientific American,* January 1990, 25.

Sekuler, Robert, and Eugene Levinson. "The Perception of Moving Targets." *Scientific American,* January 1977, 60–73.

Shapiro, James A. "The Smallest Cells Have Important Lessons to Teach." Paper Presented at the Symposium "Cosmic Beginnings and Human Ends" held in Chicago at the 1993 Parliament of the World's Religions. In *Cosmic Beginnings and Human Ends: Where Science and Religion Meet,* edited by Clifford N. Matthews and Roy Abraham Varghese, 205–24. Chicago: Open Court, 1995.

Silk, Joseph I. *The Big Bang.* New York: Freeman, 1980.

———. "Road to Nowhere." Review of *The Physics of Immortality: Modern Cosmology, God, and the Resurrection of the Dead,* by Frank J. Tipler. *Scientific American,* July 1995, 93–94.

———. *A Short History of the Universe.* San Francisco: Scientific American Library, 1994.

Snyder, Solomon H. "The Molecular Basis of Communication Between Cells." *Scientific American,* October 1985, 132–41.

Snyder, Solomon H., and David S. Bredt. "Biological Roles of Nitric Oxide." *Scientific American,* May 1992, 68–77.

Speaight, Robert. *The Life of Teilhard de Chardin.* New York: Harper & Row, 1967.

Sperry, Roger W. *Science and Moral Priority.* Oxford: Blackwell, 1983.

Stahl, Franklin W. "Genetic Recombination." *Scientific American,* February 1987, 90–101.

Stahler, Steven W. "The Early Life of Stars." *Scientific American,* July 1991, 48–55.

Stannard, Russell. *Doing Away with God?* London: Marshall Pickering, 1993.

———. *Grounds for Reasonable Belief.* Edinburgh: Scottish Academic, 1989.

Staudinger, Hugo. "Atheismus als Nebenwirkung wissenschaftlichen Fortschritts." *Glaube und Denken, Jahrbuch der Karl-Heim-Gesellschaft* 6. Jahrgang (1993): 52–66.

———. "Der Atheismus vor der Wahrheitsfrage." *Glaube und Denken, Jahrbuch der Karl-Heim-Gesellschaft* 6. Jahrgang (1993): 138–55.

Stent, Gunther S. "Cellular Communication." *Scientific American,* September 1972, 42–51.

Stockmeyer, Larry J., and Ashok K. Chandra. "Intrinsically Difficult Problems." *Scientific American,* May 1979, 140–59.

Streibert, Christian. *Schöpfung bei Deuterojesaja und in der Priesterschrift: eine vergleichende Untersuchung zu Inhalt und Funktion schöpfungstheologischer Aussagen in exilisch-nachexilischer Zeit.* Frankfurt am Main: Peter Lang, 1993.

Struyker Boudier, C. E. M. *Morgen is Het Zondag: Verkenningen in Hedendaags Scheppings-denken.* Kampen and Kapellen: Kok Agora; DNB/Pelckmans, 1990.

Stryer, Lubert. "The Molecules of Visual Excitation." *Scientific American,* July 1987, 42–51.

Swimme, Brian. *The Universe Is a Green Dragon: A Cosmic Creation Story.* Santa Fe: Bear, 1984.

Swinburne, Richard. *The Coherence of Theism.* Oxford: Clarendon, 1977.

Tanzella-Nitti, G. *Questions in Science and Religious Belief: The Roles of Faith and Science in Answering the Cosmological Problem.* Tuscon: Pachart, 1992.

Teilhard de Chardin, Pierre. *Accomplir l'homme: Lettres inédites.* Paris: Grasset, 1968.

———. *L'Activation de l'Énergie.* Oeuvres t. 7. Paris: Seuil, 1963.

———. *L'Apparition de l'Homme.* Oeuvres t. 2. Paris: Seuil, 1956.

———. *L'Avenir de l'Homme.* Oeuvres t. 5. Paris: Seuil, 1959.

———. *Le Coeur de la Matière.* Oeuvres t. 13. Paris: Seuil, 1976.

——— . *Comment je crois.* Oeuvres t. 10. Paris: Seuil, 1969.

——— . *Les directions de l'Avenir.* Oeuvres t. 11. Paris: Seuil, 1973.

——— . *Écrits du temps de la guerre—1916–1919.* Oeuvres t. 12. Paris: Grasset-Seuil, 1965–76.

——— . *L'Énergie Humaine.* Oeuvres t. 6. Paris: Seuil, 1962.

——— . *Génèse d'une pensée: Lettres 1914–1919.* Paris: Grasset, 1961.

——— . *Le Groupe Zoologique Humain: Structures et directions évolutives.* reimprimé sous le titre: *La Place de l'homme dans la Nature: Structures et directions évolutives.* Oeuvres t. 8. Paris: Albin Michel-Seuil, 1956–64.

——— . "L'Homme devant les enseignements de l'Église et devant la philosophie spiritualiste." In *Dictionnaire apologétique de la foi catholique,* edited by Adhémard D'Ales, 501–14. Vol. 2. Paris: Beauchesne, 1924.

——— . *Journal I, 1915–1919.* Ed. Nicole and Karl Schmitz-Moormann. Paris: Fayard, 1975.

——— . *The Letters of Teilhard de Chardin and Lucile Swan.* Ed. Thomas M. King, S.J., and Mary Wood Gilbert. Foreword by Pierre Leroy, S.J. Washington: Georgetown University Press, 1993.

——— . *Lettres à Jeanne Mortier.* Paris: Seuil, 1984.

——— . *Lettres à Léontine Zanta.* Bruges: Desclée de Brouwer, 1965.

——— . *Lettres d'Égypte 1905–1908.* Paris: Aubier, 1963.

——— . *Lettres de voyage 1923–1939.* Paris: Grasset, 1956.

——— . *Lettres d'Hastings et de Paris 1908–1914.* Paris: Aubier, 1964.

——— . *Lettres inédites à l'abbé Gaudefroy et à l'abbé Breuil.* Monaco: Le Rocher, 1988.

——— . *Lettres Intimes à A. Valensin, B. de Solages, H. de Lubac, A. Ravier (1919–1950).* Introduction by Henri de Lubac. Paris: Aubier, 1974.

——— . *Le Milieu Divin.* Oeuvres t. 4. Paris: Seuil, 1957.

——— . *Nouvelles lettres de voyage 1939–1955.* Paris: Grasset, 1957.

——— . *L'Oeuvre Scientifique.* Ed and comp. Nicole and Karl Schmitz-Moormann. Preface by Jean Piveteau. Vols. 1–10 and 1 vol. of maps. Olten and Freiburg: Walter-Verlag, 1971.

——— . *Le Phénomène humain.* Paris: Seuil, 1955.

——— . *Science et Christ.* Oeuvres t. 9. Paris: Seuil, 1965.

——— . *Tagebücher.* Ed. and trans. Nicole and Karl Schmitz-Moormann. 3 vols. Olten and Freiburg: Walter-Verlag, 1974–78.

——— . *La Vision Du Passé.* Oeuvres t. 3. Paris: Seuil, 1957.

Teleki, Geza. "The Omnivorous Chimpanzee." *Scientific American,* January 1973, 32–47.

Thomas Aquinas. *Sancti Thomae de Aquino Expositio Super Librum Boethii de Trinitate.* Recensuit Bruno Decker. Studien und Texte zur Geschichte des Mittelalters, hrg. von D. Dr. Josef Koch, Bd. IV. Leiden: E. J. Brill, 1955.

Thomas, James H. "The Mind of a Worm." *Science* 264 (1994): 1688–89.

Thomas, Owen. "Recent Thought on Divine Action." In *Divine Action,* edited by Brian Hebblewaite, 35–50. Edinburgh: T. & T. Clark, 1991.

Tinbergen, N. "The Courtship of Animals." *Scientific American,* November 1954, 42–59.

——— . "The Curious Behavior of the Stickleback." *Scientific American,* December 1952, 22–38.

——— . "Defense by Color." *Scientific American,* October 1957, 48–69.

———— . "The Evolution of Behavior in Gulls." *Scientific American*, December 1960, 118–33.

Tipler, Frank J. *The Physics of Immortality: Modern Cosmology, God, and the Resurrection of the Dead*. New York: Doubleday, 1994.

Torrance, Thomas. *Divine and Contingent Order*. Oxford: Oxford University Press, 1981.

Torrance, Thomas Forsyth. *The Ground and Grammar of Theology*. Charlottesville: University Press of Virginia, 1980.

Trennert-Helwig, Mathias. *Die Urkraft des Kosmos: Dimensionen der Liebe im Werk Pierre Teilhards de Chardin*. Freiburger theologische Studien 153. Freiburg, Basel, and Wien: Herder, 1993.

Tribus, Myron, and Edward C. McIrvine. "Energy and Information." *Scientific American*, September 1971, 179–90.

Trusted, Jennifer. *Physics and Metaphysics: Facts and Faith*. London: Routledge, 1991.

Turner, Barry E. "Interstellar Molecules." *Scientific American*, March 1973, 50–69.

Unwin, Nigel, and Richard Henderson. "The Structure of Proteins in Biological Membranes." *Scientific American*, February 1984, 78–95.

Urey, Harold C. "The Origin of Life." *Scientific American*, October 1952, 53–61.

van den Beukel, A. *More Things in Heaven and Earth: God and the Scientists*. Trans. J. Bowden. London: SCM, 1992.

van Lawick–Goodall, Hugo, and Jane van Lawick–Goodall. *Innocent Killers*. Boston: Houghton Mifflin, 1971.

Veltman, Martinus J. G. "The Higgs Boson." *Scientific American*, November 1986, 76–105.

Vilenkin, Alexander. "Cosmic Strings." *Scientific American*, December 1987, 94–103.

Viola, Victor E., and Grant J. Mathews. "The Cosmic Synthesis of Lithium, Beryllium and Boron." *Scientific American*, May 1987, 38–45.

Vloet, Johan van der. *De Schaduw van God: Christelijk scheppingsgeloof en niewste wetenschap*. Antwerpen and Baarn: Hadewijch, 1992.

Wald, George. "The Origin of Life." *Scientific American*, August 1954, 44–53.

Waltz, David L. "Artificial Intelligence." *Scientific American*, October 1982, 118–35.

Ward, Keith. *Divine Action*. London: Collins Religious Publishing, 1990.

———— . *Rational Theology and the Creativity of God*. New York: Pilgrim, 1982.

———— . *The Turn of the Tide*. London: BBC Publications, 1986.

Washburn, S. L., and Irven DeVore. "The Social Life of Baboons." *Scientific American*, June 1961, 62–71.

Wassermann, Christoph. *Struktur und Ereignis*. Genfer Beiträge zum Dialog zwischen Physik und Theologie 2. Genf: Faculté Autonome de Théologie Protestante, 1991.

Wassermann, Christoph, Richard Kirby, and B. Rordorff, eds. *The Science and Theology of Information*. Geneva: Labor et Fides, 1992.

Weaver, Warren. "The Mathematics of Communication." *Scientific American*, July 1949, 11–15.

Weinberg, Steven. "The Decay of the Proton." *Scientific American*, June 1981, 64–75.

———— . *Dreams of a Final Theory: The Search for the Fundamental Laws of Nature*. New York: Pantheon Books, 1992.

———— . *The First Three Minutes*. London: Andre Deutsch, 1977.

Weizsäcker, Carl Friedrich von. *Zeit und Wissen*. München: Hanser, 1991.

Westermann, Claus. *Schöpfung: Wie die Naturwissenschaft fragt—was die Bibel antwortet.* Freiburg im Breisgau: Herder Taschenbuch, 1989.

Westfall, Richard S. *Essays on the Trial of Galileo.* Vatican City: Specola Vaticana, 1989.

Whatmough, Joshua. "Natural Selection in Language." *Scientific American,* April 1952, 82–86.

Whitehead, Alfred North. *Process and Reality. An Essay in Cosmology. Gifford Lectures Delivered in the University of Edinburgh During the Session 1927–28.* New York: Free Press, 1978.

Wigner, Eugene. "The Unreasonable Effectiveness of Mathematics in the Natural Sciences." *Communications in Pure and Applied Mathematics* 13 (1960): 1–12.

Wilber, Ken, ed. *Quantum Questions.* Shambhala, Boulder, and London: New Science Library, 1984.

Wildiers, Norbert M. *Wereldbeeld en teologie: Van de middeleeuwen tot vandaag.* Antwerpen: Standard Wetenschappelijke Uitgeverij, 1973.

Willows, A. O. D. "Giant Brain Cells in Mollusks." *Scientific American,* February 1971, 68–75.

Wilson, Edward O. "Animal Communication." *Scientific American,* September 1972, 52–71.

Wilson, Stephen A. "Conformity, Individuality and the Nature of Virtue." *Journal of Religious Ethics* 23, no. 2 (1995): 263–89.

Winograd, Terry. "Computer Software for Working with Language." *Scientific American,* September 1984, 130–45.

Wissink, J. B. M., ed. *The Eternity of the World in the Thought of Thomas Aquinas and His Contemporaries. Studien und Texte Zur Geistesgeschichte Des Mittelalters.* Ed. Albert Zimmermann. Vol. 27. Leiden: E. J. Brill, 1990.

Wolpert, Lewis. "Pattern Formation in Biological Development." *Scientific American,* October 1978, 154–65.

Woosley, Stan, and Tom Weaver. "The Great Supernova of 1987." *Scientific American,* August 1989, 32–41.

Wright, Karen. "The Road to the Global Village." *Scientific American,* March 1990, 83–95.

Zurek, Wojciech H., ed. *Complexity, Entropy, and the Physics of Information.* Redwood City, Calif.: Addison-Wesley, 1990.

Zycinski, Jozef M. *The Idea of Unification in Galileo's Epistemology.* Vatican City: Specola Vaticana, 1988.

INDEX